5-7-73

BRITISH LABOUR STRUGGLES:
CONTEMPORARY PAMPHLETS 1727-1850

COOPERATIVE COMMUNITIES:
PLANS AND DESCRIPTIONS

Eleven Pamphlets

1825-1847

Arno Press

A New York Times Company/New York 1972

Reprint Edition 1972 by Arno Press Inc.

Reprinted from copies in the Kress Library
Graduate School of Business Administration,
Harvard University

BRITISH LABOUR STRUGGLES: CONTEMPORARY PAMPHLETS 1727-1850
ISBN for complete set: 0-405-04410-0

See last pages for complete listing.

Manufactured in the United States of America

Library of Congress Cataloging in Publication Data
Main entry under title :

Cooperative communities: plans and descriptions.

    (British labour struggles:
contemporary pamphlets 1727-1850)
    CONTENTS: A visit to the colony of Harmony, in
Indiana, by W. Hebert [first published 1825].--
Owenism rendered consistant with our civil and
religious institutions, by J. Hamilton [first pub-
lished 1825].--Description of an architectural model
from a design by Stedman Whitwell, esq., by S.
Whitwell [first published 1830]. [etc.]
    1. Collective settlements. I. Series.
HX630.C64   335'.9   72-2522
ISBN 0-405-04415-1

Contents

1768007

published by the Christian cooperative community society . . .
Cheltenham, Printed by T. Willey [1842?]

[Somerville, Alexander]
. . . Notes from the farming districts. No. XVII. A journey to
Harmony hall in Hampshire, with some particulars of the
socialist community, to which the attention of the nobility,
gentry, and clergy, is earnestly requested . . . [London,
Printed by W. Ostell, 1842]

Holyoake, George Jacob
A visit to Harmony hall! (Reprinted from the "Movement")
With emendations, and a new and curious vindicatory chapter.
Dedicated to the socialists of England and Scotland. By G. J. H.
. . . London, H. Hetherington, 1844.

Hunt, Thomas
Report to a meeting of intending emigrants comprehending a
practical plan for founding co-operative colonies of united
interests, in the north-western territories of the United States
. . . London, W. Ostell [etc.] 1843.

Community of Icarie. [London, Printed by F. I. Watson, 1847?]

A

VISIT TO THE COLONY

OF

HARMONY,

IN INDIANA,

IN THE UNITED STATES OF AMERICA,

RECENTLY PURCHASED BY MR. OWEN FOR THE ESTABLISHMENT OF A

SOCIETY OF MUTUAL CO-OPERATION

AND

COMMUNITY OF PROPERTY,

IN A LETTER TO A FRIEND;

TO WHICH ARE ADDED,

SOME OBSERVATIONS ON THAT MODE OF SOCIETY, AND
ON POLITICAL SOCIETY AT LARGE:

ALSO,

A SKETCH FOR THE FORMATION OF

A CO-OPERATIVE SOCIETY.

" Many schemes ridiculed as Utopian, decried as visionary, and declaimed
against as impracticable, will be realized the moment the march of sound
knowledge has effected this for our species; that of making men wise enough
to see their true interests, and disinterested enough to pursue them."—LACON.

BY WILLIAM HEBERT.

London:
PRINTED FOR GEORGE MANN, 39 CORNHILL.

1825.
Price One Shilling.

ERRATA.

—·000·—

Page 20, line 14, for thing, read things.
—— 20, —— 27, for excrescenes, read excrescences.
—— 21, —— 32, for philanthrophist, read philanthropist.
—— 23, —— 23, for philantrophist, read philanthropist.
—— 24, —— 39, for res ess read restless.

A VISIT,

&c.

Albion, Edward's County, Illinois,
6th February, 1823.

DEAR SIR,

In the month of September last I made an excursion with a friend to the celebrated German Colony in our neighbourhood at Harmony, the name of the place being characteristic of the society that is settled there. It is situated in a thickly wooded country on the banks of the Wabash, on the Indiana side, at about thirty miles from the mouth of that river. The site of ground upon which the town stands is generally flat for about a mile and a half from the river, when the surface of the country becomes hilly and pleasingly undulating. This singular community consists of about seven hundred individuals, chiefly from Wirtemburg and its neighbourhood. They have occupied their present situation about seven years, having been induced to relinquish a former establishment in a back situation of Pennsylvania, near Pittsburg, from its becoming, as it is supposed, too thickly settled to suit the peculiar tenets or policy of their society. The progress which this religious community made in agriculture and every other kind of industry when settled in Pennsylvania, was a subject of astonishment to their neighbours for many miles round, but I apprehend that their present advanced state of improvement and accumulating wealth, justly excite the admiration of all acquainted with them here to a yet greater degree. It is presumable that they have made far greater progress here than they did in Pennsylvania, from their having been much longer established, and from a consideration of the sum of money for which they sold their former establishment, compared with the vast value of their present possessions. These good people have literally made the "barren wilderness to smile" with corn fields, meadows, and gardens upon a most extensive scale. Their little town, seen from the neighbouring hills, which are covered with their vineyards and orchards, has an exceedingly pleasing appearance, the Wabash, which is here an ample stream, being seen to wind its course in front of it, and beneath the luxuriant and lofty woods on the opposite banks of Illinois. The town is regularly laid out into straight and spacious streets, crossing each other at right angles, in common with modern American towns. The log cabins are giving place as fast as possible to neat and commodious brick and framed houses, which are extremely well built, the uniform redness of the brick of which the majority of them is composed giving to the place a brightness of appearance which the towns of England are quite destitute of. Nothing, I think, detracts so much from the beauty of London, next to the irregularity with which it is built, as the earthy or mud-coloured appearance of the houses, forming so great a contrast to the wealth and splendour within a considerable portion of them. The house of Mr. Rapp, the pastor of the community, is a large square mansion of brick, having a good garden and suitable out-houses attached. The streets of the little town of harmony are planted on each side with Lombardy poplars, but as these are found to die as soon as their roots come in contact with the substratum of sand, they are replaced with mulberry trees. A town being thus planted with trees, has a very picturesque effect from a distance, it appearing to stand in a grove, beside the pleasant use of affording shade and shelter when walking about it. The town is amply supplied with excellent wells, as also with public ovens, which are placed at regular and convenient distances from each other. Their granaries, barns, factories, &c. are generally built in an exceedingly handsome and durable manner. Here too, in token of Christianity being planted, (though in its most rigid character,) amongst Indian woods which had but lately resounded with the yells of their untutored inhabitants, rises the pretty village church, the white steeple of which, seen from afar through the widely extended clearings and forests of girdled trees, seems to invite the traveller onward to a peaceful resting place. And such it is, Harmony is truly the abode of peace and industry. The society, however, possesses one principle of so unsocial and dispiriting a character, as to throw a shade over the whole scene in a moral sense, and to fill the mind with commiseration for men who can so construe any of the precepts of Christianity into a virtual prohibition of the sacred ties of the married state. The Harmonians are a class of Lutherans, who, though they do not expressly prohibit marriage, discountenance it to an extent that nearly amounts to a prohibition in effect. They profess to adhere to the advice of St. Paul, in regard to this point of morality. Upon my enquiring of one of them, a candid and amiable person, how long it had been since a marriage had taken place amongst them, he said, nearly three years, and it was presumable that none was contemplated as about to take place at the time of my enquiry. This in a community which can contain scarcely less than a hundred young persons of suitable ages to enter upon the marriage state, and surrounded with plenty secured to them upon their system of society! The Harmonians consider the single state as higher in a moral estimation than the married one, as the Catholics are said to esteem it.

As you may suppose, the utmost regularity and decorum subsists amongst them. They work easily, but their hours of labour are of the usual length of the labourer's day, being from sunrise to sunset. They are an exceedingly industrious race of people, being occasionally busy long before sunrise in some departments of their establishment, such as their Distillery, Brewery and Mills which sometimes require their attendance through the night. It is understood that they subsist upon a principle of fellowship, or of united labour and capital, all deriving their food and clothing from the common stock, every individual however being accountable for the application of his time, and the amount of the articles he has from the stores. When any one is remiss or irregular to an extent to become an object of attention, no coercive measures are resorted, to but the idle or offending person is treated with distance or neglect, which, together with verbal reproof, are found to be fully efficacious to reform. The Harmonians are, however, an extremely regular and sober-minded people, whose happiness is certainly the happiness of ignorance, the pursuits of literature being wholly neglected or prohibited amongst them. They appear to do every thing with a mechanical regularity. Their town is consequently very still, the sounds of mirth or conviviality being rarely heard within it, excepting when their American or English neighbours resort there for purposes of trade or to negociate their money transactions. Being great capitalists, resulting wholly from their industry, they are frequently resorted to by persons in this neighbourhood, who receive remittances by bills on the eastern cities, to obtain cash for them. As a society they are extremely wealthy. Having overcome all the difficulties incident to their establishment in a wilderness, they have only to improve their manufactures and extend the sphere of their operations to acquire almost incalculable wealth. This numerous community of men of humble life embraces within it several artisans of nearly all the most useful occupations of life, to the exclusion or suppression of those which they do not deem essential to their welfare. Amongst the latter, I am sorry to say they include that of a Printer, they being wholly without one, and seem fully persuaded that the employment of one, if it would not be detrimental to their peace or their interests, is at least superfluous to them. They are generally averse to communication on the subjects of the tenets and the policy of their society. It may be presumed that they are totally unused to liberal discussion, and may be considered an ignorant and priest-ridden set of people. Mr. Rapp is alike their spiritual teacher and temporal director, who is as much accustomed to superintend their operations in their fields and factories, as to lecture them on their duty, and who will sometimes spend as much time in exploring their woods in search of a particular tree for a specific purpose, as in enforcing his arguments for the peculiar doctrines of their faith. He is their alpha and omega, without whom they think nothing, do nothing, and perhaps would have been nothing. Mr. Frederick Rapp, an adopted son of Mr. Rapp the pastor, a bachelor of about forty years of age, appears to be the sole cashier and ostensible proprietor of all the produce and manufactures of the society, all bills and receipts being made and given in his name only. I am informed however that their land which is of great extent and

of the first quality, is entered at the land-office in the form of
" Frederick Rapp and his associates," which circumstance I
was glad to learn, as it indicates something like joint property
on this material point, whatever may be the fact in other
respects. The affairs of the community are not regulated by a
committee, or court of directors, chosen periodically and in
rotation from among its members, which would possibly be
deemed as "*romantic*" as the representative system of government is termed by the present emperor of Austria, but by a
few of the most influencial individuals amongst them. The
governing power seems to be composed of Mr. Rapp and his
adopted son, with the assistance of the superintendent of the
general store, the doctor, the sadler, the smith, and the keeper
of the house of "private entertainment," (the designation of
the tavern,) and perhaps a few other persons; but those
enumerated are the ostensible managers, each of whom receives
money in his particular department. Further than this, nothing
is known respecting the pecuniary arrangements of the
society. Whether the governing power of the Harmonians
has any constitutional shape is unknown, but its efficiency is
matter of astonishment to all who have surveyed the scene of
its operation. If justice prevail in the society it is well, and
they are a peculiarly respectable body of people, to be com-
passionated only for the gloomy character of their religious
opinions and their general ignorance. And if equity do not
subsist among them, and the majority are duped by the wary
and powerful few, they still appear a contented people, and to
entertain an *opinion* of mutuality of possession, though they
may not possibly have any very correct ideas or information
upon the subject. It is known that books of account are kept,
in which are entered the amount of every labourer and
mechanic's daily earnings, together with the daily amount of
the articles each has from the stores; but it is not known that
there is any general account kept of the external transactions
of the society, or of the value of grain, beef, pork, whiskey,
beer, wine, and of various manufactures that are exported from
Harmony to New Orleans and elsewhere, besides an immense
amount of goods sold by retail at their general store, the
return for all which is chiefly in specie. The Harmonians have
commercial agents in several of the principal cities of the
Union, whose purchases of merchandize being sent to Harmony, are dispersed through the surrounding country by means

of their store at home, and others which it appears they think it worth their while to possess in different towns in the neighbourhood, which latter are superintended on commission by persons not of their society. They have it already in their power to say that they raise or produce every thing necessary to comfort, with an exception only to groceries, which last however they procure in exchange for their own commodities, chiefly for sale, as it is said the people in general are not allowed the use of tea or coffee, although the heads of the community indulge in those agreeable and exhilarating beverages. The Harmonians are upon the whole an interesting body of people, but it is impossible to regard their commercial spirit without a sentiment of fear or suspicion that it militates against that purity and austerity of character which they are in other respects so scrupulous of maintaining. One might enquire what is the probable destination of this community at the distance of half a century? The principle of celibacy upon which it is governed tends nearly to its extinction within this period. Upon enquiring of the good man, the keeper of the house of "private entertainment," who shewed us about the town, if they were not desirous of increasing the number of their society, he replied, "*not by strangers;*" and upon my friend's enquiring whether they were not desirous of receiving an accession of numbers from amongst their own countrymen, he said, that they considered their own countrymen, who were not of their faith, equally strangers to them with Americans or English; and having repeated that they were not desirous of increasing their number " by strangers," he added, "*that is the answer;*" implying that the answer he had given us, was "*the answer*" to all enquiries of that nature. Our guide informed us that their number was a little above seven hundred, but that he did not recollect the exact number, which last part of his communication I thought somewhat strange in an elderly and influencial associate. With respect to the Messieurs Rapp and their coadjutors keeping books of account of the amount of their annual income by exports and sales at home, and of the value of the disposable property on hand, for the information and satisfaction of the whole of the community, I never heard that there were any kept here, but I have been given to understand that a great book of accounts which had been kept at their establishment in Pennsylvania, was lost at the time of their removal, or shortly after it; and this story is accompanied by another, which, though not surprising in itself, becomes *measureably* so, when connected with the loss of the book of accounts. The second story is, that the heads of the society never received but a small portion of the sum for which they sold their former establishment. These circumstances would be little worthy notice, did the heads of the Harmonians evince an independence of pecuniary or commercial pursuits, whereas they are notoriously keen in dealing, and appear to be arrant money-lovers. The Harmonians seem in a measure to have adopted the policy of the Roman priesthood during the ages of their greatest power, which by forbidding their fraternity to marry, preserved the power and possessions of the church wholly within itself, and prevented that relaxation of interest and opposition of sentiment in its concerns, which would have resulted from a matrimonial connection of the reverend order with the laity, and these humble sectarians preserve an insular policy to the utmost extent of their power. Their children few as they are, have but the common rudiments of an education given to them, and are prevented as much as possible from learning the English language. Mr. Rapp, the pastor, it is said, does not speak a word of English, although he has lived in America nine or ten years; and notwithstanding that his son and the other leading members of the community speak it very well. That an arch craft rules the society I would not insinuate, and am indeed far from concluding upon, but that several circumstances exist strong enough altogether to induce a fear of wrong, or to keep alive speculation, must I think, be obvious to every person who has any knowledge of the outrageous impositions which avarice and ambition, under the garb of priestly sanctity, have practiced upon the simplicity, the credulity, and pliancy of mankind. As great events sometimes spring from little causes, so small matters sometimes elucidate large ones. On the door of the house of "private entertainment" was written "grapes 12½ cents. per lb." Now I would enquire, who were to buy these grapes at 12½ cents. per lb? Surely not the poor vine dressers or working people themselves, though I doubt whether any of them could obtain any without allowing for them out of their earnings; and if the bill were put up to invite the purchases of American travellers, the proceeds from this source of sale must have been trifling in the extreme. I was struck with the paltry purport of this paper at the moment I saw it, and however it happened, it was taken down a short time after our arrival. It is this excessive spirit of trade in the Harmonians that forms the great defect, and I may say the anomaly of their character, considered as a society of rigid and puritanical christians, living remote from the political world, as one would have supposed, with a view to independence of its cares and pursuits. These people exhibit considerable taste as well as boldness of design in some of their works. They are erecting a noble church, the roof of which is supported in the interior by a great number of stately columns, which have been turned from trees of their own forests. The kinds of wood made use of for this purpose are, I am informed, black walnut, cherry, and sassafras. Nothing I think can exceed the grandeur of the joinery, and the masonry and brick-work seem to be of the first order. The form of this church is that of a cross, the limbs being short and equal; and as the doors, of which there are four, are placed at the ends of the limbs, the interior of the building as seen from the entrances, has a most ample and spacious effect. A quadrangular story or compartment containing several rooms, is raised on the body of the church, the sides of which inclining inwards towards the top, are terminated by a square gallery, in the centre of which is a small circular tower of about ten feet in height, which is surmounted with a silvered globe. The reason assigned by our guide for the erection of this fine edifice was, that the first church being built wholly of wood, is found to be so hot during the summer, when the whole of the society are assembled within it, as to be scarcely supportable, in consequence of which it was resolved to delay the building of their houses for a time, and raise a more spacious and substantial place of worship, and the one they are employed upon bids fairly to do them honor, both in the design and execution. It is much more spacious than the number of their society requires. I could scarcely imagine myself to be in the woods of Indiana, on the borders of the Wabash, while pacing the long resounding aisles, and surveying the stately colonnades of this church. Here too the Englishman is once more gratified with the sound of a church bell, which however harsh it may sometimes be thought by those who have never strayed beyond the sound of one, imparts a gratification after a period of estrangement from it, as connected with early associations, infinitely more soothing than could the most delicate strains of music. As if, however the good Harmonians could not lose sight of a gainful utility in any thing, the vaults of their new church are appropriated to the reception of stores of various kinds. In descending from the steeple of the old church, (from which a beautiful scene presents itself of the wonderful effects of united industry,) we perceived that the upper compartment of that building was also used as a store for grain, earthenware, cotton, &c. The Harmonians are said to be excellent musicians, and to make a great use of instrumental music in their worship, maintaining by the cultivation of this exquisite science and their unanimity, a two-fold claim to their designation as a society. The shortness of our stay did not afford us an opportunity of attending their religious service. I am informed that during the harvest season, the troops of reapers, male and female, leave the field preceded by music. To this I would merely say, that I wish them every happiness compatible with the repression of the all-ennobling passion of love. They seem to me however to have struck at the root of earthly joy, and I earnestly wish them every success in devising substitutes, or any means of alleviation of their cheerless situation. These good people retain their German style of dress. There is nothing remarkable in that of the men. The women wear close and long-bodied jackets, or spencers, and gipsey bonnets. They are said to be a healthy looking people, and I imagine they are so, although this was not the case at the time of our visit, which was at the latter end of September, that being generally the most trying time of the year, and a considerable number of them were sick. I must mention, that in addition to their vineyards and orchards covering many of the neighbouring hills, the Harmonians have formed an extensive garden in the form of a labyrinth, having a pretty rustic building in the centre. The mazy walks toward this hermitage are formed by espalier fruit trees, and currant and hazel bushes in almost interminable rounds. It does not appear that the people enjoy any periods of relaxation, excepting on Sundays, when they are allowed to walk about the garden, the orchards and vineyards, in some situations of which tables and benches are placed for the purpose of taking refreshment. My friend and I were shewn their cotton and woollen factories, with which we were much pleased. The products of these establishments are much esteemed by the country round. I saw some very good blue cloth from the wool of their own flocks, and good

c

cotton fabrics, such as are generally worn in the western country. A great number of men, women, and children are employed in these departments. They have a fine steam engine in use in their factories. The morning on which we were shewn about the town happening to be somewhat cool after rain, our guide who would be as cheerful as his habits of thinking permitted, observed that the air was "*entirely plea-sant*," upon which I took occasion to ask him, if he considered the climate and country of Indiana equal to those of the part of Germany he had quitted. Here however nature was true to herself, for he replied with great feeling, that the climate and beauty of Germany were so superior to those of Indiana, that the latter were not to be brought into comparison with the former. But maintaining his consistency of character, he observed, "we are happier here than we could have been in Germany, we could not have done there what we have here." I could perceive however that his native country had charms for him that he could not do justice to, and that in "expressive silence," he mused its praise. He informed us that the severity of the winter in their part of Indiana, (in about latitude 38,) is such, as to render it necessary to bury one kind of their vines, (the Portugal or red Lisbon,) by bending them to the ground, and covering them with earth; the only method of preserving potatoes and turnips here during the winter being by burying them. The severity of the winters of this part of the world forms an astonishing contrast to the great and long continued heat of its summers, uniting in this respect the cold of much higher latitudes with a heat little inferior to that of the tropics.

During our stay at Harmony we witnessed some very astonishing flights of pigeons. Such were their numbers, that they literally formed clouds, and floated through the air in a frequent succession of these as far as the eye could reach, sometimes causing a sensible gust of wind, and a considerable motion of the trees over which they flew. At that time of the year these birds congregate in the woods of this part of America by millions. Parties are sometimes formed to go to their roosts by night, when by knocking them off the trees with poles, any quantity of them may be taken.

In case you may have thought me too severe upon the Har-monians in regard to their trading spirit, an *excess* of which I think derogatory to the christian character, and more especially

11

in a society of christians who profess to live in a state of seclusion from the world and more conformably to the precepts of the gospel, I would say, I have perhaps been the more strict with them from a consideration of the consistent and dignified conduct of a society of friends situated also in Indiana, near the same river, and about a hundred miles to the north of Harmony, who are commonly known here by the name of the "Shakers," or "*Shaking Quakers.*" There is also, I am informed, another society of these friends in the state of Ohio. These societies are constituted upon a principle of reciprocal assistance and common property, and like the Harmonians refrain from marriage, but with a strictness that amounts to an absolute prohibition of it. These good people however consistently disclaim an attention to mercantile or pecuniary concerns beyond the demand of their necessities or personal comfort. They also have effected great things by united exertion, but they have no traffic with the surrounding country beyond the limits I have mentioned. They have their capacious granaries, fine mills, and machinery of various kinds, but they adhere to their object of living in christian fellowship, in a state of plenty and independence of the world. They are not merchants or money-changers, and when visited by strangers, entertain them gratis. This you will allow to be really respectable.

Having mentioned all the particulars of these interesting communities that I think worthy notice,

I remain,

Dear Sir,

Your's sincerely,

W. H.

12

OBSERVATIONS, &c.

FROM the foregoing circumstances relative to the Harmonians and Friends, it is but fair to conclude that if a society could be formed of any convenient number of families, each contributing only one hundred pounds toward a common fund, and were with this to seek an agricultural and manufacturing establishment in some convenient situation of Great Britain, Ireland, Hanover, or any part of protestant Europe, they might by the formation of an equitable constitution, and the enactment of a suitable code of laws which should always preserve the door of regress open for insubordinate or discontented members, and by the encouragement of literary and scientific pursuits for the occupation of their leisure time, attain to a degree of earthly comfort, not unassociated with refinement, hitherto unknown. Such a society would of course embrace within it several individuals of all the most useful occupations of life, and every thing would necessarily be effected for the benefit of the community upon an entire system of reciprocation; and might be conducted similarly to the manner in which public societies are generally managed. No one need doubt the practicability of this. No one indeed could doubt it, who had visited Harmony, and seen the astonishing effects of the united and systematic industry of numbers, and the numerous comforts, as well as the security derived from this enlarged system of social intercourse. The greatest internal obstacle to the welfare of a society of this kind in Europe might be the want of a religious bond of union, but surely the spirit of christianity, with all its variety of sects, ought to be equal to this. To obviate or lessen any difficulty that might arise from

difference of religious opinion, a general spirit of forbearance
and liberality would be necessary, and the erection of places
of worship convenient for every denomination of which the
community was composed, desirable; the officiating members
of which should be prohibited by the constitution, under the
penalty of expulsion, from preaching in terms offensive to, or
abusive of the tenets of christians of other sects, or laying any
stigma on any system or kind of belief whatever; on the principle that differences of religious opinion are within the
decision of the Deity alone, on whose favour and approbation
all have an equal right of reliance. The objects of such a
community would be industry, society, independence or self-
subsistence, leisure for mental culture, and rational amusements; and freedom from the solicitude, anxieties, and incer-
titude of pecuniary pursuits and possessions. The principal
obstacles to an establishment of this kind in Europe, would
arise from rent, or the high rate of the purchase of the land,
the exaction of taxes, and military service. From the last of
these however exemption might generally perhaps be purchased, and the first and second, if not too heavy, might be
defrayed from the funds, or by the sale of a portion of the
produce or manufactures of the society. America however
has every civil advantage and natural facility for such a society
to Europe.

To some it might appear irksome, and perhaps slavish, to
be obliged to regulate their conduct as members of a community, by the sound of a bell or the notes of a horn, but this
feeling could arise only in the absence of a due apprehension
of the situation, and of the circumstances of the case. Those
persons who have not property to live independently of industry must exert themselves for their support in some way or
other, and industry is pleasant in proportion to its regularity
and moderation, and the prospect it affords of being effective
of comfortable subsistence. Every person entering an association of the kind contemplated, would be sensible that it
could exist only by the industry of all its members; that by the
exertion of this, every one would be pursuing his own true
interests *as a proprietor*, by contributing to the utmost of his
ability to the welfare of the society; that as his entrance into
it was voluntary, so would his continuance in it be, consistently
with its constitution, and the experience of two or three years
would convince its members that the daily quantity of labour

and attention requisite to its concerns would be very far less than is given by tradesmen and mechanics in Europe, and in Great Britain especially, to procure their comparatively precarious subsistence. On the other hand, one might suppose a due appreciation of his situation would be calculated to make every individual cheerfully alert in the performance of his portion of assistance in a compact based on the sacred principle of equity, and that of mutuality of possession and enjoyment.

An agricultural and manufacturing community, subsisting its members in plenty and respectability upon the plan of that benefactor of his race, Mr. Robert Owen, and somewhat similar to those of the Friends and Harmonians, would be but carrying the principle of Benefit societies as far as it would go, resting it upon that of an equitable reciprocation of services amongst all its members, which, could the industry and concord of them be established, might be rendered a secure and pleasant mode of subsistence to hundreds, and in different communities perhaps to thousands.

Although this plan of society should appear to be not without objection, or even objectionable on several accounts, it may be asked, whether the evils of insolvency or bankruptcy, of dependance and poverty, or of prisons and workhouses are not greater and more numerous than those of the plan contemplated could be? Supposing such a compact to be practicable, (and with the societies of the Harmonians and Friends of America before our eyes who can doubt it?) he that was hostile to it, merely on account of its being an innovation, would be hostile to his own nature and fellow men. Such a system of society could not indeed hold together, unless a large majority of its members were persons of established principles of virtue and of matured knowledge, combined with habits of activity and industry; who surveying its objects and appreciating its advantages, were inflexibly devoted to its welfare; and who could regulate their conduct on a perfect conviction of the tractableness of mankind in all cases and situations, consistently with their knowledge or apprehension of fitness, propriety and real utility.*

---

* "On the experience of a life devoted to the subject, I hesitate not to say, that the members of any community may by degrees be trained to live without idleness, without poverty, without crime, and without punishment."

15

Some persons might object that the leisure and security attending such a plan of society would be productive of idleness, insubordination and vice; to which it might be answered that this result would depend on the previous education and habits of its members, and exclusively of the influence of their new social compact; but if there were those who acted so injuriously to themselves and the society to which they belonged, the door of withdrawment from it would be opened to

---

"Any general character, from the best to the worst, from the most ignorant to the most enlightened, may be given to any community, even to the world at large, by the application of proper means."

"Human nature, save the minute differences which are ever found in all the compounds of the creation, is one and the same in all; it is without exception universally plastic, and by judicious training the infants of any one class in the world may be readily formed into men of any other class; even to believe and declare that conduct to be right and virtuous, and to die in its defence, which their parents had been taught to believe and say was wrong and vicious, and to oppose which, those parents would also have willingly sacrificed their lives."

"All men may, by judicious and proper laws and training, readily acquire knowledge and habits which will enable them, if they be permitted, to produce far more than they need for their support and enjoyment; and thus any population in the fertile parts of the earth, may be taught to live in plenty and in happiness, without the checks of vice and misery."

"Train any population rationally, and they will be rational."

"In those characters which now exhibit crime, the fault is obviously not in the individual, but the defect proceeds from the system in which the individual has been trained. Withdraw those circumstances which tend to create crime in the human character, and crime will not be created."

"The worst formed disposition, * * * * * * * * * * * * will not long resist a firm, determined, well-directed, persevering kindness."

"The character of man is, without a single exception, always formed for him."

"Man never did, nor is it possible he ever can, form his own character."

"The kind and degree of misery or happiness experienced by the members of any community, depend on the characters which have been formed in the individuals which constitute the community."

"Hitherto indeed, in all ages, and in all countries, man seems to have blindly conspired against the happiness of man, and to have remained as ignorant of himself as he was of the solar system prior to the days of Copernicus and Galileo."

Vide "Owen's New View of Society,"
A work, which for correctness of views of human nature and society, and benevolence of design, is calculated to form the basis of a vast improvement of the condition of mankind.

them, however reluctantly, by a vote of the members, through which it would be necessary for such unwise persons to pass, before their evil example had had time to be extensively productive of mischief, but not before they had proved themselves irreclaimable to virtue and social obligation.

Some persons might also object that a community of the kind contemplated would in the course of years by the natural progress of population become too numerous for the means of support contained within it; to which it is answered, that it is not pretended that this plan of society would be wholly without its difficulties, as it is probable no human arrangement of society could be. Difficulty however, like danger and misfortune, is generally greatest in apprehension, and regulating our conduct upon right principles, we may always trust to events. In a society in which every thing was previously established on the simple and natural law of justice and reciprocation, and in which every head of a family would be equally interested in the adjustment of any difficulty that arose, the unanimity of sentiment that would exist in regard to previous circumstances would form more than half the conquest of every source of embarrassment that occured; and the one contemplated being of very gradual approach, and anticipated by the sagacity of of the senior associates, would be met in good season, and perhaps adjusted to the satisfaction and welfare of the community. The minds of men being at ease, and satisfied with the previous circumstances of their situation, it is impossible to say what sacrifices would not be offered by individuals for the good of the community, upon the occurrence of a natural inconvenience of the kind supposed, or how far a generous spirit of accommodation might be carried. If men can be found in the wide and tumultuous world to sacrifice themselves for their country, surely the associates of a happy christian and philosophic community would not be found inferior in disinterestedness. The means of support to a community of this kind would of course have a limit, and when the number of its members approached its maximum, if no other remedy could be devised, a resolution might be passed providing, under circumstances, for the withdrawment of a certain number of its members, or providing for the formation of another community in a convenient situation, toward which every facility would of course be afforded; but it is impossible to conjecture what would be the resources of a society that was animated by a sentiment of unanimity, approaching to that of obligation or friendship toward each other. There can be little doubt that human virtue would shine as brightly in this situation as in any recorded in history, and in all probability with this difference, that it would be *general* and not *isolated*. The condition being new, consequently the character of the individuals composing such a community would become altogether altered and raised, as is the case in a limited degree with respect to the working citizens of the United States of America in comparison with those other countries. My imagination is warm enough to believe that in a society properly constituted and regulated, besides being productive of a secure and pleasant subsistence, every scientific pursuit, and every elegant amusement might be participated, not only without injury, but to the happiness of its members. It would of course possess a good library, a well supplied reading room, and apparatus for philosophical research, and secure a liberal education for the children.

I can imagine evening field sports, and sometimes fêtes-champetres, in which recourse might be had, according to the taste of the parties, to various juvenile recreations, in which the grave and the elderly might occasionally join without diminution of the respect and veneration due to them. If industry were supported by virtue, it could not be rendered too cheerful, never losing sight of moderation, which is the standard of wisdom and enjoyment. There can indeed be no doubt that the Deity is most acceptably worshipped when man is most rationally or morally happy, and that he then best answers the object of his creation.

In the case of ladies and gentlemen becoming members of a community of this kind, who might not be used to manual employment of any very necessary or useful kinds, and who could not be rendered immediately or wholly serviceable to the society, such persons might be allowed to avail themselves externally to the society of any acquirements they possessed that were not required by it, upon their paying into the general fund an equivalent for their personal services, or such portion of these as were not afforded to the society. If this adjustment could not in all cases be rendered so precisely exact as some persons might require, it should never be forgotten that the community was one of reciprocal benefit, and that if a little room were left open in regard to the admission of some

D

of its members, for the exercise of liberality or benevolence, it would be of no disadvantage to the society, but probably contribute to its prosperity, as it would certainly augment its respectability and its happiness. All could not be equally useful members perhaps at first, and none could contribute more than the talents they possessed; but general application and industry would soon equalize the services of the members, and a scale of compensation to the society on a valuation of time, might be enacted more particularly for those members whose talents were deemed of inferior value, and whose circumstances required their occasional absence.

Not to anticipate any speedy or general adoption of this plan of society, it would yet be a libel equally upon human virtue and human genius to say that society can never be modelled *locally or in small detached portions,* upon principles of equity and reciprocation. It needs but a conviction of its propriety and desirableness to be attempted; and perhaps it need but be attempted perseveringly and consistently to be brought to success. It would materially lessen the chance of failure if a community were composed wholly of persons of one denomination or class of christians, as they would thereby possess the strongest incentive to agreement, notwithstanding that a religion whose bond is love ought to unite all denominations. The plan of society under consideration seems particularly applicable to persons of small property and of contracted connections; to persons who have been unfortunate in business, but who have retained their integrity; and those whose businesses may be said to be nearly superseded or dissipated in the fluctuations of trade. It is adapted to the relief of those who are unable to withstand the excessive competition, the redundancy of talent, or the pressure of the times singly; and to those who prefer tranquillity and security to turmoil and uncertainty.

Looking at the principle of trade and commerce *morally, and independently of its present general or universal necessity,* what is it but petty craft from the merchant to the pedler? The taking advantage of the ignorance or the unfavourable situation of others for the procurement or production of an article, and by the disposal of it at a profit to ourselves to draw by this means a source of subsistence or of wealth at a great expense of every feeling of fellowship, of honour and generosity. Is not, *philosophically speaking,* the toil of producing the elements of subsistence and the conveniences of life, sufficient, without the addition of art or craft in the dealings of mankind with each other? It has been said of old that, "*as mortar sticketh between the stones so sticketh fraud between buying and selling,*" and it cannot be supposed that the Deity designed that mankind should be petty tricksters upon one another rather than equal and just helpmates. Why could not the intercourse of mankind be founded on just and reciprocal principles, were it not for the monopoly of the earth, and the various corrupt circumstances and tyrannies of ancient political society? At any rate there is no natural impossibility that mankind should at a future period associate in detached portions upon a principle of reciprocal justice. They are the extremes of society as it exists that chiefly require reconciling, and being brought nearer to each other. The wealth and idleness of the one being brought to the relief of the poverty and slavery of the other. The extremes of society form its greatest deformity and infelicity. Society as it exists may be compared to a connected mass of building, the greater portion of which exhibits poverty and wretchedness of construction, a second portion of which indicates considerable convenience and comfort, and the third portion, though occupying much less space than either of the others, and especially than the first, is composed of erections of such lofty and commanding sizes as to cause the whole to appear an unsightly assemblage of irregularity and disproportion. There is no continuity of design or proportion of parts as yet in society. Society is doubtlessly susceptible of vast improvement, and when the labouring classes shall have become as well-informed as the middle classes are, great alterations it may be hoped will be effected *as the simple result of discussion*, and a more equal balance of possession and enjoyment established through the whole. It is not to be supposed that the present fortuitous jumble of dependance, and unjust and partial possession of the earth, the mere result of conquest and subjection, is the best possible economy of things. Every link in the chain of society as it exists is dependance, which is rivetted throughout by the fear of destitution. How inferior this, to what would be a rational fellowship of industry and possession, to an exclusion of want, and of apprehension for the future! Men being by nature equal, physically and morally considered, having the same wants and the same capacities for enjoyment, wherefore, it might be enquired of

those who *profess* to believe in a future state, is not the intercourse of mankind founded on principles of reciprocation and
justice, analagous to their nature and destination? It is not to
be believed that the Deity can view with perfect complacency
a state of things that sets a small portion of mankind at an
immense distance from the majority; that gives to a comparatively few individuals almost boundless means of gratification,
by which the mass are impoverished; whilst many can scarcely
obtain the elements of subsistence; and numbers are impressed
into the service of vice till they become as depraved as
human nature will admit, inflicting on the whole body of
society, with a knowledge of their crimes, a portion of their
infelicity. Nine tenths of the miseries and the crimes of mankind
result from this unequal and unjust state of thing. If injustice
and its consequent evils exist extensively in society, and
human reason can devise the means of their correction or
material abatement, wherefore should not this be attempted,
as far as it is seen and acknowledged, upon the eternal bases of
equity and reciprocation? The constant pursuit of individual
gain is at variance with the duties and affections of man, considered as a social and generous being. The opulent dealer
who extracts a large profit from the poor man; the wealthy
manufacturer who holds the mechanic to his machinery at a
price just commensurate with his individual subsistence, to
say nothing of that of his wretched family; and the rich landed
proprietor who retains those who till his fields in a state of
penury and pauperism, are excrescenes on God's earth, which
he gave to all mankind. Individual condition in humble life in
Europe, and especially in Great Britain, has constantly to withstand what is to it the two-fold evils of advancing machinery
and increasing population, rendering it daily more precarious
and more scanty. Witness the frequency and increasing extent
of the combinations and strikings of the operative classes. And
what could be more rational and honourable than an attempt to
construct society, *though locally and upon a small scale,* upon a
plan of common property and benefit, aloof from the petty con-
cealments and intricacies, the selfishness, the jealousies, the
proverbial absence of friendship, the casualties and opposing
interests of ordinary commercial life, which in proportion to its
success would be productive of peace, goodwill, security and
contentment. Such a plan of society would tend most materially and directly to soften the passions, and consequently to

encrease the enjoyment of life; would remove the evils of dependance, also those vast sources of distress insolvency and bankruptcy, and family dissensions arising from the unequal distribution of property; and would have a powerful tendency to check the ravages of insanity and suicide, which more frequently result from pecuniary embarrassment than any other cause. As society exists, the journeyman shoe maker or taylor has infinitely the advantage of the man of education and refinement, who through misfortune is reduced to poverty; and the cook or housemaid has infinitely the advantage of her mistress, if the latter is through any calamity brought to indigence. How many respectable females are rendered pennyless through the commercial misfortune, imprudence, or dissipation of male relatives, to whom their property was entrusted! And how many men are from the fluctuations and vicissitudes of the commercial world reduced to a situation in comparison with which that of the journeyman artisan *in employment* is enviable! The distress of the humble poor is frequently obvious to the sight, besides being rendered so to the ear, but the difficulties and sufferings experienced in middle and genteel life are silent and unseen. Misfortune however may be said to be proportionate to the sensibility of the unfortunate; and the utmost splendour of commercial life is but splendid dependance, which is far inferior in real dignity to moderate competence or self-subsistence, however humble. That which is wanting to society is a foundation in equity to which all might appeal, and from which all might derive support by the performance of an equitable quantity of labour. As society exists, the condition of every individual not born to hereditary property is perfectly fortuitous. Cannot this defect be remedied? Shall it never be remedied? The statesman says no; the philanthrophist, that it ought to be, *if it be practicable.* As society exists mankind subsist by individual ingenuity and address, and by the advantages which one individual obtains over another by whatever means, instead of associating upon a principle of natural equity befitting rational beings, which would put vicissitude and want and distress at defiance. If Christendom were truly christian, there would exist this spirit of justice and of concord. The christian world however will never fully deserve that name until society be modelled upon and governed by its precepts, to the neglect or non-effectiveness of civil and military government, to which latter powers christianity has hitherto been considered merely as an adjunct, and not as that divine code of laws which should supersede all others that are opposed to it, as the products only of human weakness or depravity. When the christian world becomes really christian, armies will cease to be marshalled to settle its disputes, to check the progress of knowledge, or crush its efforts of improvement. Literature will not be curtailed and fashioned by censorships, like trees by the shears of a whimsical gardener. A congress of wise and good men from all its parts, (not of belted chieftains,) will settle the first in peace, and welcome and foster the last.

Human nature being not merely ductile, but its ductility being almost without limit, the basis of an improved system of society would be the effect of a general perception of error in the common estimation of wealth and power. True wealth is self-enjoyment; true power, the command over one's-self; and no perception of individual property and power as they exist, (which generally afflict by the weight of anxiety they entail,) could equal the enjoyment that would result from the consciousness of being the free and equal member of an equitably constituted society, which would be proportionably relieved of vice and the numerous infelicities attending the existing intercourse of mankind. History is decidedly hostile to the opinion that individual enjoyment is the general concomitant of power, notwithstanding that the love, and consequent pursuit of power is the general foible of mankind. "Uneasy lies the head that wears a crown," and arduous are its duties if faithfully and honourably performed. The eminences of power and wealth are doubtlessly like other objects of human pursuit that have merely personal gratification or aggrandizement for their end, being more attractive and promising at a distance than satisfactory or pleasurable in the possession. A period may indeed arrive when the resources of ingenuity in manufactures and commerce may fail to such an extent as to render an adjustment of the condition of mankind locally or nationally, upon principles of equity imperiously necessary, as those resources have long failed to the purpose of general subsistence without the vast aid of the poor laws, those wretched supports of indigence which just enable it to limp along or to prolong its sufferings. A period may arrive when from the increased numbers of mankind manual labour shall of necessity supersede the use of machinery, as the latter is now permitted or rather stimulated for purposes of revenue and commerce to operate to the injury and deprivation of millions. When manufactures may be so diffused, improved and simplified in their production throughout the commercial world as to render the shiftings and refinements of commercial treaties, and of import and export regulations, of little or no avail; when national independence or self-subsistence shall be deemed the standard of security and respectability; and when human knowledge may have attained that maturity of growth as no longer to tolerate the existing crudities of the commercial and political world. That human society is in a state of great immaturity is evident, or mankind would not be subject to all the evils attendant on the vicissitudes and fluctuations of the political and commercial world. Nor would the vast majority of mankind be miserably dependent on the minority. This cannot exist when the former shall be as well informed as the latter, when knowledge shall shed its rays like the meridian sun. It does not indeed exist in the United States of America which seem destined to reform both the political and social system of Europe. Nearly the whole continent of America now invites to a better order of things. Its desert regions from nearly one end of it to the other inviting the philosopher and the philantrophist to aim at a better construction of human society; a construction less opposed to the equality of natural right and of natural wants, and better adapted to moral improvement and social enjoyment.

In regard to the different degrees of enjoyment experienced in two situations of the established form of society, it may be enquired which generally appear to possess the greatest share of enjoyment, those persons who are immersed in business to the whole extent of their property, or those whose competence is ascertained, and who live a retired life? I imagine that in nineteen cases out of twenty, the latter situation is by far the preferable one, and that most persons would allow this. If so, then would that be the best system of society that should the most nearly assimilate to this preferable situation, consistently with the welfare of all its members. If man be a social being, society should be universally a source of support, of improvement and happiness, instead of being as it is in innumerable cases, a source of destitution, of depravity, and consequent misery; and that would be the best plan of society that was the most equal and reciprocal, and consequently the most rational and virtuous. It has however been the lamentable conduct of statesmen, (though in some cases no doubt unintentionally) to degrade and brutalize human nature to the utmost, to render it familiar with privation and suffering, and every moral corruption. If revenue have been collected and armies kept on foot, private condition with the artisan and the labourer has been too generally a matter of little moment. A certain extent of destitution has indeed been considered by eminent statesmen as an essential circumstance of political government, seeing that without that source of impressment into its service its strongest arm of power could not be maintained. But if society be a good in its natural tendency, it may be enquired, whether it be sufficiently perfect; whether it cannot be rendered more perfect, more equitable, and consequently less productive of misery? If society be susceptible of improvement upon natural and equitable principles, then would that be the preferable system of intercourse in which the selfish, the violent, and malignant passions would be least liable to be agitated; in which the turmoil of pecuniary and political pursuits would be quashed; in which the elation and depression of mind attending the vicissitudes of fortune would be subdued into a moderate and even pleasurable quantity of beneficial employment; in which the acquisition of knowledge, and the various enjoyments of society would have the freeest scope; in which the sacred tie of marriage would be allowed to take place at suitable ages unobstructed by considerations of property and the frequent avarice of parents; in which the most deplorable circumstance of society as it exists would not have place; and in which the education of youth would all form primary and essential objects of the care of its members. If there be reason in this, both virtue and humanity bid us hope that a gradual improvement in society, commensurate with the progress of knowledge and of the true economy of life, may take place. Nothing further is wished or contemplated, as it would not be reasonable to set a man or a number of men to grope for a treasure in the dark, or to make experiments that might result in their injury or destruction. But if the foregoing observations are warranted by truth and the real nature of things, then may one day the restlesss votaries of ambition and of wealth in Europe borrow valuable instruction from the societies of Harmonians and Friends in America, or from societies constituted upon similar but

improved and equitable principles, adapted to all the purposes
of moral and refined society and every human relationship.
All persons of habits of business must be sensible that it is a
desirable thing to abridge the hours devoted to it within a
space to allow of a due attention to domestic concerns, to
personal comfort, to the instruction of children, to reading, to
scientific pursuit, recreation and the enjoyment of society, all
which objects are greatly obstructed by the enormous portion
of time devoted by tradesmen to their businesses in order to
support their numerous responsibilities; and journeymen
artisans and labourers in employment have no time whatever
for these desirable and necessary objects, except on Sundays;
all which circumstances however would be most materially
and beneficially attained upon the equitable and rational plan
of society contemplated, which would also as naturally tend
to check the selfish and sordid affections as the existing form
of society contributes to excite them. What could be more
proper than for various artisans and agriculturists after the
work of the day was over, and they had had time to refresh
themselves at home, and to attend to various matters, to meet
as inclination prompted in a reading room or library, for the
purpose of reading or conversation on subjects of physical
science or any others more interesting to them, instead of
living in ignorance and poverty, neglecting their families from
necessity, and from bad habits and associations, wasting their
little leisure time, their money and health at public houses?
The plan of society under consideration is simply an extensive
and equitable partnership in all the essentials of life, or a complete and perfect Benefit Society, based in the equal or proportionate stake of all its members, in which the social feelings
would be more freely and constantly exercised than in the
present form of society. Though it be allowed that the present
state of society in Europe is commensurate with its progress
in knowledge, and that it is a great amelioration of that of the
Gothic or Feudal ages, it does not take place when that highest of all
the sciences, *the science of human life in society*, shall be better
understood and more justly appreciated in its enjoyments and
its objects. The present form of society in Europe is merely
a modification or amelioration of Feudalism, be that modification or amelioration great or little, and the problem for the
philosopher and the philanthropist of the present day is,

E

whether society be susceptible of a basis and superstructure in equity, consistently with the natural equality and dignity of mankind.

If then reason, equity and humanity be allied against ancient political society with all its tyrannies and usurpations, the question is, whether the former shall always be overborne by the crude assemblage of circumstances derived from the infancy and pristine ignorance of mankind; or whether that form of society or settling of things which conquest or brute force, aided by superstition, impressed on the weakness and ignorance of mankind, shall always prevail over that which reason would dictate, which equity and humanity demand, or which a council of philosophic friends of mankind would prescribe, acting upon the present or future knowledge of mankind? Shall improvements and discoveries be constantly going forward in physics, and none be made in society, or the art of living in society? And notwithstanding that prejudiced persons are apt to scoff at all plans for the amelioration of the condition of mankind as merely visionary or Utopian schemes, it is consolatory to reflect, that the opposition alluded to is, in some instances, no purer in its source than was that of the Roman clergy against the reforming doctrines of Erasmus and Luther; and no more founded in nature or truth than that of the Spanish nobles against the geographical principles of Christopher Columbus.

It may remain for the writer of the foregoing to assure his readers that no part of it is intended in any manner to wound the feelings of individuals of any class or station of life whatever. Individual excellence is to be found in every rank and walk of life, and is perfectly compatible with great imperfection in the frame of government and that of society generally, which imperfection is deducible from the circumstances of their origin and progress. It is incumbent on the privileged orders of society only to bear their ascendency with meekness and liberality, it not being the fault of any individual belonging to them that he was born to a title not known in moral estimation, or to the possession of thousands of acres of the earth under a system of things which denies to the vast majority a square foot. Although the iron sword of an ancestor or the lavish gift of a conqueror includes but a slender *moral* title to the possession of an estate which would afford thousands of fellow-beings subsistence, it is not to be expected that the hereditary possessors of the earth will yield their monopoly of it until they shall be presented with what they may deem an equivalent in a greater degree of moral and social happiness, resulting from equity being established as the foundation of society. The privileged orders of the present generation and those for some ages past are altogether innocent of the monstrous disparity of circumstance deducible from conquest and priestcraft acting upon the ignorance and weakness of mankind. The error or crime of the case is attributable only to the system, and not to any class of individuals who are the subjects of it. It is for the present generation only to take care that the " *march of sound knowledge*" be facilitated to the utmost. That improvement be not confined to physical science merely; but that it be admitted to modify, or remodel society, as the pressure of political circumstances on individual condition, or more correct views of human nature or of the economy of life may suggest.

The writer when in Philadelphia, in June, 1823, had] put into his hand by an acquaintance, (an opulent farmer and grazier from the west of England, who was then seeking an establishment for himself and an extensive connection in the United States,) a pamphlet written by a Mr. Brayshaw from Scotland, who had then recently arrived in America for the purpose of making a tour of the western states, with a view to ascertain a situation for the establishment of a society upon the principle of an equitable participation of labour and capital, from which the following is an extract.

" According to the present form or construction of society, the interest of every individual is placed in opposition to the interests of other individuals, and in opposition to the interests of society at large. In my own opinion, by carefully tracing effects to their causes, I shall be able to prove that this opposition of interests is the fundamental cause of the greatest part of the evils which now afflict or ever have afflicted the human species; and I think if I succeed in this point, I shall be warranted in concluding that if it be possible to give such a construction to human society as shall have the effect of uniting the common interests of mankind, by making the interest of the whole the interest of every individual, and the interest of every individual the interest of the whole body, such a state of things would remove the causes of the evil, and banish the greatest part of the miseries which at present afflict mankind."

A

SKETCH

FOR THE FORMATION OF A

SOCIETY OF MUTUAL CO-OPERATION

AND

COMMUNITY OF PROPERTY,

TO BE COMPOSED OF TRADESMEN, FARMERS, CLERKS, MECHANICS, &c.
INTENDED TO BE ESTABLISHED IN THE STATE OF NEW YORK.*

———◆———

Art. 1. It is proposed that the Society shall in the first
instance consist of about a hundred families, exclusively of
single members.

2. That the capital to be introduced by every adult male
member be not less when arrived in America and at the
settlement, than £11. 5s. (50 dollars,) nor more than £900.
(4000 dollars.)

3. That the whole of the property of the Society be divided
into shares, and that a share be equal to the smallest subscription, viz. £11. 5s.

4. That the less opulent members shall have the opportunity
by their industry of increasing their property in the society in

---

* This outline of a self-subsistent community was made by the author of
the foregoing pages at the suggestion of a friend from New York, where a
few gentlemen contemplated the formation of a society of this kind, toward
which it was proposed that every one designing to become a member should
contribute a plan or certain articles; since which time, and within a few days,
he has been fortunate enough to meet with Mr. OWEN'S "AMERICAN
DISCOURSES, &c." and the "ARTICLES OF AGREEMENT OF THE
LONDON CO-OPERATIVE SOCIETY," in which publications the principles of this plan of society are detailed, and its advantages and general
attractiveness rendered apparent.

proportion to that of the other members, and that an equitable adjustment of the value of time be made for the whole of the members.

5. That the affairs of the Soeiety be conducted by a rotatory committee, or board of management, of all its members in succession, which committee or board of management to be chosen monthly, quarterly, or half yearly. To consist of —— members.

6. That the capital of the Society, after the purchase of the land, the expence of the *first* clearing, fencing and building, (this to be done by natives,) the purchase of cattle and other live stock, implements, machinery, &c. be vested in the United States Bank, in the names of all the members of the Society.

7. That every male member of the Society shall engage to employ himself in any and every manner that shall at any time be determined by the existing board of management; that there shall be no exclusive employments; and that every male member be eligible to every employment or office to which he is nominated by the managing board or committee for the time being, or by the election of not less than two-thirds of the members of the Society

8. That it is a radical principle of this society that labour of every necessary or useful description is honourable; that true respectability consists in integrity of character and utility of conduct. That what must be done by some may be done by all. That idleness, as opposed to usefulness and to honesty is despicable, and to be abhorred.

9. That the constitution of this society be enacted in every article by at least three-fourths of all the members, and that not less than three-fourths of all the members be at all times competent to alter or amend it.

10. That it shall be allowable for any number of the members to practice or follow any trade or calling required for the benefit of the society; and that the artisans of any particular trade do instruct as many of the other members of the society therein, as may be desired by the existing board of management; in return for which the members so teaching, will themselves receive instruction as the wants or circumstances of the society require; reciprocal service for the benefit of the whole being the principle of action throughout the community. In some cases the thanks of the society may be voted to an

individual who evinces a particular readiness, activity, or perseverance in this respect.

11. That the value of time devoted to the concerns of the society in whatever trade, calling, or office, be considered uniform and equal amongst all its male members; and that the average length of a day's work required by the society, exclusively of time for meals or refreshment, throughout the year be eight hours, excepting on particular emergencies when it may be extended to any length required. That it be considered at a subsequent period of the establishment whether the term of eight hours' labour per day may not be reduced to six.

12. That every male member do learn to practice some one necessary or useful trade or calling, in addition to the performance of his duty as an agriculturist or other labourer; that domestic manufactures in as great a variety as possible may be constantly going forward.

13. That no exception whatever shall be taken, or objection made, on account of the religious persuasion or opinions of any member of this society. That the expression of opinion be as free as air. That moral character be solely looked to, this being indispensable to the welfare and happiness of the society collectively and individually.

14. That the wives and children of members be allowed to work at any business or calling that they may be desirous of, at regulated prices and on regulated terms. That the wives of members have the right of voting and of expressing their opinons at all general meetings of the society, and that the females elect each other to all the departments of female employment of the society.

15. That the children of the members be educated upon the Lancasterian plan, and that their education be rendered as liberal and philosophic as possible; to the exclusion however of the retarding and profitless burthen of the dead languages. That every arrangement be made to facilitate the society, recreation, and instruction of the infant children of the members.

16. That the principles of the society be in the strictest sense equal and democratic; that equity and wisdom, and not property may govern. That to this end, as the interest of the proprietor of one share will be equal to that of the proprietor of five or ten, considered as the whole of their vested property respectively, and in a regard to the welfare of their families in

the society, that the rights of the members be in all respects equal, that all votes be equal, and that no member have more than one vote upon any question or occasion whatever.

17. That all disputes, misunderstandings, or dissatisfaction arising between members, be settled by arbitration, the arbitrators to be chosen by ballott, either from the existing board of management or from the members in general.

18. That the society have the power of expelling any member for continued idleness, misconduct, or immorality, by a vote of not less than three-fourths of the whole of the members; and that the property of such individual be valued and paid to him at the time of his quitting the society.

19. That no member of the society shall go to law with, or sue another member for debt, or upon any account whatever; the doing which, shall be deemed on the part of the individual an act of self-expulsion from this society, which, if necessary, shall maintain the defendant's cause.

20. That the society collectively, may purchase the property of any member that may be desirous of withdrawing from it, but that members cannot sell or transfer their shares to each other, the whole of the property, with the exception of household furniture, clothing, books, plate, &c. being the property of the society. That the property in shares of every member being vested in the society, be disposable only by the society at a general meeting; and that a majority of not less than two-thirds of the whole of the members be requisite in all cases of the sale of shares. This restriction is enacted solely to prevent partial interests and obligations; the servitude of the less opulent or poorer members upon the others; and all doubtfulness, perplexity, or confusion in respect to immoveable property, and its consequent disputes.

21. That as a true and equal economy should govern every circumstance of the society, it be enaced, that no more horses or cattle shall be kept by the society than are necessary or useful. That no member shall keep any horse, cow, sheep or pigs for his private use without making a fair allowance to the society for such part of their keep as is derived from the society's property.

22. That the horses, cattle, sheep, pigs, fowls, ducks, geese, &c. the property of the society, be equitably used and participated by all the members; and every article of consumption, when necessary, rated at the time's market price, and every

family debited with the quantity or amount of its demands or consumption; which debit, together with that on account of wearing apparel, &c. be regularly placed against the amount of its earnings, and the balance placed to the account of capital in the society's stock of every family once in every year.

23. That regular and correct accounts be kept of the society's property, and of all its transactions, both internal and external.

24. That convenient stores be kept of all the society's property for disposal to its members, or for sale to the public; and that the primitive and fair principle of barter upon a valuation by the quantity of time and labour employed in production, be acted upon to the utmost extent, both within, and without the society.

25. That every member shall devote his time as regulated by the society to its concerns and interests, and be resident on its land.

26. That after the daily employment of eight hours in the service of the society, every member be wholly at his own disposal, and may employ himself for the remainder of his time in any manner that his inclination may prompt. That the products of the private and extra industry of the members be offered to the society at fair prices, and if purchased by it, that the parties be credited by the amount, or should the society not purchase such produce of the extra industry of its members, that the latter be at liberty, after having offered it to the society, to dispose of it out of the society for their own private benefit.

27. That any member wishing to quit the society may at Christmas in each year give written notice of such wish, upon receiving which, the society must within a month after, make an election of either purchasing the share in the society's stock of such individual and family, or of accepting a substitute for him, subject in either case to the approval of not less than two-thirds of the whole of the members.

28. That a law be enacted to settle and determine the mode in which the widows and children of deceased members shall succeed to their property and be retained in the society, rendering to the widows and children of worthy members the utmost protection, sympathy and kindness; as also the manner of payment to such widows and children as may be desirous of withdrawing from the society.

29. That a piece of ground be enclosed and kept sacred as a burial ground, for such of the members as may prefer being interred within the society's land. That grave stones be erected, and the ground kept in the utmost order. That all funerals be performed by the society and without expense to the afflicted family.

30. That every member of the society do occupy for himself and family in permanency, a cottage and garden, comprised within about a quarter of an acre of ground. That the cottages of the society be built detached, (or two together, if deemed preferable,) all of the same size, and upon the same plan, convenient for a family.

31. That the cottages of the society be built so as to form a spacious square, open at the angles, and open also in the centre of each side, of sufficient width to form streets, in order to provide for the increase of its members without crowding the square. That the square forming the village have a circular enclosure within it, in the centre of which, to be erected with all possible neatness, a Building for Public Worship, and the various purposes of the society. That the enclosure be laid out into walks, planted with fruit and other trees, furnished with benches, and kept with all the neatness of a London square. The enclosure to serve as a play-ground for the children, and for the evening walks and recreations of the members. That the storehouses, granaries, factories, workshops, tannery, brewhouse, barns, stables, cattle-sheds, stack yards, &c. &c. be arranged in the outer square beyond the gardens of the village, and having a good road all round between these and the front of those buildings and appurtenances; which road to be connected with the inner square by streets formed from the angles of both squares, and others from the centre of the sides of each. It is presumed that this plan would embrace contiguity and general convenience, at the same time that offensiveness of all kinds would be removed to a desirable distance. It would perhaps be desirable that the central building were divided on the ground floor into two compartments, and that one of these were exclusively appropriated to religious purposes, the different denominations into which the society might divide itself, occupying it alternately, or by a wise expansion of christian fellowship, or of a sentiment of unanimity, resolve to know no differences of sect, but to use it in common, to read the scriptures in common,

and to allow every reader or officiating member to expound, and to express his opinions, without controversy. An upper spacious room might be made to answer the purposes of a library, a reading, lecture, and school room; and be used for the evening amusements of the members. A small tower furnished with a clock with four faces and a bell, would be a desirable addition to the village Hall, and if the roof or tower were railed round it would form a pleasant observatory.

32. That no member be admitted into, or retained in the society in the separate or exclusive character of a minister of the gospel. That this office be free to all the members, and that it confer no privileges whatever.

33. That the growth of the most useful kinds of roots and vegetables be as much an object with the society as the cultivation of grain, by which the time and labour of the members in raising vegetables in their gardens will be materially lessened, and as by this means a more abundant supply of food for the cattle and live stock will be provided, particularly for winter use. That the cultivation of fruit trees be also an object of attention with the society.

34. That the society's stock be valued, and all accounts appertaining to the society and to individuals be settled and balanced once in every year, and all surplus capital invested in the stock of the United States Bank in the names of all the members.

35. That in order to adopt and preserve the best economy in the society, agricultural, manufacturing and domestic, a friendly correspondence be maintained with all other similar communities as far as circumstances will allow, and that a deputation of two members be occasionally made to visit Harmony or any other community, for the purpose of obtaining any particular information that the society may require.

————

The author of the foregoing sketch would be permitted to explain that he does not suppose that a society formed upon its principles would constitute a perfect *ELYSIUM*, he being fully aware that troubles, vexation and imperfection rest upon every thing human; but he would express it as his decided opinion that a society of honorable individuals, of regular business habits, each having the welfare of his family and

35

that of the society at heart, could not fail of being productive
of immense security, comfort and advantage to its members.
The compact would be simply an equitable partnership in all
the essentials of life and means of happiness.   The foregoing is
designed merely as an outline to be corrected and perfected
by the joint labour of the associates and the results of experience.

FINIS.

Plummer and Brewis, Printers, Love Lane, Eastcheap.

OWENISM

RENDERED CONSISTANT

WITH OUR

CIVIL AND RELIGIOUS INSTITUTIONS,

OR

A MODE OF FORMING

Societies for Mutual Benefit

ON

RATIONAL AND PRACTICAL PRINCIPLES,

WITHOUT THE ASSISTANCE OF THE RICH, OR THE NECESSITY OF BORROWING ONE SHILLING.

Addressed to the Working Classes.

By JAMES HAMILTON,

AUTHOR OF THE HAMILTONIAN SYSTEM.

LONDON:

PRINTED BY G. SCHULZE, POLAND STREET;

AND TO BE HAD OF ALL BOOKSELLERS IN TOWN AND COUNTRY.

—

1825.
Price Sixpence.

TO THE JOURNEYMEN MECHANICS.

FRIENDS AND FELLOW CITIZENS,

THERE is nothing learned, nothing profound, nothing metaphysical in the discourse which I intend addressing you this evening; it would therefore be more pleasing to me, and less fatiguing, to offer you the substance of it, in the extempore language of my heart, than to present it you in the form of a written speech.*—There is, however, so much danger of misrepresentation, the subject has already been treated by so many, and is in itself, so truly important, that the fear of leading you into error, or of being misunderstood by you or by the public, has induced me not only to write, but to print the observations which a desire to promote your happiness individually, and the general good of my fellow men, have suggested.

This mode of address has at least this important advantage over extempore speaking, that every person who hears this discourse, and thinks it worth his future consideration may, for sixpence, read, examine and reflect on it at his leisure.

---

* It was intended to make this pamphlet the subject of a public lecture.

OWENISM

&c., &c., &c.

MY own existence, or the light of heaven, does not appear to me more evident than that every man, the moment he is born into this world, has a natural, indefeasable right to have his wants supplied till he is able to work, and that, when able to work, if willing, he has the same natural right to convenient food, clothes and lodging. Every creature that God has made comes into the world in the enjoyment of these rights, and no other creature but man is deprived of them while it exists. To each of the innumerable classes of beings which the Deity has created, he has usually allowed one species of food, and one mode of attaining it, for which instinct is in each an infallible guide ; but to man, endowed with reason and the knowledge of his Creator, he has given all other creatures for food, besides the means of supplying innumerable aliments from the earth. Labour is indeed enjoined on man, but labour is to man a blessing, without which existence would be insupportable ; his existence, is, therefore, made to depend on it : but with labour his supplies of every necessary and comfort of life are tenfold greater, and more secure than those of the creatures subjected to him. Man in his natural state, and without the assistance of accumulated experience, combining his talents with those of his fellow men, might provide himself with food, clothes and habitation, infinitely beyond his utmost wants, and still have more than two thirds of his time to devote to his own instruction, to the promotion of his own happiness, to the perfectibility of his nature, and the extension of his knowledge. It is, however, a melancholy truth, that few exam-

1**

ples of combination or association for such useful
purposes, are found among men. But in all ages, we
find man combine with man for the purpose of destroying his fellow, and the talent and industry used on
such occasions, and the success of them, demonstrate
what he might do for his own happiness, if a like degree
of talent and industry were used to promote it. This,
however, is not the case. But our object is not to find
fault with man in any of his relations, but to point
out his powers, and the means of using these powers,
not as heretofore, to mutual injury, but to mutual
good. To this end, let us enquire into the present
state of society; not according to the theories of economists or politicians, who seem to think the evils
sustained by the greater part of mankind, inherent in
their nature and beyond the power of remedy, but as
men alive to the wants of our fellow men, and to
the hope of relieving them.

As men having the use of reason, and speaking from
the evidence of our senses, what do these senses declare
to us with regard to our relative situations? And first,
as to the working classes? Those whom I have characterized as being able and willing to work? Have they
universally a superabundance of all the good things of
life, and sufficient leisure for the improvement of their
intellectual faculties? Their labour is indubitably more
than sufficient for these purposes, does it produce this
effect?

In answer to this, we have the evidence of all our
senses, that the working classes, those by whose labour every comfort of life is produced for those who
do not work, are themselves the most wretched of God's
creatures, insomuch, that the dog, the ox, the swine,
the fowls of heaven and the fishes of the sea, are in
comparison with great numbers of them, in situations
truly enviable. Upon a more minute enquiry, we find
that a family of the man, his wife and three or four
children, subsist, on an average of the working people
of England, on about ten or twelve shillings per week;
that, if there are many workmen who earn more, there

are thousands, nay tens' of thousands, who earn less, and who, from the circumstances of their situation, have this sum only wherewith to pay for food, lodging, covering by night and day for five or six persons; instruction or provision for accident or old age, are entirely out of the question; in all these cases, they become almost inevitably a burden to the rich. We find that, besides this class of men, able and willing to work, and deriving from their labour a miserable existence, there are thousands and tens' of thousands of others, once able and willing to work, but from sickness or old age, or vice, the usual consequence of poverty and ignorance, are now in poor houses, work houses, penitentiaries or prisons, begging their bread from door to door, living on the wages of prostitution, or the uncertain gains of theft and robbery, a burden to themselves and to society, the disgrace and infamy of the human race—to these we must add a like number of orphans abandoned by their parents, unable to provide for them, and some hundreds of thousands whose sole employment is to kill their fellow men at the command of their officers, and who for doing this or being always ready to do it, are assured without work, a habitation, food and clothes. Such is the state of ninety-nine hundredths of the human race. These are what I have called the working classes of society, that is to say, those whose labours alone produce all the comforts of the other one hundredth part, to whom we will now refer. This one hundredth part consists of kings, princes, nobles, clergy, gentlemen, merchants, farmers, masters of manufactories, and master tradesmen, officers in the army and navy, instructors in the different sciences, factors, brokers, stewards, &c., &c., all these possess the comforts of life to such a degree that it may be asserted with truth, that the far greater part have them in greater abundance than Solomon in all his glory—they are literally clothed in purple and fine linen and fare sumptuously every day. I speak of the very lowest of this one hundredth part, as to some of the higher, there are individuals who consume in a single supper, or lose on a single throw of the dice, as much as would provide

abundantly for a hundred families a whole year ! such a
nobleman has estates kept solely for his amusement,
which, if given up to garden tillage, for the benefit of
the working classes, would provide for a thousand families ! nor is this state of things likely soon to end ; the
inequality of fortunes becomes greater and greater every
day. The poverty of the poor becomes every day more
difficult to redress ; the riches of the rich almost naturally augment. In our time the estates of most of
the noblemen of Great Britain have nearly doubled in
value, and hundreds of new nobles have sprung up with
fortunes as large as the old. Nay the riches of all these
must augment if they do not wantonly squander them.
At the moment I write, the British nation is on all
hands allowed to be in the most prosperous situation
she has ever known, the national wealth has augmented
one hundred fold within the last century, and at this
moment the capitalists of Britain having lent their millions to all the princes of Europe, even to satiety, are
obliged to travel into another hemisphere, to find some
one willing to hire a part of their treasures : but all
this is only true of the one hundredth part I have just
described, for all this prosperity has not added one
ounce more of daily food to the scanty pittance of the
sons of labour, nor a particle of clothing to cover his
nakedness and shield him from the inclemency of the
weather.

Such is society, such is man in the most favored, the
most truly polished, the most truly enlightened, the
most religious, the most moral, the most wise, the most
liberal, the most generous, the most charitable, the most
free nation under heaven! what is his situation every
where else ?

It was necessary for you, my friends, that I should
lay this picture before you without palliation on the one
hand or exaggeration on the other ; it was necessary
that you should see and feel that, while your labour produces to others all the necessaries and comforts of life,
you are yourselves wholly deprived of the latter, and
have only a very scanty allowance of the former. While
it is demonstrable that the labour executed by you,

would be more than sufficient to produce a superabundance
of both for every human being in these realms ; and that
this superabundance, as it is impossible to consume it
rationally, is now squandered in the maintenance of every
species of vice and folly, and in the production and
nourishment of every infirmity of body and mind in
many of those for whom your labours are exerted.

We come now then to this grand question : Is this
state of things, so evidently contrary to reason, to religion, to the happiness of all, is it *just ?* because if it
be unjust, if the rich have no right to their riches, the
shortest and simplest way would be to take them from
them ; I hasten to answer the question—It is MOST JUST.
—It is indeed, contrary to the happiness of all, even of
the rich, but it is in perfect conformity to the rules
of justice between man and man, and with this only have
we to do here.

Let us prove this—However general be the poverty
of the working classes for whom I write, there are no
doubt, among you some few who have derived from their
parents or relatives, some little sum of money, a piece
of land, cabin, &c., there are others who giving up
every enjoyment and determined to save something from
the little they earn for the purpose of assuring their sub-
sistance and that of their family, in distress or old age,
have, after months or years, scraped together a few
pounds. With the possession of this property, they
may be assimilated to the rich, as they possess more
than their present wants require, do you think it would
be right and just to deprive them of it ? certainly not.
—Suppose that by a continuance of such a course of
life for 15, 20, or 30 years, during which they have
toiled with incessant application and given bread to
thousands, they amass a considerable fortune, do you think
it would be right to deprive them of it then ? certainly
not—suppose that fatigued by years and labour, they
at length resign their business to others, and retire to
enjoy for a very few years the fruits of their industry,
shall we despoil them of it then ? by no means—suppose
a person of this class die, and leave a property to his son,

shall we take it from this latter and turn him out on the
world as destitute as was his father when he began it ?
certainly not—who then would labour ? shall we take
it from the grand-son, or the great grand-son ?
by no means, this would be a horrible injustice—so it
would, my friends, but so is the property of all the rich
of this country and of every other, with few exceptions,
acquired, either by actual personal industry or inheri-
tance, and if you think these modes of acquiring riches
a just, a legitimate title to keep them, there is no hope
of obtaining *justly* a participation *in* the riches of others,
farther than you now enjoy it; nay *let* us go farther,
suppose a man amass wealth by fraud or knavery, if
the law do not take cognizance of his actions and punish
him during his life, the son to whom his wealth arrives
in regular succession has a just and lawful title to his
riches. Thus it is, that from the prince on the throne,
who, whatever and whoever were his ancestors, has himself come to the enjoyment of it in regular succession
according to the laws of the realm, to the lowest of his
subjects, the man who by personal industry, the favor
of others, or both, possesses riches, is justly entitled
to hold possession of them, and whatever be the wants
of the poor man, he cannot justly lay those wants at
the door of the rich, or accuse him of the poverty or
wretchedness of his situation.

Having acquitted the rich on the score of *justice and
equity*, let us try them now on the score of charity and
benevolence.—Have the rich wholly abandoned the poor ?
have they refused to succour him in his distress ? on
the contrary, we are obliged to acknowledge that hundreds of thousands of pounds, are every year *voluntarily*
subscribed, besides many millions *legally* paid, to meet
his different wants ; the land is covered with hospitals,
with asylums, with benevolent institutions of every name
and nature, to provide if *possible* for every want of
every class of the poor. But the millions thus yearly
expended, though they indubitably diminish the cases
of extreme necessity, yet the number to be relieved,
passes even the powers of the rich, without overturning

all the existing laws of society, and doing injury instead of good, by attempting to relieve the great mass of society from the necessity of working, which we have begun by asserting, is not a curse but a blessing, and which, if removed momentarily by a general division of riches, would cause immediate, inevitable and universal confusion and destruction. On the score of *benevolence* and *charity* as well as on that of justice and equity, we must therefore also bring in a verdict of full and complete acquittal of the rich ; nor can we reasonably expect more from them than they have done and continue to do.

But a remedy has been proposed whose application depending on the rich, and having been rejected by them, would seem to invalidate this verdict. Mr. Robert Owen has spent several years in propagating a plan which he assures us would bring a remedy to every evil, would banish poverty, ignorance and crime from the world, and bring in an universal reign of plenty, peace and happiness. His proposal is, that the rich should give up their property to the poor, or at least such a part of it at first, as would enable the poor to get the remainder afterwards, or render it useless in the hands of the present proprietor, and in the mean time to become their partners not only in trade, but their inmates and daily companions, living with them under the same roof, eating at the same table, clothed with the same costume, partaking of the same occupations, enjoyments and amusements, and in all things living with them on a footing of perfect equality ! That is to say, that the different characters of the rich, whom I have described as having become such by a course of self denial, virtue and useful industry, or those who have derived their riches from parents who owed them originally to like causes, should voluntarily relinquish the fruit of so many years' labour, and all the advantages of their situation and education, the refinements of social life and intellectual advancement, and become the companions of those, whose ignorance, idleness, drunkenness, or other vices would have rendered them objects of contempt and abhorrence in the very lowest state in which they or their ancestors had ever found themselves ! such persons by Mr. Owens' plan, they were to constitute their partners in their *own* property, and with such, dividing their toils and their labours, condemn themselves and families to dwell in habits of friendship and intimacy the rest of their lives ! Such was, in a few words, the proposition of a man esteemed for his benevolent intentions ; and who, on the credit of these intentions, obtained a patient hearing from thousands, who, while they hailed with delight the general idea of remedying the miseries of the poor, could not think that object could be justly accomplished by depriving the rich of their property by fraud or violence, and who had sense enough to perceive, that they would never give it up spontaneously.

The plan failed, but as it may be again revived, as there is even now an *operative society* in progress which Mr. Owen assures us he will return to this country, for the purpose of organizing, it may be worth while to enquire into the probable consequences of such a scheme when brought to maturity.

Mr. Owen contemplates, if I mistake not, forming communities of about 1500 or 2000 persons with a borrowed capital of one or £200,000 ; let us take the smaller number, 1500 adults from the lowest class of society, without education and consequently without those principles which are usually derived from it—let us suppose these men transplanted *at once* from labour and misery, to affluence and comparative ease, working four or five hours only per day instead of twelve, possessing fine clothes, fine apartments and every luxury of meat and drink. Mr. Owen assures us that a man in such circumstances would immediately become sober if a drunkard before ; an honest man, if a thief ; filled with charity and compassion for his fellow men, even though before he had been a brawler, a striker, a very Thurtel. Only surround him, says Mr. Owen, with different and *favourable* circumstances which shall do away the interest he has to be vicious, and that moment the natural goodness of the human heart will shew itself, and the

individual before a devil, becomes an angel of light—so
says Mr. Owen. But what says experience?—About
forty years ago, a hatter, of the name of Taylor, who
had a shop on Tower-hill, got £10,000 in the lottery—
did he use it according to Mr. Owen's theory?—immediately on the reception of the news, he threw his hats
out of doors to the populace, whom he also plentifully
regaled with porter—indulged in every excess for one
year, at the end of which, having spent every shilling, he
was obliged to begin hatting again. He was only one,
suppose 1500 men, taken from a much lower sphere of
life and raised at once to conscious affluence, who is it
that is acquainted with uneducated human nature, will
believe, that they could resist the temptation to make a
wrong use of it? who is it can believe that they would not
ruin by their irregularity, drunkenness and even dishones-
ty, the establishment founded on the hope that they would
labour even fours hours a day? Well but, says Mr. Owen,
we will educate them, when? when they shall have already accomplished all that could be hoped from the most
perfect education? I have heard of no idea, no plan of
teaching adults, and if not taught, and if not trained to
discipline, to right principles, to right ideas, to real and
general information of men and things, before they are
put in possession of riches, or are rendered their own
masters whether to work or not, it appears to me but too
probable, that they would use their liberty to gratify the
very worst propensities of their nature, and at best would
resemble much more the hatter above mentioned, than the
new and rational creature surounded by new and favourable circumstances as depicted by Mr. Owen. As a man of
business, wishing to derive a fair interest for my money,
I would not therefore take a share in such an establishment, and I have much difficulty in believing that men
of business generally will be found to embark in it.
Benevolent men should I think be counted on still less;
what should we think of that man's benevolence who, on
Sunday evening should enter the different brandy shops
of this city and present every son of labour, he should
there meet, five shillings, in hope that they would im-
2

14

mediately become sober and take it home to their suffering families ? Should we seriously think he had rendered
them a service ? but if he should come the week after,
armed with a law process, to compel them to return it,
should we not think him a monster of cruelty ? It would
however be only the counterpart of men lending to associations of mechanics unprepared for the reception of
wealth. In every point of view in which Mr. Owen has
proposed his plan to the acceptance of the public I
conceive it impracticable, irrational and mischievous.—
But while I thus deliver my opinion of the scheme as
proposed by Mr. Owen; justice, truth, and I will add
inclination, oblige me to acknowledge that a more
sublime idea never entered into the heart of man than
the general principle of the " *co-operation of the working classes for mutual benefit.*" To Mr. Owen is the
honour of this idea due, *he* has proposed it, *he* has called
the attention of mankind to it for years. It is the plan
of bringing this idea into effective operation, as proposed
by Mr. Owen, to which I object—not to the principle
itself. And it was only after reasoning with Mr. Owen
and his friends, after combatting his scheme and endeavouring to shew the fallacy of it for above two years,
recommending and entreating him to organize the idea on
some plan consistent with received ideas, with our institutions, civil and religious (of all which his scheme is plainly subversive), that I resolved to attempt the herculean
task myself ; to detach the precious principle of mutual
co-operation from the personal plans and personal opinions of Mr. Owen and his followers, and endeavour to
apply it to such a combination of labour, talent, intellect and means as should not have the government of
the country as well as every man of property, influence,
or virtue in it for its enemy ; as should not launch the
uneducated artizan into ease and affluence all at once,
as should not nurture in his breast, the idea of his being
able to live without working; but combining his gradual
acquisition of wealth, with his gradual acquisition of
knowledge, and both with moderate labour, should make
his education and change of circumstances go hand in

hand and his acquisition of wealth, progress with his fitness for its reception. Besides, I conceive it important to the success of any scheme for the amelioration of the condition of the poor, that it should be the consequence of their own good conduct, and not brought about by the power of the rich.—In the scheme which I am about to propose, the artizan is required to exert at the outset, order, economy, industry and a general moral conduct, founded not on a vain and false philosophy, but on religion, the only true source of a right conduct, and he can continue to possess the good held out to him, only by a patient continuance in the practice of these virtues for years. It would be absurd to take the vicious as the subjects of an experiment, the success of which is to depend on their own virtues and good conduct. In short, I consider vice the fundamental cause of all the misery of man, but leaving the task of extirpating it where it has taken root, to others, I endeavour to prevent its introduction into the society I wish to form. I take uneducated men, because I cannot procure any other willing to work, and because I possess the means of educating them in a shorter time and by a simpler and more effectual process, than any other man living.

The intention of this discourse is not to discuss the principles of good or bad systems of education, but the mechanic is perhaps a stranger to the discussions which have taken place, during the last two years, relative to the Hamiltonian system, and may not be sorry to be put in possession of the following facts.—On the 16th of May last, a few benevolent and enlightened individuals, with a view of ascertaining the effect of the system of teaching which I profess, subscribed £200 towards defraying the expense of boarding and educating for six months, ten boys, who were then taken from a charity school of the lowest order, and put under my care. The boys were examined by several gentlemen called together for that purpose, and found to be ignorant of every language under heaven—they could with difficulty read the English testament, and had never read any thing else—they were questioned as to the meaning of the most common words, in the English language, such as " Grammar," and " Latin," and had never heard of either.—It is, I believe, intended to authenticate the progress of these boys, by a public examination at the end of six months. In the mean time I may be allowed to state that they know more French, Italian and Latin than is usually acquired on the common plan in three years. They translate the commentaries of Cesar, the Recueil Choisi and Rolandi's Anedotti, the two first especially, with a degree of facility and accuracy of grammatical analysis of which the schools offer few examples, after any length of time whatever.

I had calculated the expence of these boys at £500, but notwithstanding the loss they have already occasioned me, the desire of rendering more palpable the difference between the common mode of teaching, and that which I profess, makes me ardently wish to keep four or five of them six months more. In that time they would acquire three languages more, the Greek, German and Spanish, making with their mother tongue, seven languages in all; I do not say they would have a perfect knowledge of any one of them, their age, intellect and previous ignorance forbid this, besides, a perfect knowledge of any language can only be attained by much reading, and they neither have read nor would be able to read in the following six months more than their class books—but these class books would be so numerous, and they would know them so perfectly, that I am conscious I do not err in believing they would know more of these languages in that time, than is now acquired or could be *generally* acquired in our schools in ten years' painful and disgusting study.—I say *could* be acquired in that time, for we all know, nothing of this nature has ever yet been accomplished in any length of tuition, and will probably never be even attempted while the present school system of ordering to learn instead of teaching pervades this and the other nations of the civilized world.

While thousands are every day subscribed to the endless charities to which I have before alluded, shall these five boys, thus brought so far on their way in the road of science, be obliged to return to the wretched employments of their parents, because there are not found in Britain, seven more individuals (for no more formed the first subscription) as generous as the first ?—I trust the rich will forgive this appeal, which I believe will not be a vain one, as it will offer another opportunity of redeeming the pledge I have given, that they do for the poor in every position and on every occasion, the utmost that can be hoped from them. It is not for me, I want not to *gain* by it, but 'to make the experiment beneficial to the subjects of it as well as to the nation at large ; subscriptions will be received at Messrs. Smith, Payne and Smith, at Messrs. Willis, Percival and Co., or at 62, Gower Street.—It is probable few of the bankers would refuse the trouble of it.—I return to my subject.

True it is, I intend to make the members of the society pay for their education as they pay for every thing else connected with their prosperity as a company, and it will be the glory of this society, that they pay for every thing, that they owe every thing to their own exertions, that the rich contribute not one shilling. But in making the artizan pay for the education he receives, do I not give up all idea of disinterestedness ? I would ask 'in return, what obliges me to disinterestedness ? it is not here required of me. By the combination of industry and talent into which I introduce every member of the society, he possesses ample means of paying for his education, nor is it to be presumed that he would prefer having it gratuitously ; whether the extra remuneration I require be unreasonable or unjust, may be gathered from the following fact. My pupils generally pay five shillings a lesson of one hour, and at that price I have more than any other teacher, and yet I am willing to devote my time to the instruction of persons whom it will probably be more difficult to instruct than my pupils generally at the rate of two pence an hour !—for one shilling a week, for six lessons, amounts to no more.—I now proceed to develope the plan of the association I propose.

2**

I have heard that the fortune of the first Mr. Horrocks thus began, he was a journeyman muslin weaver in 1793, and was, with thousands of others, thrown out of work at the commencement of the French war; but he had saved £10 from the produce of his previous labour; with this he bought cotton and manufactured coloured bordered handkerchiefs; not being able to sell the first parcel he manufactured, in the country, he came up to London and had them sold by auction; they left him a handsome profit: so, after making an agreement with the auctioneer to sell as fast as the goods arrived, and to be permitted to draw for the amount as fast as they were sold, he returned to the country, and in the course of two or three years manufactured, it is supposed, above one hundred thousand dozens of them. Beginning with so scanty a capital, he employed in a short time several thousand workmen, from whose labour he amassed a princely fortune. Now, if Mr. Horrocks, instead of waiting till pushed by necessity, to reflect on his own powers, instead of waiting till he was deprived of work, had, in conjunction with ninety-nine other steady men, began this scheme of manufacturing six months before, could not these one hundred men, have effected the same thing with an infinitely greater probability of success? And would it not be more useful to the nation at large to possess now one hundred families in comparative affluence and respectability, than one colossus of wealth, however estimable his public or private character may be? The Arkrights, the Peels and a hundred others, have amassed fortunes in nearly the same way as Mr. Horrocks. Now if the workmen, instead of working for these gentlemen, had worked for themselves, would not the same result, or even a much greater, as regards wealth, have been produced, if the business were conducted with the same propriety and order as in the hands of one person. Here then is what is to be sought, such an union of time, labour, talent and capital, as will enable five hundred persons or more to conduct for their own account and emolument, a business, or several businesses, which they now conduct for the interest and emolument of their masters contenting themselves to receive scarcely one tenth of what they produce. At least Mr. Robert Owen, who is himself one of those persons who has been enriched by the labour of others, and whose calculation may therefore be fairly relied on, asserted in his last lecture at the Mechanic's Institution, that the workman generally does not receive one tenth of what his labour produces, and if, as I think it but fair, we add the power of the steam engine to that of the workmen employed to give that power effect, I think he does not essentially err. Such an union does not appear so difficult, as to give the members of it such an education as may assimilate them to the present possessors of wealth, and be a security for their making a proper use of it—but this also, I conceive, may be accomplished.

In order that the simplest mind may comprehend my plan, instead of five hundred, let us take for example, one hundred taylors, good workmen, now in full employ, unmarried, from the age of twenty to thirty, of good moral characters, handsome of person, and willing to obtain and pay one shilling per week for a liberal education, and four shillings per week for the formation of a partnership fund or capital. Let us suppose these men associated under the direction of one enlightened head or partner, and the business conducted by a committee of their own body. Journeymen taylors earn thirty-six shillings per week ; they would not find it difficult to live for five shillings per week less. The four shillings per week lodged in the hands of the head partner, and by him in the hands of a banker, each week, would at the end of three months amount to £260.

With £260 in hand, and a certain revenue of £20 weekly, exclusive of full pay as journeymen for themselves, the head partner would now state their case to the public, and propose to work on such terms as would interest the public in their behalf. A committee of five, chosen from a knowledge of their superior talents and good conduct, and who, during the three preceding months, had most profited by their teacher's instructions, would act as the ostensible agents of the company for perfecting the orders received. They would buy their cloths for cash only, and sell *only* in the same manner, they would charge a profit of 5 per cent on the cloths, journeymen's wages only for making, with the addition of from five to eight shillings on a suit of clothes, according to their fineness and value. *The books of the society would be always open to the public, so that every individual who chose to buy his clothes from them would have the conviction that there was no delusion; that he had every thing on the terms offered him, that is to say, 20 per cent cheaper than he can now procure them.* I think it cannot be doubted that a society of this nature would almost immediately obtain a sufficient patronage to occupy the whole company of one hundred hands; but they would *begin* only, by taking from their present situation, a *few* of the partners, the rest would be taken as the business increased. The time would, however, soon arrive when the whole would be fully occupied. One hundred good taylors fully occupied would manufacture one hundred and fifty suits of clothes per week, leaving an average profit on cloth and making of eight shillings per suit, and producing £60 a week; each workman receiving exclusively his usual pay of journeman's wages, out of which he continues to pay weekly to the general fund four shillings, making with the above sum £80 per week; from which the rent, advertising, and other general expenses, say £10 per week (in order to provide for sickness if any) are to be deducted; £70 a week would therefore remain to the credit of the general fund, which at the end of one year would amount to £3,640! From the moment that all the partners would be employed for account of the association, one hour per day would be diminished from their hours of labour, for the purposes of education, and this, at the end of eighteen months, would be found sufficient to make every individual of them good English scholars, and to give them a knowledge

of at least two other languages, besides the acquisition
of general information, by hearing lectures on history,
geography and other sciences, attending courses of physical experiments, reading, &c., and the attainment
of the less important accomplishments of refined life,
music, drawing, dancing, &c., as each might be inclined to cultivate them. I have said a society of one
hundred persons would possess at the end of one year
from the time of its complete organization £3,640 at
their banker's. But it would be wrong to let this sum
remain idle there; as soon as a sum of £500 was collected, premises should be hired sufficiently large to
lodge and board the members comfortably, and render
their education more easy; this would also diminish
their expences considerably, as the members would pay
neither for lodging nor furniture, which would be provided from the general fund, and thus having their food
cooked together, and buying their provisions wholesale, it is evident they would save 50 per cent.

The next use of the capital would be, the purchase or
hire of a farm; this well stocked, would in a little time,
furnish drink, vegetables, flesh and fowl in abundance,
but to enjoy these things as well as the other advantages
of their continually accumulating riches, the aid and
co-operation of other trades now become absolutely necessary. To build, in town and country, convenient
residences and workshops, to fertilize the farm, and draw
from it all the resources possible; bricklayers, carpenters, smiths, weavers, farmers, gardeners, &c., become
necessary and ought not to be *hired*. Now it would
have been just as easy for the head partner to *begin* by
associating to himself an equal or proportionate number of each of these different trades, as with a hundred
taylors, for with whichsoever of these trades he might
begin, he would almost immediately find, that for a
perfect society, a reunion of all the trades is absolutely
necessary; that far from being in each other's way, as
in the present state of society is often found to be the
case, there would, on the contrary, almost immediately
result from their union, such advantages, as the imagi-

nation is really startled to pourtray for fear of entering into what is called the romantic part of Mr. Owen's system, a very millennium of social happiness. This much, is at least sufficiently obvious, that applying the same principles to one hundred carpenters, who would, under the direction of their head partner and a committee of five, chosen, as from the taylors, work for the public for journeymen's wages, and a very small retribution by way of profit, it is evident I say, that this new company, affording a like security for the honorable direction of their labours, would meet the same patronage, and derive the same advantages, as the one we have described. The same may be said of a company of bricklayers, smiths, &c., but the reunion of all these different trades, would alone enable them to effect one great principle of the association, to do all within themselves, by *partners*, and as far as possible, neither *to hire the services of any person, or to go in debt.* It being an undeviating principle of the association here recommended, a principle of vital importance, *never to take, or give credit.*—The taylor must be paid, on bringing home his cloathes ; the carpenter, the bricklayer, the smith, &c., at the end of the week.

In this simple, straight forward scheme, there is no need of capitalists: the mechanic has his fortune in his own hands ; if he is wise, he will not borrow one shilling. The rich man who comes into society with the poor, comes in as a creditor, he must have power, emolument and privileges different from others and thence the destruction of that PERFECT EQUALITY which can alone render the association here alluded to permanent, useful or happy. I have mentioned the taylors as a body of men less likely to realize a fortune by united efforts, than any other, in order that demonstrating the practicability of it, by their example, bricklayers, carpenters, silk and cotton weavers, smiths, cotton spinners, machine makers, farmers, gardiners, &c., may attempt the same easy and efficient mode of escaping from misery, ignorance and vice, and rise to independance, instruction, comfort and affluence. I do not hesitate to declare my opinion that the man who becomes the member of such a society as I have depicted, carried on, on principles of rectitude, honor and religion, lays a better foundation for the good education and happiness of his children, than he who leaves to each an independent fortune; the latter will be ever subject to 10,000 chances, the former has the guarantee of 500 well informed, affluent and honorable families; and let us remember, that while we are grateful to Mr. Robert Owen, for bringing up the idea of communities, they are when undertaken on rational principles nothing more than the renewal of the first christian societies, who had all things in common, and realized the happiness of all. In forming them, let us have these societies in view, let us be careful as they were, whom we receive. What man of sober habits, would wish to become the partner of a drunkard? who would be the associate of a liar, a cheat, an impostor, an extortioner, a man without religion, without principle? honest religious men of good reputation for sobriety and industry, should *alone be received*, and should any others contrive to come into it, let it be provided by a fundamental law that a majority of all the members voting the exclusion of any particular one, that one shall cease to be a member, but will have the privilege of selling out to a person approved by the society. Men of bad principles are willing enough to embark in business with honest men, but honest men should be careful how they associate with such characters, it never fails to become their ruin. In such a society the scientific, social, religious education of the members themselves, and their children is, after the attainment of necessary food and clothes, the most urgent, the most important want, the most sacred duty. Now if they are of different sentiments in religion or if many have no religion at all, this would become very difficult. In order to conciliate every body, the principles communicated to the children, would under pretence of being liberal, become loose and relaxed.—Let then the communities be all of one profession; church of England with church of England,

methodists with methodists, presbyterians with presbyterians, catholics with catholics, jews with jews. There
appears however, no very great inconvenience in admitting into the same community, members of the
church of England, and methodists, between whom
there is no essential difference. The moral and religious
habits of the quakers already formed, would render
them most valuable members in such a society. These
three last would be likely to agree with the general
doctrines to be expounded to them, and in the other
views of scientific or social education. Having elucidi-
dated my plan with regard to a small number, of one
trade only, I return to the elucidation of the plan in a
reunion of different trades, to the number of about 500
unmarried, healthful, well made men, from twenty to
thirty years, which is the society I project. Why I
take such men in preference to others, is plain enough.
The weak, the deformed, the diminutive, the sickly,
the burdened with families are really much more to
be pitied than these, and need more immediate relief
from association, if association can procure it; but the
society I propose to establish, is not a charitable institution but a manufacturing and commercial company. It is
indeed intended to point out to the working classes, a
remedy for all their evils if they will adapt the principle generally, but in order to insure the success of
the first experiment, I must *choose* my partners. Now
if I choose the sick, must not the funds of the society
instead of increasing the riches of the society, go to
their relief ? the same may be said of those burdened
with families, &c. Besides, *riches*, which a society
like this must almost of necessity create, are a very
uncertain advantage in the hands of the ignorant. I
choose, therefore, men susceptible of instruction, because
their intellectual improvement is the most important
part of my plan. I choose them without families that
we may not risk having their families to educate before
the society be in a comfortable situation to do it.
It is intended to fit the members of this society for the
right enjoyment of riches by a liberal education before

they come into the possession of riches, and if they were previously married, and married to ignorant or perhaps vicious women, this would become very difficult, if not impossible ; but, after giving them this education and riches, it is also intended to provide for them virtuous, beautiful, and accomplished wives

I return to the details of the primitive organization of the society, and in order to shew the facility with which this may be effected I suppose that there are at this moment ready to enter the association

> 100 taylors, such as I have described,
> 100 bricklayers and plaisterers,
> 100 carpenters and joiners,
> 50 smiths, of all kinds,
> 100 silk weavers,
> 50 of all other trades, hatters, shoemakers, cabinet makers, &c.

_____

500 unmarried healthful men.

from 20 to 30 *now fully employed,* and likely to be so ; of moral, religious and industrious habits, none other to be received.

Each of these first gives his name as candidate, so as to allow time for enquiry into his character.   If approved in the first instance by the head partner, to whom application is to be made, and afterwards, by the committees appointed for this purpose, he is received as a member, and pays weekly five shillings, of which, one for his education, and four, towards the partnership fund. The first payment will be. made on Saturday the 12th of November, from which day the partnership will date, and every member received after that day, will have to pay up the arrears of five shillings per week, till the day of his reception. These 500 men, by the act of association, *guarantee to each other convenient food, raiment, habitation and instruction for themselves, their wives and their children in sickness and in health for life, together with a full, perfect, and equal participation in all the rights, benefits, im*

3

*munities, privileges, advantages and comforts of the
society, as the fundamental principle of their union,*
of which no individual can be deprived but for positive
crime, such as reiterated drunkenness, habitual swear-
ing, theft, idleness, or other crimes of like mischievous
nature ; and after a fair trial and the vote of a majority
of his partners. By the first of January there would be
a few hundred pounds in the bankers' hands, this would
suffice to begin the operations of the society *as journeymen to the public* in the mode mentioned with regard to taylors. A large house, in a central situation,
should be now taken which would serve in the beginning,
as a warehouse, and for the meeting of the committees
appointed to agree for work, to appoint the men to effect
it and to oversee its execution ; till such a house be taken, the committees of the different trades, would meet
at the house of the head partner, who immediately on
the formation and signature of the act of partnership,
by from 60 to 80 partners would publish the prospectus
of each set of workmen, and endeavor to obtain orders
for them to commence the first Monday in January.
There is reason to suppose, that by that day, the full
number of mechanics of all descriptions would be filled
up, and in that case, the weekly payment to the partnership fund would be at four shillings per week
for 500 members, £100—supposing, that on the average of the three following months, 250 of the partners
have employment from the society, the profit on their
work, exclusive of the four shillings per week, would
amount at eight shillings per week, per man, to £100
per week, which for 13 weeks, would produce a total
sum of £2,600. A lot of ground of at least *one acre*
should now be purchased, or taken on lease and built on,
or if there exist a building, it should be fitted up to the
purposes of the partnership, by the formation of immense
halls for dormitories for the whole partnership, a kitchen,
dining, school and assembly rooms, and lodgings for the
head partner and his family, (every member of which
would assist in the education of the partners), the whole,
with such a front as should command respect. The so-

ciety wou'd use the building in time, as warehouses and show rooms, or a general bazaar for all their manufactures. The next month would be enough to organize the cooking, to prepare iron or wooden bedsteads, with a straw and woollen mattrass to each, so that each man should have his separate and comfortable bed ; the summer would be taken to render this dwelling comfortable as far as real substantial conveniences could make it, and to establish an excellent table for every member on the cheapest possible terms, buying every thing wholesale, and for ready cash. I have now calculated the result of four months from the commencement of effective operations, and have supposed only half the number of partners employed by the society ; from this moment, say from the 1st of May 1826, we may count 500 partners fully employed ; for I entertain not the slightest doubt, that this society would obtain an almost instantaneous preference from the public over any private master. Who is it, that knowing he can have a dozen honest and conscientious bricklayers, excellent workmen, willing to work for journeymen's wages, with the trifling addition of one shilling and sixpence a day for each, under the direction of a company associated on moral and religious principles, responsible for the effective performance of their duty, will not prefer them to the measuring system of the present day, in which they pay at least treble journeymen's wages ? but should the person hiring, prefer to have his business done by the piece, this will be also undertaken, but always considerably under the regular prices, only that a proportionate part of the work be paid at the end of every week, the company keeping no running accounts, and having no dealing, that by any means can implicate them in law suits or disputes.

The public will always have the choice of the workman's working by the day or the piece, or job, but always on terms lower than can be obtained any where else. For the objects of manufacture, hats, shoes, furniture, or silk goods, the same invariable rule will be preserved, the prices charged will always cover, and only cover the journeymen's wages and one quarter more than the amount of such wages for risk of goods laying unsold, rent and other expences, defects from time, and losses of every nature.

Mr. Owen asserts, that the producer does not receive the tenth part of what he produces ; here the public enjoys the whole benefit of this disproportion, the producer contenting himself as usual with journeymen's wages, the company taking only a one fourth more than such wages, and giving up to the public, be the object of manufacture or workmanship what it may, the remainder of the profit usually taken on every article of comsumption.

Thus promising the public, and thus really and truly effecting and continuing to effect, I risk nothing in calculating that, from the beginning of the fifth month, May, 1826, the whole number of five hundred hands will be in full and effective operation. The profits will then be weekly four shillings subscription, say £100

Profit on the labour of five hundred men at eight shillings per week 200

Weekly £300

From the first day of May, 1826, the net revenue of £300 a week would fall into the coffers of the partnership, each member of which would besides receive his journeyman's wages, have his lodgings gratis, and his food and clothes superior to what he had ever enjoyed at one third less than their usual cost.

His instruction has gone on in the mean time. From the moment the partnership house is in order, one hour per day of the journeyman's labour is diminished, and this hour, and at least another with it, are devoted to the study of the English language first, and then to that of the other languages ; courses of lectures on the different sciences will also be organized, and such other modes of rational instruction and amusement found out for the partners as shall induce them to make it an undeviating rule to pass their evenings at the establishment, and no where else.

Thus established in comparative comfort and happiness, with the revenue I have mentioned, the head partner and committees will be on the look out for a large farm, at least five hundred acres, if possible within ten miles of the city, and, at all events, commanding a water communication with it. To find this and agree on the terms, &c. may take three months more, and so much will be necessary to collect a sum sufficient to carry the bargain into effect, to give security to the proprietors for the rent, and to stock and furnish it: but in three months from May, 1826, the society would have nearly £4,000 in hand. The farm should be purchased, or at least taken on a lease of ninety-nine years. It would almost immediately suffice, to furnish the whole society with vegetables, beer, milk, butter, eggs, fowls, &c. which they might either pay for at a low rate, and thus increase the funds of the society, or receive gratuitously, so as to leave them their wages for clothes, instruction and the formation of a library and philosophical apparatus, as might be determined by a reunion of the committees of the different trades, or by the general assembly of all the partners to be held once a month at the partnership house.

A building of six hundred feet by sixty, of three stories besides the ground floor, which should be entirely composed of halls and assembly rooms of different descriptions, would be necessary for the comfortable habitation of five hundred families. After having determined on the plan and site, a section of one hundred feet would be immediately begun and finished in the shortest possible time—during this portion being built, which would not occupy more than two months, the society will advertise its intention to receive as partners five hundred girls, or as many as there may then be unmarried partners in the society, from sixteen to twenty years of age, of handsome person, (none under five feet one inch), of an unblemished character, of moral and religious parents, of moral and religious sentiments and conduct themselves. A committee of enquiry, consisting of the head partner, the minister attached to the association, and one member from each of the trade com-

mittees, would make on this head the strictest, the severest
perquisition, and the slightest stain, nay the slightest suspicion of stain, ought to be enough to exclude the candidate, however recommended. These five hundred
young persons would be received into the new building
as soon as ready, and Mr. Hamilton and the females of
his family, with assistants, would immediately begin
their education; it should correspond with that given
to the males: first, the English language, to speak and
write it with grammatical purity, to write and count
well, to read a number of good English authors, so as
to give them a taste for literature, and a general degree
of information and instruction on all subjects of usual
conversation. The French and Italian languages, music
and dancing, not so much for the exercise of this latter
art, as for the ease of person and manner which it almost
infallibly communicates. With these outward accomplishments, religious instruction, so as to fit them for
good wives and good mothers, so as to enable them to
become in time the instructresses of their children, and
for this it may even be thought useful to teach those
who may have a taste and facility for them, the Greek and
Latin languages; for though these languages are indubitably not worth the time and money they now cost,
yet when they can be attained in a few months' pleasing
study, and at a trifling expence, they should be acquired
by every person who can come at them. But the
whole time would not be given up to study, eight hours
a day they would work at tayloring, millinery, plain
sewing, straw-bonnet making, and other branches of
useful industry, so as not only to pay their board and
education, (the latter as for the men, one shilling per
week payable out of the society's fund,) but even
to increase the funds of the society, and allow it to
clothe them. This course of education would be pur-
sued during nine months, during which their female
teachers and governesses would never quit them night
or day, and would consequently mark the slightest deviation from a right conduct; and if that deviation
should be thought to indicate a vicious mind, it would
be privately arranged to place the delinquent some

where else, or return her to her parents. With these precautions, a virtuous and accomplished companion for life would be assured to every member of the society who should choose to use the privilege here afforded him, and thus would he himself by a course of eighteen months' instruction and discipline, be prepared to enter upon a state of life where happiness so essentially depends on the virtues and accomplishments of those who enter into it.

During this course of education for both sexes, the parties would never see each other, the girls never go out except with their governesses, and always veiled. But as soon as the building is perfected, of which the plan is already made, providing a bed-room and parlour for every couple, besides kitchens, dining and assembly rooms of all descriptions, when I say all this is provided, all the partners will assemble in the great hall, serving for church, the ladies on one side, veiled, and in uniform dresses, the men also in the costume of the Hamiltonian Society on the other, and after sermon and prayer to invoke the blessing of the Almighty, and to entreat him to arrange the marriages of these people, for their mutual happiness, and their several good, the head partner and the minister, assisted by the foremen of all the committees, will put the written names of the men in one box, and the written names of the girls in another. Then withdrawing to some distance from each other, the head partner after mixing up the names of the men, will draw one out and proclaim it aloud. The minister immediately draws out the name of a girl from his box, when the persons so called, come forward, and receiving their tickets or written names, immediately walk arm in arm out of the church into the square or lawn appointed for this purpose; if content with the decision of heaven, for such, it is conceived lots so drawn, indubitably are, they return and seat themselves together in a certain part of the church, appointed for that purpose. If not contented with their lots they throw their tickets back into the boxes whence they were severally drawn and returning each to his and her former places among the candidates, their lots will be drawn over again with the same ceremony as before until all be content.— Should the whole terminate and yet one or more of the gentlemen not have found a mate, he or they return to the town establishment and the supernumerary girls remain in the country, until the renewal of this ceremony to be appointed by the society. The marriage of all the others is celebrated at the same moment, and immediately after the drawing, and to each pair, a parlour and bedchamber are allotted, according to the number of their tickets drawn for the marriage.

Having thus united my partners with virtuous, beautiful and accomplished companions, having placed them in the possession of wealth, acquired by their own labour, with minds enlightened by useful science, unadulterated by the detestable sophistries of those who would deprive us of the noblest incentive to good actions, the truest spring of real and substantial happiness, religion, possessing not only all the necessaries and comforts of life in abundance, but enjoying such a conviction of their duration as leave them at ease with regard to the happiness of their children, we may now commit them to the direction of their head partner, committees and monthly general assemblies, and to the care of that providence, which, it is hoped, first suggested the idea of such a union, and afterwards afforded the means of bringing it into effect.

I am aware, that such a mode of uniting people in marriage, may appear fanciful and romantic to many, who will not fail to ridicule such a lottery of wives, and thence, perhaps, scout the whole plan. But to those who would be inclined to consider it in this light, I would oppose an experience of the world as long as theirs, and perhaps as much observation, and from both I see no reason to suppose that a marriage thus formed, may not be rationally expected to produce as much happiness as those we see formed every day.—Sure I am, that there are thousands, who would give half their worldly substance for the liberty of exchanging their present lot, for a ticket in this new lottery. After all, here is no force, a well educated and accomplished wife, a virtuous and healthy if not beautiful woman is provided for every partner; if she should not please, he draws a second, a third or a fourth time, and may at length reject all.—To have unmarried partners of either sex, is not considered a misfortune, but it would be considered one that a woman partner should marry an ignorant and vicious husband, or that a man partner should marry an ignorant and vicious woman—in either case, the peace, happiness and prosperity of the society would render it necessary to oblige the man, to sell out and to declare the woman no longer a partner—for as she has brought nothing into the society, she can have no right to sell.—Neither is it intended that this or any other regulation mentioned in the project should be so absolutely determined before-hand, that the will of of the whole body when united, may not change it, on due consideration and conviction of the utility of such change. Perhaps some mode might be contrived, on which the young people might see each other without danger, as at a weekly dinner or tea party, and so arrange their future union, without having recourse to lots. But on presenting the plan of a community, it was necessary to make provision for every circumstance that could be obviously foreseen, and, though I would chearfully submit to the decision of the whole body a point which concerns their own happiness so essentially, yet is it the most ardent desire to promote that happiness, which has suggested the plan here given.

As the society will be governed by its committees and head partner, as an executive and permanent counsel, and the whole body meet once a month, to have an exposition of the general state of the society from the head partner, and receive the accounts of the different committees, it is not necessary to enter into the details of its government, or to form bye laws before they become necessary. But it may not be improper to consider the light in which this company, such as I have described it may be looked on by society at large. It will doubtless be hailed with pleasure by all parties; it can excite the jealousy of none; it will be useful as far as its influence extends to every rank of society, it will relieve from, and secure the public against the combination of a class of middle men, who preying alike on the journeymen and the public, fatten on the spoils of both. It will lower the price of every article which the company manufacture, and give bread to numbers, who now want it. — Government, necessarily hostile to to Mr. Owen's system, as subversive of all government, would see with pleasure the formation of a society, whose first principle is submission to " the powers that be," all whose views are in accordance with the established institutions of this country, and whose success must necessarily augment the general wealth and happiness of the nation.

Such societies (for they may be formed on very different plans) will solve a problem at all times interesting, but which at this moment is a matter of real anxiety to every rank.—Is, or is not the education of the poor, beneficial to them ? Is it, or is it not injurious, or at least dangerous, to the interests of the rich ? knowledge, is I think, on all hands allowed to be power, and combined with genius, is undoubtedly an immense power. This was the lever by which Mahomet, Cromwell and Bonaparte, rose to be the greatest men of their time, but it is only beneficial to man, in the hands of those, who have neither interest or inclination to make a wrong use of it.—Imagine an able bodied man, living, or starving, with a wife and children on twelve or fifteen shillings per week, who, while he is conscious that his daily labour combined with that of his fellow workmen, enrich the master who employs them, is equally conscious that his participation in the benefit of that labour is unequal and unjust, would not power in the hands of such a man be dangerous ? Now suppose power in the hands of half a million such men, is not the idea sufficient to make us shudder ? but the fear of losing the pittance they receive, would keep them quiet ? possibly it might. However, if such a stagnation in trade, as we have all seen repeatedly, were to compel the masters to discharge half the number, what argument would be sufficient to persuade 250,000 such men, to behold with tranquil apathy, their families starve in the midst of surrounding plenty ? the laws of distributive justice would be cobwebs in such a case, an universal insurrection of all the working classes, led on and combined by 250,000 men of education, would be the inevitable consequence. Constituted as society now is, however unpopular the doctrine, I conceive, the fears of the rich to give the poor more education than is sufficient to enable them to understand rightly, the laws of god and man as far as they are concerned in obeying them, are well grounded and rational, and, though I applaud the efforts of those men who now so so zealously promote the education of the working classes, I would, nevertheless, respectfully submit to their consideration the institution of societies which, by assuring them the means of comfortable existence, may take away every temptation to make a wrong use of their knowledge.

On the other hand, let us conceive these 250,000 men not working for masters, but divided into communities, constituted, not on the atheistical and world-turned-upside-down principles of Mr. Owen, but in the mild and gentle spirit of christianity, on principles preservative of every good we have among us, and attempting or thinking of reform, only in their own life and conduct, increasing in knowledge only in proportion as the interest they have in the peace of the country increases, possessing not individual, but common wealth, sufficient in every case to secure them a comfortable existence, with moderate and healthful labour. What interest would such men have in insurrections or revolutions? none could make their situation better; they would have every thing to lose, they could gain nothing; their whole might and influence would therefore be opposed to every appearance of commotion, and would in every case be infallibly effectual; they would constitute an eternal and insuperable barrier between the rich and the poor, and be a perpetual security to the former for the conduct of the latter. The individuals of such communities, while they would enjoy plenty, peace and comfort would in nothing else resemble the rich, and could neither excite their envy or their jealousy; the community indeed would be rich, but no individual of it would possess either power, riches or influence.

Such is the form, and such the principles of those associations into which I invite the working classes to enter, the first of which, as the education of the members constitutes an essential feature, I have ventured to name " HAMILTONIAN."

If it be the opinion of those persons whose efforts to serve the working classes have justly conciliated their confidence and esteem, that this form and these principles are likely to produce the results I have described, or at least something approaching to them, they will doubtless use their influence to promote the formation of such societies; they will give their countenance and aid to the experiment I am about to make, they will pry into its nature, mark its progress, and enlighten the public with regard to it. Mean time, they will tell the mechanics who come within their reach the nature of association, they will point out to them the difference between association and combination, the latter is the fertile source of wretchedness and misery, and must draw down inevitably on those engaged in it, the severity of the laws ; the former is replete with every good, has every man for its friend, and brings a speedy and effectual remedy for every evil.

Conceiving therefore, that individual and general good can only result from the formation of such a society, and believing that the system of teaching, which myself and children have introduced into this country, affords very great facilities for the accomplishment of the object which such a society ought to have in view, the individual happiness of its members, by the acquisition of wealth and knowledge, I shall from this day receive at my house, 62 Gower Street, from 7 till 9 o'clock in the evening, the names of those individuals who are disposed, to become members of " THE HAMILTONIAN SOCIETY FOR MUTUAL BENEFIT AND INSTRUCTION." As soon as 50 or 60 persons shall have subscribed their names, committees will be formed, and the public made acquainted with the progress of the society.

Printed by G. Schulze, 13, Poland Street.

ERRATA.

In the title for *consistant* read *consistent*.
Page 16, for *Cesar* read *Cæsar*.
Idem for *Anedoti* read *Aneddoti*.
Page 36, line 11, efface *so*.

POSTCRIPT.

The Taylors having been first named in order to illustrate the nature of the projected association, I perceive I have, with regard to the weekly subscription, attempted to make their measure fit every other trade, this is not just: they pay four shillings out of thirty-six, that is, one ninth. Every other mechanic will therefore be received on the same footing as the taylors on paying weekly one ninth of his full journeyman's wages, be it what it may ; if only nine shillings, and the trade he professes be such as the society may probably stand in need of, he will be received on paying one shilling per week to the partnership fund, and one shilling as the others for education.

The society guarantees to all its members, as far as consistent with its situation moral, local and pecuniary, every necessary comfort and even luxury in food, clothes, furniture, &c. which the members themselves collectively may deem expedient, and to all its members without distinction, in perfect equality : but the journeyman's wages is the peculiar property of each member, and it will always remain precisely as it was before he entered the society, and be regulated by the same laws, and, after his marriage, the work done by his wife, if susceptible of evaluation, will also be added to his journeyman's wages. Each member of a committee receives one fourth more than the journeyman's wages of his trade, and the foreman of each committee of five, one half more, the other foremen in proportion.— The head partner receives no journeyman's wages, receiving one shilling per week from each member of it during his life ; but on his death, his widow and those of his children assisting in the education of the members and their children, will be each entitled to journeyman's wages in lieu of the one shilling per week, unless it should be thought proper to continue to them the care of the education department. On the death of the present head-partner, a head-partner will be elected by a majority of the society with such a salary as the respectability of the Society may render expedient, partaking besides of all the other advantages enjoyed by the other members for himself and family.

DESCRIPTION

ARCHITECTURAL MODEL

FROM A DESIGN BY

STEDMAN WHITWELL, Esq.

FOR

A COMMUNITY UPON A PRINCIPLE OF UNITED INTERESTS,

AS ADVOCATED BY

ROBERT OWEN, Esq.

HURST CHANCE & Co. ST. PAUL'S CHURCH YARD,

AND

EFFINGHAM WILSON, ROYAL EXCHANGE.

MDCCCXXX.

Price 1*s. or Coloured* 1*s.* 6*d.*

DESIGN

for a Community of 2000 Persons founded upon a principle

Commended by Plato Lord Bacon and Sir Thomas More.

and combined with all the advantages of scientific discoveries down to the present time.

Engelmann & Co lithog

EXPLANATION OF THE PARTS NUMBERED ON THE PLATE.

1 Gymnasiums or Covered Places for Exercise, attached to the Schools and Infirmary.

2 Conservatory, in the midst of Gardens botanically arranged.

3 Baths, warm and cold, of which there are four for the Males, and four for the Females.

4 Dining Halls, with Kitchens, &c. beneath them.

5 Angle Buildings, occupied by the Schools for Infants, Children, and Youths, and the Infirmary ; on the ground floors are Conversation-rooms for Adults.

6 Library, Detached Reading Rooms, Bookbindery, Printing Office, &c.

7 Ball room and Music rooms.

8 Theatre for Lectures, Exhibitions, Discussions, &c. with Laboratory, Small Library, &c.

9 Museum, with Library of Description and Reference, Rooms for preparing Specimens, &c.

10 The Brew-houses, Bake-houses, Wash-houses, Laundries, &c. arranged round the Bases of the Towers.

11 The Refectories for the infants and children are on each side of the Vestibules of the Dining halls

12 The Illuminators of the Establishment, Clock-towers, and Observatories, and from the elevated summits of which all the smoke and vitiated air of the buildings is discharged into the atmosphere.

13 Suites of adult sitting rooms and chambers.

14 Suites of Chambers, which may be easily and quickly made of any dimensions required ; Dormitories for the Unmarried and Children.

15 Esplanade one hundred feet wide, about twelve feet above the natural surface.

16 Paved Footpath.

17 The Arcade and its Terrace, giving both a covered and an open communication with every part of the building.

18 Sub-way leading to the Kitchens, &c. and along which meat, vegetables, coals, &c. are conveyed to the Stores, and dust and refuse brought out.

DESCRIPTION OF THE MODEL.

***

Extent and Position.

THE area of ground occupied by the Buildings, Promenades, and Gardens of the Establishment would be about thirty-three acres; that of the enclosed quadrangle twenty-two acres, nearly three times as large as Russell Square.

It is proposed that one of the diagonal lines of the square should be so placed as to coincide with a meridian, and, if possible, to range with some remarkable points or objects of the distant country. This would ensure an equal distribution of light and darkness, sun and shadow among the occupants of every part of the edifice; and be convenient for astronomical and geographical reference.

It is desirable in most cases that the scite of
land selected for this purpose, should be in the
vicinity of a stream, ample enough to supply the
domestic purposes of the establishment, to secure its
drainage, and furnish power sufficient for the mills
and other manufactories necessary or convenient
for the accommodation and prosperity of the inhabitants.

———

General Arrangements.

THE Building to be disposed in a quadrangle
measuring one thousand feet on each side; divided
    Externally, into
        Dwelling houses,
        Central public buildings,
        Angle ditto.
    Internally are disposed the
        Baths,
        Public Refectories,
        Kitchens, Breweries, &c.
        Stores, Offices, &c.

Botanic Gardens.

Gymnasiums.

surrounded by a Cloister or covered Arcade for
general communication.

———————

Arrangements of the Dwelling Houses.

THE dwelling houses are situated on the extended lines, between the central and angle buildings, upon each side of the quadrangle; and
occupy the ground and the first floor stories, they
are divided into two sets of a Sitting room, Chamber, and Water closet each. They have ready and
convenient access to the offices, by means of Covered ways, at a lower level than the general
entrance from the Esplanade; these form also the
separate and private entrances to the Cloister or
Arcade surrounding the whole interior of the
quadrangle; and by means of Bridges of communication, over the Covered ways before-named,
connect the staircase of each house with the Terrace
over the cloister, forming a general access from
every house to every part of the establishment.

The Dormitories.

THE ranges of apartments over the dwelling
houses, are proposed to be occupied as Dormitories or Sleeping rooms, for unmarried persons and
children; having no connection with the dwelling or private houses below them. They are
approached from the great staircases in the central and angle buildings. This story is so contrived that the whole, or any part of it may, at
any time be thrown into vast apartments, or be
subdivided into chambers of the most minute
dimensions.

Temperature of the Interior——Ventilation——
Light——Supply of Water——Drainage
——Basement.

THE whole of the Interior, but most particularly
the Dwelling houses, to be warmed and ventilated
upon the most improved principle, and the tem-

perature maintained at an agreeable degree of heat in the coldest and most variable seasons, by means of Air-warmers; the whole of which, with the arrangements for the service of hot and cold water to each apartment, at all hours, the lighting with gas, and other scientific means of reducing domestic labour, to be constructed in the general basement, which extends under the entire range and over the whole extent of the Buildings; Access to which is obtained from the central and angle buildings, so that it may have no connection with the dwelling houses.

Central and Angle Buildings——Staircases.

THE central buildings are occupied on the ground or terrace floor, by the grand entrances to the quadrangle, and in these and the angle buildings, are the great staircases communicating on each side with the dormitories, over the private apartments, and the Public Rooms contained in these Buildings.

Public Rooms in the Centres and Angles.

In these buildings are contained the Libraries, Museums of Natural History, &c. Theatre for Lectures, Exhibitions, Ball and Concert Room, Reading Rooms, Conversation Rooms, Rooms of Management, &c. &c.

———

Central Public Buildings inside Quadrangle——
Offices, &c.——Public Refectories.

Passing through each of the grand Entrances, a raised Platform, with which the Cloisters are connected, leads to the central public buildings within the quadrangle. The Hall or Vestibule of which is approached by flights of stone steps of large extent. On each side the Vestibule are disposed the Dining Apartments for infants and children; the Vestibule itself leading to the great Hall or Public Refectory, a noble and extensive Saloon, open to the roof, lighted by seven lofty windows on each side, and in which every means of reducing the labour of service is proposed to be adopted: particularly the service of the dinner, &c. from the public Kitchens under the Refectory, this is proposed to be performed by mechanical means, in a rapid, quiet, and cleanly manner; the different utensils removed by the same process; and the apparatus to present, in the Refectories, the appearance of handsome sideboards in recesses.

The most perfect System of Ventilation, so important in Apartments of this description, is proposed to be introduced.

In the rear of the refectory, and opening to it, are rooms for the glass, table linen, spices, and other condiments, &c. &c.

Basement——Sub-way to Basement.

THE Basement is approached by inclined planes, leading under the principal carriage entrance to the public Kitchens, and Store Departments.

This entrance or approach is sufficiently capacious for the admission of carts, &c. to supply the various kitchens, stores, breweries, gas works, &c. &c. all of which are concentrated near these four central points, from them branch off railways, meeting each other, and forming one complete circuit of communication throughout the whole establishment, on which carriages will convey the supply of fuel, provisions, &c. to the different depôts, without interference with the dressed ground, Esplanade, or with the dwelling part of the establishment, and by the same Routes all refuse material is removed.

In the Basement of the Inner Central Buildings, under the great hall and refectories, are the public Kitchens, Sculleries, Larders, Offices for the distribution of stores, &c. &c. and around the bases of the towers are disposed the Breweries, Gas-works, Wash-houses, Laundries, Steam works, for the supply of the kitchen, &c. and other apparatus for carrying away all smoke, and vapour, the whole of which is collected at these points, and carried upwards through the great shafts of the towers; means of access to any part of which for necessary repairs, cleansing, &c. can at all times be had, and spacious accommodation for those so employed.

The vaults for the stowage of malt liquors, fuel, and other heavy stores, are of extensive and spacious dimensions, and situated in the vicinity of those places where their service is most immediately required.

Towers——Illuminated Dials——Distribution
of Light from the Towers.

THE towers which rise from the four internal central buildings, are intended, (in addition to to their uses as stated above,) to form .observatories, and for that purpose a commodious spiral staircase surrounds each of them, springing from the roof of the rear building, which is designed as their base. About midway upon each shaft, are placed dials, illuminated at night by gas, visible at all hours in all parts of the internal area and buildings. The gallery which forms the observatory upon each tower, immediately surmounts the parapet of the same, which parapet is pierced with a series of arched openings, at the back of each of which powerful reflectors are placed; gas burners being introduced here, the light is distributed downwards, in all directions, and the space between the corbels supporting the parapet is left open for the same purpose. By these means, independent of any other light, that from the towers will be sufficient to illuminate the whole Quadrangle and the rooms which look into it, and these four points will be from their elevation, (about two hundred feet,) so many beacons to the surrounding country, marking distinctly the position of the building to a very great distance.

Cloister or Arcade, and its Terrace.

THIS runs round the whole internal area, and forms the boundary of the gardens; on the ground it will be a kind of continued alcove, surmounted by a terrace of the same extent, both furnished with seats, and serving as delightful places, either for retirement from bad weather, or for social purposes. From the arcade and terrace a direct communication is made to every part, particularly to the baths, gymnasiums, and gardens. It will be observed, that by means of the cloisters surrounding the inner quadrangle, the most perfect communication can be maintained with every part of the establishment in bad weather, without exposure ; while the terrace over it affords equal access, and a delightful promenade, under more favourable circumstances.

Gymnasiums.

THE angles of the inner area of the quadrangle are occupied by the gymnasiums for the Infants, Children and Youth of the community, and for the Convalescents of the Infirmary; these are accessible by covered ways, from the cloisters and alcoves at the angles of the building.

Baths.

To each of the four main divisions of the general building are annexed warm and cold baths, for the separate accommodation of the male and female members of the community. These distinct buildings are placed on each side the central internal public buildings, and are approached by the covered ways from the cloisters, and the terrace over them. These baths will contain accommodations of a novel and peculiar character, uniting the privacy of retirement with the exercise of extensive general baths.

Pleasure Gardens——Conservatory.

THE quadrangle is intended to be laid out in shrubberies, flower gardens, and pleasure grounds, scientifically arranged, that the gratifications of the garden may be combined with new accessions of information, and the means of inculcating precepts of order at every step. The walks to be so disposed

that each shall form a vista, terminating with some
object or part of the building, of a varied and
pleasing character; the centre of the grounds
to be occupied by a Conservatory, of about one
hundred feet in diameter, for the reception and
cultivation of exotics, to be warmed and fitted
up upon an improved and novel plan.

The Esplanade and Approaches.

THE Esplanade surrounding the general edifice
to be one hundred feet wide, and laid out in
lawns, and other pleasure grounds, with a Promenade, defended by a parapet, and overlooking
the surrounding scenery of the Establishment
and country. This Esplanade it is proposed
to elevate above the level of the adjoining land,
and to connect it, by means of a wide and
gently ascending road, forming an Approach for
carriages, &c. proceeding to the establishment.
Steps of communication will present themselves
at every angle, and at other convenient points of

18

the Esplanade. The four fronts of the whole structure to be furnished with fruit trees, trained upon
trellis, and the tract of land upon which the establishment is placed to be cultivated for agricultural
purposes, for the supply of the community; regard
being had to preserve a picturesque effect, as far
as the interests of the establishment will permit.

EXTRACT

FROM

Mr. J. M. MORGAN'S LETTER

TO THE

BISHOP OF LONDON.

THE organization of a community of united and
equal interests, where individuals are trained and
educated from infancy in accordance with that
principle, is, of course, not new to your Lordship; who probably, in common with other
scholars, have, in your earlier days, first admired
the beauty, and then lamented the impracticability,
of the schemes of Plato, More, and Bacon. But
although those great characters were unable,
through the insufficiency of knowledge and experience in their respective eras, to perfect a system, yet their general principle was true, and
has at length assumed a practical and durable
form. It is not, however, to be supposed, that
the present generation, with all its acquired habits,
opinions, and injurious passions, their ignorance
or partial knowledge, can be qualified for a superior constitution of society, much less can we suppose that the different classes could be at once
amalgamated.

Should your Lordship not admit the possibility of establishing a community where the private and public interest shall be so united, in the mind of each individual, as to become the undeviating rule of his conduct; or, admitting the correctness of the principles, you deem any attempt to act upon them premature; permit me to suggest four distinct and separate plans, by which each class of society may derive great advantages, without the surrender of their present habits and opinions; and whether considered as an advance towards a superior state of society, or merely as an improvement of the present, I think they will be found unobjectionable, and if sanctioned by your approval and patronage, would soon gain acceptance with the public.

The first plan for the higher and middle classes of society, I have recently circulated in the following

SUGGESTION,

For a Club upon an extended scale, for the attainment of all the objects of superior Society, in the immediate vicinity of London.

If a College, of the size of one of the largest squares, were erected, surrounded by a park and gardens, and sufficiently capacious for the accommodation of four hundred families, whose incomes did not exceed £200, and each family paid a rent of £100, the rental would amount to £40,000, requiring an outlay of £800,000. This sum might be raised by shares, which would afford a safe and profitable investment, even for those who had no desire to become occupants.

It is perfectly demonstrable, that each family, expending the remainder of their income (£100 per annum,) under such arrangements, would derive far greater advantages than could be yielded by an income of £600 per annum, in an establishment for one family only ; for, besides procuring, in a superior degree, their present objects including education for their children, they could have libraries, theatres, and philosophical apparatus for lectures, music and ball-rooms, baths, gymnasia, and whatever belongs to the highest physical and mental cultivation.

The same economy, though with less advantages, would obtain, in an outlay of £400,000, for an equal number of families, with £100 per annum.

But, if an income of £500 were expended upon the same principle, the advantages would equal those of an individual establishment of £5000, as the benefits increase in a greater ratio from the increased expenditure.

It is equally demonstrable, that those collisions of interests, or incompatibilties of disposition, which militate against the friendly union of two or more families in one dwelling, would, by the comprehensiveness of the establishment, be entirely avoided ; while the privacy of separate houses, or of two apartments for each adult, male and female, with the choice of taking their refreshments in them, or in the grand dining-hall, collectively, or in different parties, together with the right of leaving the Society at a quarter's notice, would afford the same liberty as is now enjoyed.

Under this plan of combined expenditure only, there is no necessity for *productive* employment— unless, for the sake of beneficial exercise for themselves and children, the members should desire to cultivate their own gardens.

A model of one of these colleges is now placed in the saloon of the Colosseum in the Regent's Park. By the description it will be seen how much the economy of the arrangements abridges, and renders agreeable to the young, employment in the domestic offices. Children delight in being occupied, especially in numbers, and when they understand that their employment is useful, there is scarcely any domestic service, which the youth between the ages of seven and sixteen, with all the aids which modern science afford, would not with ease, and as an amusement, perform ; while, in reality, it would become an essential part of their education, in the true signification of the term. Families with limited incomes could thus dispense with servants altogether.

However extraordinary may be the pecuniary advantages of the foregoing plan, they bear no comparison with its moral effects. It combines the pleasures of a town and country residence, without the disadvantages of either; the accommodations and intelligent society of the former, with the fresh air and exercise of the latter; to the advantages of a private, are united those of a public education, and of an university. The clubs hitherto established have had the effect of excluding one sex, before too much separated, from the intellectual pursuits of the other. This plan brings them forward, and gives them a voice upon subjects no less interesting to women than to men, and in a knowledge of which, their participation is absolutely essential to the wellbeing and happiness of society. Perhaps there could not be found a more salutary restraint upon the conduct of adults, than the frequent opportunities that would be afforded them, of witnessing the process of education, and the progress of the children; nothing so well calculated to teach them to seek improving pleasures, and to entice them from horse-racing and gaming, as to be called upon to deliberate upon projected improvements in instruction. Increased attraction could be given to scientific inquiry by

magnificent orreries, the large globes lately exhibited at Paris, superior solar microscopes, and
other aids to philosophical illustration, and such as
no private fortune, however splendid, could command. The powerful impulse which such exhibitions and aids would have in stimulating the useful
curiosity of the children, must be obvious. The
concerts also could be conducted upon a scale of
magnitude, and with an effect, beyond the reach
of any private entertainment.

This association would also enable the children
of the middle and higher classes of society, to enjoy the benefit of an infant school, which has
hitherto been confined to the working classes.

THE second plan, for the labouring classes, is as
follows :—

Squares to be erected within two miles of London,
or within a more convenient distance, for the residence of those employed during the day in the
cities of London and Westminster. If four proprietors agree to build a square, each may undertake
one side, which would remain separate and independent property; or if eight united, then half
the side of a square would belong to each landlord.
This arrangement would do away with any risk of
partnership. At the upper end of the square,

large school-rooms should be built; the ground floor to be used as an infant school, the upper floor for children more advanced.

The expense of building these rooms could be borne jointly by the proprietors, or if built by one person, he could let it to the inhabitants.

These apartments, light, convenient, and airy, and equally independent, would be taken by the working classes, in preference to the close and unwholesome rooms in narrow dirty alleys, where the children, if not an incumbrance to their mothers, are running about, without superintendence, in the streets. Under the proposed arrangements, the children, when not engaged in the schools, would be playing in the square, and at all times within sight of their parents or teachers. One of the inhabitants could receive the rents weekly, having a small compensation for his trouble.

The school-rooms would be used for lectures in the evening, and a small library could be attached; in short, almost any object of general interest, such as their benefit sick clubs, and other societies of mutual assistance, could be there formed.

The contiguity of this building to their own dwellings would enable their wives and children to participate in the instructive amusements of the evening, which would be well calculated to supersede the attractions of the public house.

There they could establish their own stores, and in a short time, bake their own bread, and brew their own beer, and perhaps supply the neighbourhood. This arrangement would be found advantageous, not only in the vicinity of cities and large towns, but also in the agricultural districts, as distinct gardens could be allotted to each family, and even separate cottages, provided they were sufficently near for the children to be under the continual observation of their parents or instructors, and near the school.

In the Rev. Daniel Wilson's reply to a request of the parishioners of Islington, to take the chair at a meeting convened for the purpose of forming " A Mutual Assurance Society," by which the labouring classes can assist each other in old age, sickness, and infirmity, is this judicious remark :— " For it is impossible, I think, not to see, that if two hundred or more persons will form a society for mutual aid, on correct principles, each one will know, that whenever he falls sick, he shall have two hundred friends to hold him ; and that during the years of health, he will have the gratification of affording to others the aid which he requires from time to time himself." And why should they not unite for the preservation also of health, as well as for the recovery from sickness, for sanity of mind, and for all the objects of rational existence? It is this comprehensive union that is wanted for the suppression of vice, and for the support of virtue.

THERE still remains another class which requires attention—those who are willing and able to work, but can procure no employment. If the plan of united interests is objected to, they must have separate allotments of land, and be allowed to supply their own wants, with that just regard to their feelings, which every principle of humanity or of true religion can suggest. The efficacy of this mode of relief has been fully confirmed by the success of similiar experiments in Holland; the details of which have been too long before the public to need any commentary now. Their efficacy, however, will be found far inferior to small communities of mutual assistance, in which the individual and general interest are united.

Neither this nor the preceding plan for the working classes already employed, will, of course, admit of arrangements upon such a scale of convenience and grandeur as the model represents. As soon, however, as a knowledge of the true principles of society are generally diffused, there is not an individual of the most exalted rank, who would not desire to have his children educated in a community of united interests, in which artificial, frivolous, and degrading distinctions are unknown, "for the Northumberlands, Devonshires, Bedfords, Staffords, Grosvenors, and Lowthers, are not in possession of a tithe of the real wealth, knowledge, virtue, and happiness, which under the direction of a science fixed and certain in all its results, may be secured through all coming generations, for every individual*."

The fourth measure proposed by Mr. Morgan, refers to the employment of the churches for instruction and lectures in the week-day, and is not so immediately connected with the objects for which the model has been designed.

* Mr. Owen's Lecture delivered at Almack's Rooms.

Plan

OF THE TOWN.

1.2. Warehouses
3 Slaughter-yard
4 Stables
5 Streets
6 Houses for Tanners
7 D.º for Bakers
8 Store-houses
9 Cemetery
10 Canal

11 Island
12 Factory
13 Warehouse
14 Temple of Wisdom
15 D.º of Happiness
16 Government Hall
17 Garden of Pleasure
18 D.º of Praise.

Colonnade

No. 9.

No. 3

No. 7

No. 18

J. Thimbleby, inv.ᵗ

S. Woodhouse, Fecit.

Published for the Author by W. Pickering, Vol. 1.

MONADELPHIA;

OR,

THE FORMATION OF

A NEW SYSTEM OF SOCIETY,

WITHOUT THE INTERVENTION

OF

A CIRCULATING MEDIUM.

"The love of money is the root of all evil." I Tim. vi. 10.
"This is the message that ye heard from the beginning,
that ye should love one another." I John, iii. 11.

BY J. THIMBLEBY.

BARNET:
PRINTED FOR THE AUTHOR,
AND W. BALDOCK, BOOKSELLER AND STATIONER;
AND W. FORD, BOOKSELLER, 69, WOOD-STREET,
CHEAPSIDE, LONDON.
1832.

ENTERED AT STATIONERS' HALL.

BARNET:
PRINTED BY W. BALDOCK.

NOTE.—A critic, in the COURT JOURNAL, having thought fit, amongst several witticisms with which he honoured the Prospectus of this Work, in an article entitled "No money Club," to object to the title chosen for it; the reader is referred to Lee's Introduction to Botany, (4th edit. Rivington, London, 1810) p. 60, line 10, where he will find that the word "Monadelphia," expresses *a single brotherhood*.

TO THE READER.

Reader, I do not address you for the purpose of deprecating criticism; or, to beg a
protection for my work which it does not
deserve. I wish to be tried by the merits of
the case. I am not unaware, that the man who
attempts to overturn an old system, sanctioned
by time, and fortified by prejudice, runs the
risk of being assailed by every weapon which
calumny and ill nature can supply. It is
nevertheless the duty of every good man, to
act, speak, and think, fearlessly, for the welfare
of his fellow creatures. That I have this, at
least, at heart, I hope the following pages will
testify. I have endeavoured to lay down a
Plan, by which man may be made happy;
and I think it will be his own fault if he is

b

not. In making pure Religion the basis of my system, I have essentially differed from those who have gone before me: and I hope that the plan submitted to your notice, will have some claim to attention; as it unites the spiritual welfare of man, with his temporal happiness.

The importance of the subject merits a much more extended discussion than the present: but it was my wish to bring the price of the Work within the reach of the poorest classes of society. Should a discerning public, over-looking the defects of the author, patronize it for the sake of the good which it is my hope it will diffuse, I may feel encouraged to resume the subject at a future period.

INTRODUCTION.

MY fellow man ! whether rich or poor—high
or low : whether thou wast born on the fertile
plains of Asia, or in the deserts of Siberia :
under the burning zone of Africa, or on
the never-melting snows of Lapland : whether
thou supposest thyself a free-born Englishman,
or art really the vilest slave on the face of the
earth : this treatise equally affects all.   In it
behold a prospect of that day, which soon will
succeed this long night of error and misery !
Yes, it will be found to embrace every
means of producing the most superior happiness to the whole world, by founding on
the firmest basis, a project, which will erase
from the mind every error; will concentrate
into one point the diversified opinions and prejudices that now exist with regard to religion,
root out every misery from society, and make
men really free; will establish truth, and, in

B

short, will effect every blessing which the mind of man can comprehend.

In order to bring home to the mind more fully the superiority of this, my system, I will endeavour to point out clearly the misery of the present one, and the cause of that misery : confining myself to known facts, admitted by all. Who will deny that men are generally "every one against his fellow"? Turn your attention to the American Indians, to the horrid cruelties which they exercise towards their fellow men : to the Savages that inhabit the islands of the South Sea—the numberless tribes that are ever warring against each other, along the coast, and in the interior of Africa— besides innumerable hordes in different parts of the world, where civilization is unknown;— heaping upon themselves slavery and wretchedness. And what is the cause of all this? One individual marks out a boundary, and calls it his own : a stronger than he covets it. This produces war, and all its horrors.

But why confine myself to uncivilized nations? Do war and misery, slavery and wretchedness, belong to them alone? No.

Even in Europe (the most enlightened quarter
of the globe,) these horrors are equalled, if not
exceeded.   Behold the despot! whose will is
law, tyrannizing over those for whose protection
he ought to sacrifice his life; murdering some;
incarcerating others for life in gloomy and unwholesome dungeons; and wresting from his
subjects the fruit of their hard earnings; his
aristocrats keeping the deluded peasantry in
the worst state of ignorance and slavery !

Again, behold the nation striving to obtain
that freedom of which her more powerful
neighbour has deprived her; her fair fields de-
luged with the blood of thousands, and misery
and wretchedness hovering around her devoted
inhabitants ! Even if she gain her freedom, what
dark prospects present themselves! her land
laid waste, her towns levelled with the ground,
and her treasury exhausted.   Look upon other
states, some of their inhabitants rolling and
revelling in riches, while others are starving
with hunger !

Would that I could pass over England,
my dear native country, but I know too
well the misery that surrounds all classes of

society in England's envied isle. My readers
too, will be Englishmen; they will feel more
acutely the wretchedness of the system by
which they are galled; they will see that ere
long that system must have an end—is fast
wearing away. The convulsions that at this
present time are shaking the nation, prove it.
Men's minds are becoming more and more enlightened, while education is reflecting from
her mirror, truths that cannot be controverted.
Yes, my countrymen, a new era is about to
appear, when the light of heaven will no more
behold the Right Honorable rolling in his carriage, while his fellow-mortal knows not where
to find his next meal: will no more behold the
pampered rich man wrenching from the poor
the produce of their labour; no more behold the
man who once moved in a high sphere, sunk deep
in poverty, viewing with despair his wife and
children starving around him, without the power
to alleviate their distress : will no more behold
the man who has toiled through the greater
part of his existence to gain a scanty livelihood; in the decline of life, when time has
bleached his locks, and old age has robbed him

of most of his bodily powers—at a season too, when nature requires support and attention — obliged to be the inmate of a workhouse; where, perhaps, an unfeeling master tyrannizes over his sufferings: neglected—forgotten— suffered to die, without one friend near him to receive his last wish, or close his dying eyes.

As I have begun to view the misery men are now suffering, allow me to direct your attention more particularly. Enquire of the man who has titles, honours, and riches, if he is happy! No: for he is the victim of hope, of fear, and of doubt. The canker-worm of care, may be preying on his vitals, rendering the blessings he possesses tasteless and insipid. Ask the man of independent fortune, who feels not the weight of public affairs, if he is happy! No: there too care will be found embittering his life. Time may rob him of all his independency, and he may become one of the poorest mortals that breathe. Ask the merchant, or the tradesman; the professional man, or the poet; the schemer, or his dupe; the farmer, or his labourer; and you will find none happy in the true sense of the word. Hope and fear, doubt and care, are the inmates of every breast.

Take a view of the different scenes in our great Metropolis ; consider the sinks of infamy with which it abounds. See men who might have been the most useful members of society, plunging themselves into a vortex of dissipation, to support which they use every unlawful means ; preying upon their fellow men; shrink-ing from no crime; no action so base but they would glory in the performance of it; and at last, justly suffering the penalties of their coun-try's laws, against which they had so often offended.

Reader, when a mind that is susceptible of those feelings which bespeak love to man; a mind that deeply sympathizes with the evils to which he is now subject; when such a mind views the abject misery inflicted on those whom man is bound especially to protect, it sickens with horror; it loathes a world in which the acme of wretchednesss is experienced by the weakest and loveliest of nature's works. O man, consider! what must be the state of that system in which the most beautiful part of the creation are degraded, debased, and made the victims of man's worst passions.

Take a view of the many filthy hovels, and equally filthy alleys, the abodes of poverty and vice : your soul will be harrowed at the prospect. Attend at our police offices, and your ears will be astounded at the crimes which man can be guilty of. Take a general view of the labouring class ; behold most, if not all, sunk into the lowest state of ignorance, victims of want and distress. Degrading thought ! that in this island of boasted *freedom* and refinement, of arts, and of sciences, there are thousands removed but one gradation from the brute !

I have now taken what may be called an individual view of the misery experienced under the present system: but if I extend that view to political concerns, another and a wider field is opened to me. Consider the millions which are expended in support of a system, that with all those millions spent, can neither lessen vice nor reward virtue : that cannot deduct from the cares of man, but rather increases them.

Who will deny that the use of machinery,

instead of adding to the comfort and convenience of man, too often increases his misery? Who
will deny, that there is land now lying waste,
which would support thousands, while thousands are starving? that Religion, which ought
to make man happy and sinless, is made to
increase crime and render him wretched? that
education, instead of enlightening the mind,
is entangling it in a labyrinth of doubt,
perplexity, and prejudice? Thus does the
present system of things turn blessings into
curses; while men, instead of co-operating
together for each other's good, allow selfishness
to actuate every motive, thereby increasing the
general misery.

My readers may here say, I have glanced
at the bad features of the present system only;
and have not in any way considered the good
which results from it. But I will ask them,
Where is the good? They may tell me to consider our philanthropic and benevolent societies; that there is no distress, in which even
the poorest sufferers may not somewhere find
relief. They may remind me how we have
risen above other nations in arts and sciences.

May point out the liberal and beneficial laws by which we are governed; laws, such as no other country can boast of : may instance our charity schools, where the poorer classes are clothed and educated,—our religious freedom, by means of which man may worship God in any way he pleases,—our naval and military establishments, to watch over the safety of the state,—our parliament, to attend to the rights of the people,—our police, to protect,—our prisons, to deter the robber from attacking our property,—and a thousand other benefits which we are enjoying. I acknowledge all : I will allow that we are experiencing blessings to which other nations are strangers : but let me ask, Are not Englishmen also, generally, suffering the miseries which I have described above? No one, I am sure, can deny that those miseries exist. How imperfect, then, must that system be, that, with all its acknowledged blessings, cannot secure any lasting happiness to man.

Having fully demonstrated the badness of the present system, and its insufficiency to give genuine happiness to any mortal, I next proceed to enquire into the cause of that insufficiency, that I may the better be enabled to provide a remedy for it. My fellow man, the primary cause of all thy distress, thy troubles, thy cares, and thy misery, is INDIVIDUAL PROPERTY ; or, the CIRCULATION OF MONEY! two evils, which may be considered as synonimous ; and which, before thou canst experience any degree of real earthly happiness, must cease to exist.

Start not at the idea—say not that it is impossible! Do not treat me as a visionary, and so throw the book aside, but read on : consider, and well digest it. I defy any man to prove that it is impossible to exist without money. The abolition of money would pave the way for the extension of the Christian Religion in its utmost purity; and, consequently, secure the real happiness of every human being on the face of the earth. Men's minds would then rise rapidly to that enlightened state, in which nothing that might add to the well-being of society would be left unaccomplished; for while I look upon man as a superior being, created for great and noble purposes, I feel certain, that, by the help of his Creator, he can and may effect them.

If there was no individual property, there would be no ambition. And what is ambition? Some of our authors do their best to make it appear a virtue; but, throw aside the flimsy veil with which they strive to cover its deformity, and it will appear in its true shape, covetousness and envy undisguised. One man sees another placed in a high situation, envies him, and covets his honors. This we miscal ambition! Kings covet each other's territories; and the lives of millions are, without compunction, sacrificed to gratify one man's *ambition !* Yet historians and poets hold up to succeeding generations an Alexander, a Cæsar, or a Buonaparte, not as one of the greatest murderers the world has produced; not as an example to deter others from acting, or wishing to act like him; but as an example to excite in the young mind that horrid sin, ambition.

But, if there was no individual property, there would be no wars ! And what an invaluable blessing is peace ! Again, if there was no individual property, no man would be richer than his fellow, and consequently there would be no tyranny, either civil or religious, to paralize the efforts of mankind: no oppressor to trample with relentless fury on the innocent and the helpless.

If there was no money, there would be no theft; no inducement to deceive: for the comforts of all would be equal. Reader, it is money that brings the old man to a prison: it is money that makes the town swarm with prostitutes, and brings poverty and disease into the abodes of misery: it is money that engenders ignorance: money is the parent of vice: through money the honest man beholds his wife and children starving around him, without the power to help them: through money the man who holds a confidential situation, with every prospect of happiness before him, is led to rob his employer, and ends his life upon the gallows: it is through the love of money that the man who allows himself to be involved in gambling schemes, is quickly ruined—seeks to drown his cares in drinking—becomes the outcast of society, the pity of some, and the scorn of others; until, unable to bear up under his troubles, he, at last, rushes unprepared into the presence of his Maker.

If money then produces so much evil, the abolition of it must naturally be productive of good. I have shewn it to be the cause of all the evils with which men are afflicted. I have now to lay before my readers the means to be used to abolish those evils. To accomplish this, I shall point out a system that will produce real happiness : a system in which men's necessities may be fully supplied : in which they will have no care for the future, either for themselves or their offspring, with regard to food or clothing : in which disease and all its dreadful ravages in a little time will cease : and in which every thing will harmonize, so as to produce the most beneficial results.

To give a clear idea of the nature of the system to which I have adverted, I will briefly open the principle of it to the mind, before I proceed to enlarge upon it in detail. Suppose a shoemaker, who had made a pair of shoes, wanted a loaf of bread; I would not advise him to take them to a baker, and ask him to give a loaf in exchange for them, because that might only create confusion. The baker might not want the shoes; or the shoemaker might consider his shoes worth more than a loaf of bread. But I would desire the latter to take his shoes to a warehouse appropriated to that purpose, and the baker should bring him bread ; and so on with regard to any other trade. The tailor, when he had finished a garment should also take it to the warehouse: the hatter should do the same. In this warehouse should be different departments for all kinds of goods, both manufactured and unmanufactured; and when the tailor or the shoemaker were in want of materials to work with or upon, they should go to the department in which those materials were kept, and take them. When the baker or butcher found his clothes worn out, he should go to the clothing department, and fit himself with a new coat, shoes, or hat, as he might want. So it should be with all trades or classes of men. Each man should do his utmost for his fellow-creatures, and should receive in return from the public property, every necessary. The baker and the butcher would daily supply him with food; and in regard to clothing, at any time when he found himself in want, he would go immediately to the warehouse and supply himself.

Having thus slightly explained the ground-work of my plan, let me entreat the careful attention of my readers, to the systematic development of it, which is comprised in the following pages.

DEVELOPMENT.

It has been shewn, in the Introduction to this work, that all the misery to which man is subjected under the existing system, is to be attributed to Invidual Property, or the Circulation of Money. To abolish these evils, must, therefore, be the first step towards effecting a change for the better; and the second, to substitute a new system, in place of the present one, pure and efficacious in its principle, simple in its construction, and replete with all that is requisite to combine the real and permanent happiness of individuals, with the best interests of society at large. The basis of this system must be BROTHERLY LOVE. Individual Property must be succeeded by equal participation in the general stock; and the use of a Circulating Medium by a reciprocal exchange of the necessaries and conveniences of life. To carry this desirable object into full effect, it will be necessary to adopt a systematic plan : and the following will, I trust, be found to embrace all that is necessary to the gradual progress of mankind, towards that much-longed-for summit of earthly happiness, which should bound the wishes of the real christian, on this side the grave.

THE TOWN.

A town should be built which would contain 6,000 persons. It would be required, that round this town, there should be sufficient land to maintain that number of inhabitants. I do not mean that this plan could not be carried into effect by any less number of persons : for if only 200 persons were all actuated by the same motives, it might soon succeed.

This town should be constructed in a square form, with a projecting square at each corner; (vide engraved Plan) and should consist of 18 departments : viz. No. 1, a warehouse for the reception of manufactured goods, to which the different trades should bring the produce of their labour, and from which they would receive their necessary clothing. No. 2, a warehouse, divided into two parts : one for raw materials, the other for materials wrought up into cloth, cotton, leather, &c. No. 3, a slaughter yard, containing stalls for cattle, melting houses for candle makers, &c. No. 4, stables for horses, for the convenience of the inhabitants, either for pleasure or business. No. 5, streets, or rows of houses, for those who require workshops. Each row of houses should be inhabited by one trade. No. 6, houses for tanners. No. 7, ditto for bakers. As the health and comfort of every person should be chiefly considered, the ovens should be entirely separated from the dwelling houses. No 8, storehouses for poultry, butter, eggs, fish, vegetables, &c. * No. 9, burying ground, or cemetry ; it should contain a chapel, where solemn praise should be given to God, for his mercy in taking another soul to heaven. No. 10, a canal, which would afford recreation to youth,

* To ascertain the exact quantity of provisions required for the society, read J. R. Edmond's Practical, Moral, and Political Economy.

and serve to bring corn, &c. into the town; it
should branch off in the centre, leaving an island,
No. 11. No. **12**, a factory, for the manufacture
of such goods as require fire or water.
No. **13**, a warehouse, for the receipt of iron,
lead, and copper ore. No. **14**, temple of Wisdom; the two wings for the education of youth,
the centre for those who study the fine arts,
composers, doctors, and astronomers. No. **15**,
temple of Happiness: part of this building
for the reception of those who have arrived at
that age, when they would wish to retire from
toil, both mental and bodily; the other part
for those who prefer leading a single life. No.
16, the government hall. In this building the
governors of the society are to assemble, to
discuss the welfare of the community. No. **17**,
the garden of pleasure, for all persons to resort
to, from three in the afternoon, until ten in the
evening. In this garden, every thing that is either the work of Art or Nature, should be brought
into requisition, to make it really the seat of
innocent delight. The sublimity and grandeur
of Nature should be exhibited, in her rivers, her
rills, cataracts, grottos, and groves; and

the pleasing and admirable effects of Art, shewn in her fountains, bowers, illuminations, and transparencies. Here should men realize their loftiest ideas of all that is sublime and beautiful, of all that they consider attractive and lovely. It should also contain four halls, those of statuary, science, mirth, and concord : and a colonnade, where the astronomer could display to his audience the wonders of the heavens ; the naturalist, those of the earth ; and the composer delight the senses with the effects of music. No. 18, the garden of praise, which should be planned so as to excite the sublimest feelings on entering it. It should contain a promenade, and a temple for worship. There should also be a collection of beasts, birds, and fishes, so arranged as to give the best possible effect ; and a similar collection of the choicest botanical productions. In both of the gardens should be cottages for those who attend to keep them in order.

It would require a society consisting of between 6,000 and 7,000 persons to allow my system to bear upon all its points : viz. 3,000 persons about the age of 21, with their wives, and 50 persons about 40, with their wives. The young men to work, and the middle aged men to be considered as regulators.

The town being thus supplied with inhabitants, and provided, in every respect, with the means of affording them habitations, sustenance, clothing, and recreation, I proceed, in further development of my system, to consider the necessities of the Society, or Brotherhood, with regard to the important questions of Government, Education of youth, and Religion. I shall first speak of

GOVERNMENT.

MAN, under the present system, is a mere machine. He is enslaved, degraded, and debased. He has no power to act of himself, but is surrounded by circumstances which act upon him; and is compelled to receive impressions and to imbibe prejudices, quite inimical to his real good. Nature, who from month to month, and from year to year, pours her blessings into the lap of man, in many instances pro-

duces misery instead of happiness : so
much has he disorganized and perverted his
best means of enjoyment. To give him real
happiness, the darkness of ignorance must be
chased away by the light of knowledge. He
will then be able to discern truth from error :
will soon remove the bad circumstances that
now surround him, and be no more the slave of
ignorance. Reader, remember I am addressing
all classes of mankind ! Then, Britons ! open
your eyes, and view the mean, the paltry powers
which now enslave you,—which grasp you
with a hold so firm, that you say it can never be
loosed ! Ignorance has placed you in a dun-
geon, shutting out the light of Truth and Reason;
has given you that bauble, gold, to dazzle your
understanding with its lustre ; and placed over
you, that monster, Prejudice, who has bound
you in his iron chain. My friends, arise !
watch the moment when Prejudice is least upon
his guard, and allow Reason and Truth to throw
their cheering light upon you. Soon will you
then cast away the treacherous metal ; soon
will you tread it in the dust. You will detest
it as an " abominable thing." If you act thus,

Prejudice will give way to Truth, and Ignorance to Knowledge. The danger will vanish, and you will be surprised that you have been so long enslaved by powers so despicable and so detestable.

The government of the society formed under this new system, should be vested solely in men of every profession who have attained the age of forty. Men's minds at this age arrive at a point, when if properly brought into action, they will produce the most beneficial results. It would be one great end of this system to make men really free. I do not speak of that ideal freedom which men now boast of: there is not one man in a thousand, who has ever experienced the happiness of being perfectly free. Indeed, in the present system, all men are slaves, either to circumstances, their passions, or their prejudices. In this system on the contrary, it will be seen that men, from their birth to their death, would experience the most perfect freedom; and consequently, when they had arrived at the age of forty, would be allowed to act as they pleased; to work, or not to work; to attend to the management of the society or not, at their own will and pleasure.

The principal concerns which they would have to attend to, as governors, would be, the bartering of goods manufactured in the town, with strangers; the warehouses, that they might be always properly supplied with manufactured goods, and materials for the manufacturer; any inconsistency in the conduct of the inhabitants, in order that it might be rectified: all the buildings, so that they might be kept in proper repair; the regular distribution of provisions; and the general wants and comforts of all.

It will be seen that every man would have the prospect of one day becoming a governor; and consequently, have the strongest inducement to attend to the orders that the governors might see it necessary to issue, for the welfare of the community. Thus, if any of the departments required a fresh supply, or tenders were sent by strangers for the barter of any commodity, of which there was not a sufficiency, after the subject had been debated in council, printed notices should be sent round to all; and

E

as every men would be required to employ his
time or talents, for the general good of the
society, all would at once see the expediency of
furnishing the necessary supplies.   Still no restraint would be put upon any one : every man
would be left to act by his own free will,
without any danger to the public welfare; for
the system of education which I shall propose
hereafter, would so act upon the mind, that
employment would be considered a pleasure, and
not in any way a toil.   Every man, whatever
might be the trade or profession in which he at
any time became engaged, would receive from
the public stock whatever he required; clothes
to wear, food to eat, and physicians to attend him
when ill: and would enjoy pleasures which
but few have now the possibility of doing,
with the certainty of being provided for in
old age, and the prospect of eternal bliss hereafter.

I would ask the advocates of the present
system, What could men require beyond than
the above? What advantage is it to have more
than we can possibly make use of ?   If society
was properly formed, one man could always

produce more than sufficient for himself : then why not let the surplus of his production go towards equalizing those blessings, with which, under the present system, the idle class are satiated, whilst the productive class have it not in their power to partake of?

It was not to Adam alone that God gave dominion over the "fish of the sea, and fowls of the air," but to Adam and his *posterity*; and, consequently, all men have, by nature, an equal right to participate in those bounties which Providence so lavishly bestows. By what authority, then, does one man arrogate to himself those things, which, if properly equalized, would confer happiness on all mankind alike : but which, those who possess in superabundance do not really enjoy, while those who have them not, are miserable for the want of? so that in both cases they are rendered the very reverse of blessings. Many a rich man, through the whole course of his life, has not performed one good action; his own sensual gratification being the only spur to all his exertions, while his possessions (sufficient, perhaps, to support twenty men) have not been obtained through

his own industry, or talents, but inherited from
his forefathers; by whom they were first
received from a Sovereign, who had wrested
them from the original possessor, by means of
that species of wholesale robbery which men
call war. Thus we should often find, that the
rich, the mighty, and the idle of the land, are
in possession of that, which in justice belongs
to those, whose labour has brought it to a state
fit for production.

And I would ask, if it is not also a fact, that
but few men of genius, have realized that prosperity to which their exertions entitle them.
Their minds deeply intent upon some grand or
notable discovery, cannot be supposed to be at
all engaged in the accumulation of money, and
therefore they become the victims of interested
persons, who make a property of their abilities.
The man of genius is mostly doomed to struggle with poverty, while the man of no intellect,
but of a low and sordid mind, is reaping all
the benefits derived from their talents. Thus
is genius trod in the dust, till at last, crushed
to atoms by the weight which it is unable to
shake off, it leaves this world of darkness and
wretchedness. But to proceed.

A certain number of governors should attend at the warehouses, daily, from ten till three o'clock, to receive manufactured articles from the makers, and to answer the application of those persons who required materials or clothing. Each department of the warehouses should be superintended by such of the governors as had previously been engaged in the line of business to which it was appropriated. Thus, the shoe department should be under the control of shoemakers; the hat department under that of hatters, and so on.

The females of the society should be employed to make the linen garments, and such articles of furniture as require needle-work; and would receive from the warehouse, the goods and necessary implements for that purpose. They should also make their own clothes, and dress according to their ages. The fashion of their dress should be extremely simple, yet such as to render them lovely and desirable. With regard to the distribution of provisions, the governors should see that the slaughter yard and provision warehouses were properly supplied; and that the inhabitants received their provision daily, and at proper hours. It should be taken round by the butchers and bakers, in machines for the purpose; so that every family might have their choice. Each person would be required to take a sufficiency of provision on the Saturday, to last till the Monday following; as no work whatever would be allowed on the sabbath.

Every youth, when arrived at the age of fourteen, would be required to choose some trade or profession, that he might learn to be useful to his fellow man; but after such trade or profession was learned, he would be allowed to act as he pleased.

At three o'clock, those who felt inclined, might quit their work, and follow such recreations as they liked. The Garden of Pleasure would be then opened, where each one might amuse himself as he thought proper: some in conversation, or walking: the young people in dancing, or other healthful sports: some persons might attend to the orations, or music, and others wander over the garden. The governors should also take care to vary the amusements, that the mind might not be tired by sameness. I have before observed, that, in this garden, Nature and Art should vie with each other, to produce the greatest possible diversity of entertainment.

Men would also be allowed to travel at pleasure : but, in the infancy of the society, would be required, at their return, to give an account of the good they had done, or the benefits they had received. As the society advanced towards maturity, such would be its superior state, that its inhabitants would have no other motive to quit their peaceful homes, than the pure one of benefitting their fellow creatures.

When men arrived at that period of life at which old age begins to creep on, and they found their strength decaying fast, and their faculties getting weaker and weaker, having done all in their power for the good of their fellow men, they should retire to the Temple of Happiness; where their latter days would be passed in calmness and serenity. No cares for their offspring would trouble them ; no fears for the future would disturb their minds in the contemplation of the delightful idea, that they were only leaving this world for a better.

The other part of this building should be appropriated to those who wished to live a life of celibacy. The females who inhabited it would be required to attend to the comforts of the aged, and to keep the building in order and cleanliness. Young girls from the age of fourteen, till marriage, would be required to assist those married people who had no children : (except the eldest, who would remain with her parents :) but their labour would cease daily, at the regular hour of three.

With respect to the union between the two sexes, the parties should make their wishes known to the governors; who would thereupon appoint them a dwelling house, and see it properly furnished for their reception. The parties should stand up in the temple on the sabbath day, and openly take each other for man and wife. If they afterwards found, that, from difference of tempers, or any other cause, they could not live happily together, they should be allowed to separate, and repair to theTemple of Happiness. Thus would all unhappiness, with regard to marriages, cease.

As it is impossible to be happy without

health, the health of the community should be
the chief point considered. The study of
medicine, chemistry, and surgery, must, therefore, be particularly attended to ; and it would
be requisite that the medical professors should
notice attentively the habits of their patients ;
so that they might as much endeavour to prevent disease, as to cure it when contracted.
In order to facilitate this object, each medical
man should be appointed to preside over a
certain district, which he should visit daily,
and which should be limited, so as not to be
burthensome to him.   In cases of emer-
gency, he must call in the aid of (at least) two
other professors, (or more, if necessary) for the
purpose of consultation.   Should the patient
eventually die of a disease that baffled their
united skill, they should open the body previously to interment, and endeavour to discover
the cause of death ; and if any medical
professor, in the infancy of the society, by
neglect, improper medicine, or not calling in
timely assistance, occasioned the death of a
patient, expulsion from his office should
directly ensue ; and he should be required to

F

quit the town in two days. In order to improve the study of medicine, each professor should be desired to keep a journal, in which he should enter the particulars of every case that occurred in his district, and his treatment of it; which journal should be produced at the meeting of a medical board, (convened once in every month) for the inspection of all the professors who composed the said board.

As all the necessary comforts of wine, spirits, broth, gruel, panado, sago, arrow root, jelly, &c. would be freely dispensed, on the requisition of a medical man, it would be necessary for each professor to see that no improper use was made of them, but that they were applied to the best advantage.

With regard to beverage in general, the opinion of the medical professors should be taken, as to quality, the quantity to be allowed to individuals, and the regulation of the supply.

The chief object of this system being to do away with a Circulating Medium altogether, merchants should be engaged to supply the town with raw silk, raw cotton, wool, hemp,

flax, timber, metals, coals, and every other species of material required: which they must
exchange by barter, for the manufactures of
the town. The merchant should draw up his
terms of barter, which should be laid before
the council of governors, and, according to
their decision, be acceded to by the society,
or rejected.

EDUCATION.

Upon the education of the rising generation,
from the time of their entrance into the public
school, at four years old, till their arrival at the
age of fourteen, I should place my chief hope.
To prove the utility of my plan of instruction,
and to bring the difference between it and the
existing methods home to the mind, I will endeavour to point out to my readers, the wrong
notions which are necessarily infused into the
infant mind, under the present system.
Children who abide with their parents till they
are twelve or fourteen years old, naturally imbibe all the false notions, prejudices, and other

evil qualities, of those about them; and as parents among the poorer class are mostly uneducated, and drunkards, (and indeed, indulge in every other species of vice,) the effect is dreadful to the young mind; depravity becomes firmly rooted in the heart; and the conduct of the parents continues to operate upon the children, till they arrive at maturity; when they walk in the same path : often in a worse. The same may be said of all the gradations in the nation. According to the situation in which the child is placed at his birth, he imbibes the pride and ambition of the first class of society, the narrow prejudices of the second, or the vices of the third. I will now turn your attention more fully to the different circumstances, notions, and prejudices, which are at present brought into action in forming the infant mind, among these three classes.

The first class, will be first brought under consideration. Bred up in a state of pride and luxury, taught to look down on their fellow mortals, as merely subservient to their pleasure or their profit, and to consider individual property, as the only means by which they can derive any happiness, they see, without remorse, their fellow creatures suffer the evils of poverty, while they are revelling in superfluity, or plunging into dissipation.

Very few of this class prove superior to the rest of mankind, in regard to intellectual faculties : a great proof of the insufficiency of their education to produce that benefit which is expected from it : on the contrary, it too readily instils into their minds, those bad principles, of which they very often make a boast.

We will now take a view of the second, or middle class of society. What innumerable evils has a child here to contend with ! His ideas are hardly formed, ere he is taught to consider money as the most valuable earthly possession. Nursed under the too tender eye of a parent, till five, six, or seven years old, his little passions fostered, instead of being rooted out, he is sent to a boarding school; where, if he should not meet with a good instructor, his mind becomes inert, or open only to bad impressions. Having myself experienced the ill effects of a boarding school education, the master of which was incapacitated, either through engagements or inability, I am enabled to write feelingly. The child is sent to the school, with his mind alive only to the fear of punishment, or the hope of reward, which act upon it, so as to beget innumerable evils; making education a toil instead of a pleasure. The master has, perhaps, numerous scholars; many are therefore unavoidably neglected; and the consequence is, that those who are quick and ready, though idle, may receive reward, while those who are slow, though industrious, receive punishment. Again, no attention is paid to the youth's future prospects; but his most valuable time is sometimes spent in learning that, which will be totally useless to him through the whole of his life. In other instances, he is obliged to learn that for which he has no inclination; while that which would be most congenial to his feelings, and in which, therefore, he would make most rapid progress, is never taught him, and the youth becomes indifferent to learning. Again, the master, instead of cultivating a due respect and esteem from his scholars, sometimes gives undue license to one, and uses severity towards others : this excites a spirit of insubordination in the school, which not unfrequently ends in open rebellion; so that many children who are anxious to learn, dare not, for fear of the larger boys. Thus they receive the rudiments of education, without the least knowledge of its fundamental parts.

The child is at length introduced on the great theatre of life ; taught to make riches his chief aim; to look upon every man as deceiving him ; and to do his utmost to deceive others, in his turn.

Under this head, we will also consider the amusements of children, and prove that they are equally bad in principle. Few of them do any more than engender bad propensities. Children are allowed to play games of chance, which naturally lead them, first to cheat, then to lie and steal; and arouse all the bad feelings of the heart. A few of their amusements, it is true, have the effect of adding vigour to the body; but none add vigour to the faculties. It is by a judicious employment of the season of relaxation from study, that the body may be invigorated, the mind enlarged, and the ideas expanded, to far greater extent than intense study would ever admit of.

We now come to the children of the third, or poorer class. As soon as the infant arrives at the knowledge of right and wrong, (indeed, while in the arms,) he is taught to look upon money as the means of supplying his wants. This naturally creates in him a wish to possess it, which, as his age increases, produces the worst effect upon his morals; and his depraved nature, unreformed by education, leads him to steal, lie, and deceive, in order that he may obtain money.

Besides these evils thus acting upon the three classes of society, envy, malice, and discontent, unite in steeling the mind against the admission of the finer and more generous feelings, and lead gradually on to those horrid acts of depravity and cruelty, which disgrace mankind; while they break asunder the bonds of brotherly affection, which can alone hold society together.

Equally the same may be said of modern female education, which engenders pride, vanity, the love of dress, and many other evils, ending, too often, in prostitution, and all the dreadful vices connected with it.

Thus do we behold the faculties of the mind destroyed, or cooped up, through the improper education of youth. No wonder, then, that we move very slowly on with regard to the arts and sciences; whereas if the young mind was allowed to expand freely, we should behold the sciences advanced to perfection, and the arts cultivated so as to produce great and wonderful effects on all created beings.

My readers will again say, that I have been partial ; that I have considered the evil, and not the good. I reply as before, there is little good emanating from the present system; for if one man rises above his fellows, it is not the effect of education, but of his own natural genius. Every mind has a peculiar organization, the development of which, should be the chief end of education ; and which, when properly brought into action, will inevitably lead to the most beneficial results.

G

Having pointed out the errors of modern education, and the ill effects arising therefrom, I shall call the attention of my readers to an improved system, by which I hope to remedy all the evils complained of, and to promote the happiness of all men, through the whole course of their lives.

The part of the town appropriated to the education of youth, would be the two wings of the Temple of Wisdom; one wing for boys, and the other for girls. These wings should each consist of an hospital, sleeping rooms, dining and education halls, kitchens, &c. The education halls should be appropriated to reading, writing and arithmetic, drawing, music, dancing, and the languages, in such a manner, as to allow each pursuit to be carried on, independently of any other. In the centre of each wing, should be a school library, with a lecture room over it. The large ground should be planned out for the recreation of the children, and furnished with baths, and various machines, such as the lever, pulley, wedge, screw, and other philosophical contrivances, disposed in such manner as to invigorate their bodies, and at the same time fix the first principles of science in their minds, so that amusement and instruction might be combined.

The instructors should be persons of the most amiable disposition; deeply sensible of the responsibility of their office, and convinced that the welfare of the community must depend upon their skill and diligence; and the future happiness of each child on the superiority of their instruction.

There should be three divisions of boys; the first, comprising those from four to six years of age : the second, those from six to ten : and the third, those from ten to fourteen. The first division should be placed on the girls' side; as it would devolve on the female instructors, to unfold their tender minds, in the first instance. One of the chief objects in view, should be to instil love towards each other; this should be effected, not only by formal instruction, but by the tenderest attention being constantly paid to them. No idea of reward or punishment should be allowed to enter their minds, that they might not be tempted to tell an untruth

by the hope of the one, or the fear of the other.
The children in each division should be clothed
alike, that there might be no cause for envy.
Instruction should be, as much as possible,
combined with amusement: no force
whatever should be used; no task imposed;
but the infant mind left entirely free. They
thould be taught only one prayer to their
Creator, and that should breathe the language
of praise; no idea of punishment in the
next world, should be allowed to harrass
them.

At the age of six years, they should be
placed in the second division, and removed to
the boys' academy, where the rudiments of the
different branches of education should be laid
before them, in the simplest and most amusing
manner. The masters should regulate their
conduct, watch their minds, and carefully
observe the bent of their ideas; so that the
latter might be expanded in such a way as to
be of the greatest use to society. This division
should attend to their studies from seven in the
morning, till noon.

At the age of ten, they should have more

liberty ; a room should be allowed them, as a study and sleeping room. They should attend to the lectures on History, Astronomy, Religion, Mathematics, &c., so that the ideas which had previously been formed in school, might be perfected in all their bearings. This division should attend to instruction, from one o'clock till six. The utmost freedom should be allowed, from the age of six till fourteen, so that each particular talent might take its right course.

Their sports, it has been observed, should improve the mind, while at the same time they served to invigorate the body. Professors should attend during the play hours, to give explanations, and render the most trivial sport, a pathway to science ; by illustrating the theory of the trundling of a hoop, the rolling of a ball, the projection of a stone, or the flying of a kite.

With regard to clothing, each division should be dressed in a simple, but separate uniform ; light, elastic, and in no wise calculated to incumber their bodies.

We now come to the female department. This, as has already been stated, should occupy the other wing, and be fitted up in the same manner as the boys'.

The importance of female education has never been sufficiently considered: but how necessary it is, that this should be of a very superior order, when we consider that it naturally devolves on woman to form the infant mind. Disinterestedness, purity of thought, and a firm resolve to live only for the happiness of their fellow creatures, form the basis on which I would build female education; and on this basis I would raise a structure, comprising every branch of learning, that would be most fitting for the important station the pupil would expect to fill. The silly superfluities, and useless attainments, the pride of dress, and love of ornament, (the dregs of savage life) which mark the present age, should be viewed with contempt; leaving room for nobler feelings, which alone should be called into action.

To habituate them to domestic affairs, they should be required to attend to the Temple of Wisdom; to keep it in state of cleanliness; to cook the provisions; and wash and make all the clothing for themselves, and the boys. Their instructors should be persons strongly impressed with the importance of the leading points of my system; and should always remember, that they are rendering the greatest benefit to man, while filling the station of instructor to children of either sex.

The noble doctrine of Universal Brotherhood, should be systematically and deeply impressed on the minds of youth of both sexes, from the earliest dawn of reason; together with a filial reverence for age, as the only distinction in society entitled to respect.

All the children should attend at the Gardens of Pleasure and Praise, to wait upon their elders. How delightful, on such occasions, would it be, to see well educated children exhibit that retiring grace and modesty, which would then be natural to them!

Six medical professors should reside in this temple, (three in each wing) for the sole purpose of attending to the whole establishment.

At the age of fourteen, the children, both male and female, should visit the trades, manufactures, &c., and be allowed to select such trade or profession, as might be most agreeable to them.

The other parts of the Temple of Wisdom, should be set apart for men of genius, whatever might be the point to which that genius was directed. It should be planned out with studies, libraries, and other conveniences for them; and they should have every thing allowed them that was necessary to the proper development of the powers of their minds.

That all men might receive the reward due to their exertion, the fruits of their genius should be exhibited in the Garden of Praise.— There the Sculptor should place his statues; the Artist his paintings; the Poet should recite his verses; the Astronomer open to all, the beauties of the celestial world; the Composer delight with his music; and the Elocutionist prove the utility of the efforts of some genius, who had too much modesty to do it himself. Thus would all men of genius meet with the applause due to their talents.

In the Temple of Wisdom should also be the

Printing Offices, that Authors might have their works printed and distributed round to the inhabitants, and thus receive their just meed of praise.

RELIGION.

I have now to speak of Religion, the greatest blessing possessed by man, yet by man made the vehicle of injustice, deception, rapine, and murder. Under the mask of religion, men have inflicted on each other the greatest injuries, and converted the blessing into the worst of curses. This misuse of religion arises solely from the circulation of money ; for if no money existed, there would be an equality, and consequently those feelings which now spur men on to commit the worst of crimes, would then most decidedly wither away.

To erect on the basis of the existing christian establishments, a superior system, pure in all its points, and remarkable chiefly for the simple regularity of its construction ; having no dis-cordant parts, but so harmonized, that men's

H

minds might rest upon its doctrines with perfect tranquility ; in which no mystery, nor doubts might exist, to cause a difference of opinion upon those minor subjects, which (though in themselves of little or no importance,) so frequently excite the most complicated disputes, would indeed be a " consummation devoutly to be wished," and it would be my object to bring the society as near to that " consummation " as this life would allow.

I shall first give a glance at the christian religion as it now exists. How very few act up to its doctrines in every particular ! Indeed, what man, in the present system, is so placed, with regard to circumstances, as to be enabled to live according to its dictates ? What differences of opinion exist ; producing the greatest variety of ill will and prejudices ! What a wretched perversion of true religion, to unite it to civil concerns ! When religion is the brightest ray transmitted from heaven, to give light and happiness to this world, to make it an instrument in the hands of kings and princes to mis-rule their subjects, is a crime of the deepest dye. When the mind wanders over the history of past events, it is lost in horror to find, that men have made religion the means of deluging the earth and seas with blood. The fanatieism of one man, the religious bigotry of another, or the ambition of a priest, has produced all the accumulated horrors of war upon war, and pestilence upon pestilence.

Short sighted, miserable men ! what has all your fanaticism, your bigotry, and your ambition produced, but the worst of misery to your fellow mortals ! But we need not look back to history, it is sufficient to look at the present time, to prove the extent of the ill will aroused in the minds of men towards each other, while eagerly grasping at that shining metal, which dazzles the understandings even of the teachers of religion. Behold an Archbishop, tempted by the love of gold to break that commandment which he has sworn to teach, and feasting on his twenty, thirty, or forty thousands a year; wrenched by the stern decree of the tithe law, from the earnings of the industrious or the poor ! Do we not hear of prosecutions for non-payment of tithes ? Do we

not see men dragged from their wives and
children, and cast into prison for the same cause?
It is this which brings the established religion
into contempt ; it is this which produces
Atheism, and Deism, and above all, dissenters
from the establishment ; it is this that produces
the ill will, the uncharitable feeling, and hatred
one to another, which now pervade all classes
of mankind with regard to matters of religion.
Nor are, as I have said, even its ministers exempt from the baneful effects of the love of
money.   Those who are styled "priests of the
most high God," whose business is to propagate
his truth, and to set an example of the contempt
in which the " unrighteous mammon " should
be held by every follower of him, who said,
" lay not up for yourselves treasures upon
earth," stand in hourly danger from its con-
taminating influence : and the different ecclesi-
astical offices from Archbishop to Curate, on
account of the superfluity or lack of riches,
which distinguish those who hold them, instead
of raising in their minds the pure, meek, and
humble spirit of religion, serve but excite
pride, envy, and covetousness.

And when the different sects of religion are analyzed, we find them mostly actuated by the same spirit. For some worldly benefit they are hypocrites; they assume religion, either to conceal crime, or to obtain gold. Few are actuated by the genuine spirit of religion; selfishness pervades their minds. The wish to be thought greater or better than our fellow men, produces most of the ideas that are found to direct or control the ruling passion in every breast.

Religion, viewed generally, according to the present system, is only assumed : few really feel the power of it; and those who do, through the demoralizing effects of the present age, are too often drawn back to their former vices. Forms and ceremonies are still adhered to : some really useless; enslaving the mind, engendering pride, and, too often, producing the worst effects upon men in general.

Let it be observed, that I have not included in the foregoing sketch of religion as it now exists, any other than that of Christ. I defy any man who has read theScriptures to dispute, that in them are to be found the most beautiful

and perfect laws. The religion of Christ, as
pointed out to us in the New Testament, is
most simple, and would, if duly observed by all,
produce the most beneficial results. Yet,
under the present system, that religion is so
perverted, as to cause the many evils I have
described, and the many diversified opinions
which now exist among men. The question
may be asked, What is the reason of this?—
there must be some grand point of that religion
which is entirely neglected; and through that
neglect we are now suffering. Yes, my reader,
there is a point, a command, which men appear
to consider was never in existence. Indeed, I
have been told, even by the wise and good,
that in the present state of things, it is impossible for men to obey the command. (How
strong an evidence in proof of the wretchedness and fallacy of the system!) The command
given by our Saviour, to love our neighbour as
ourselves, and to do unto others, as we would
have them do unto us; when once properly
implanted in the human breast, would produce
all those happy results to which we are now
strangers; would set in order the vast machi-

nery of nations, which is now wholly deranged, and harmonize those discordant jarrings, that are every where to be found. The bad passions and miserable feelings that are ever rising in the human heart, would die away; and in their place would spring up all that is benevolent and philanthrophic. When this was accomplished, a new era would flourish on the earth. Then let Brotherly Love be implanted in every mind—let its delights be opened to all by the preacher ; sung by the poet; and drawn on canvas by the painter; as the first steps towards a renovated state of society.

As religion, acting strongly upon mens' minds, has hitherto been made the means of producing innumerable miseries, so would I make it act in future, that no sacrifice should be considered too great, when brought into competition with the good of mankind. Extreme love to God and to our fellow man, will alone produce the purest and simplest religion. No forms or ceremonies are needed to debase or shackle the mind ; no pomp to foster pride, nor superiority to excite envy : but it should enlighten the mind, and elevate it to a celestial joy.

A s, in the new system, there would be no sin, the fear of punishment in a future state, would be erased from the mind ; and consequently praise alone would be given to God, for giving us in his mercy a Saviour, who at that blissful period, would pour out the residue of his spirit, so that his kingdom should come, and his reign be over all the earth.

Youth, at the age of ten years, when the mind could comprehend the nature of the great plan of redemption, the great benefits and blessings they were receiving, and the wretched state of human nature, that required so great a sacrifice, should have these truths so brought home to their minds, as to lead them deeply to reflect upon the greatness of God, and the goodness of the Saviour: this should be so done, that it might not produce any wish to live under the old system, but only to look upon it as a state of misery, from which mankind had happily escaped.

At the age of fourteen they should be permitted to converse with men of superior age, and allowed to attend the solemn service that would be performed in the Garden of Praise, and partake of the sacrament, which should be regularly administered every sabbath, in remembrance of the great sacrifice, through which they experienced so much true happiness.

At each corner of the Garden of Praise should be erected a Temple: and to these temples all should resort on the sabbath : as men would require no warnings nor threatenings, with respect to the future consequences of sin, no other service would be needed, than solemn and heart-felt thanksgiving and praise. Every one should be taught the power of harmony in his youth; so that the most sublime and solemn effect might be produced, both by vocal and instrumental music.

In the course of the day, those who wished to return thanks to God for benefits received, should, at certain hours, rise and offer up their prayers: and any pair who wished to be united, should come forward, publicly exchange their vows with each other, and solemnly unite, in the presence of the whole congregation.

One day in every week should be wholly devoted to God. No work whatever should be done by any person on that day; it should be

a day on which all should turn their thoughts
to that world to which we are hastening; where
it will be an eternal sabbath.

All men would see the necessity of daily
praise and prayer; and it would be seen that,
in the new system, "old things" would entirely
"pass away, and all things become new."
Every sin would be rooted out, and lost in the
change; every thing that the eye now sees,—
empires, cities, and towns,—would disappear as
the system advanced; sciences now in their infancy would be brought to perfection, and
sciences yet unknown, discovered; so that
every thing we now have an idea of, is as
nothing to what would then take place; my mind
cannot encompass the effects it would produce,
for when it tries to grasp at a small portion of
its superiority to the present state of things,
it is lost in the contemplation. Within the
new system would be found the most perfect
state of real happiness, which the finite mind
could comprehend—even that kingdom promised in Holy Writ. Reader, do not consider
that I am going too far: do not suppose me a
fanatic, or a visionary! Do we not, in the Lord's

prayer, pray for that kingdom? Do we not
read in the Scripture of such a kingdom, promised in the plainest terms? How is it to be
brought about? By the agency of man. The
greatGod will, in his mercy, place this within the
power of human means to accomplish. For He
has spoken, and it shall be accomplished. Then
let man, in gratitude, use the means now offered
him, to effect this noble object, and quickly
shall,

> "——the kingdoms, the kingdoms of this world,
> Become the kingdoms, the kingdoms of our God."

I feel no hesitation in saying, that even if
but twenty men were to join, and act upon the
principles here laid down; and, according to
their circumstances, train up their children
entirely in pursuance of my system of education, they would lay the foundation of God's
kingdom, and their children would form a part
of it.

For the further advancement of Religion, as
the basis of this system, persons should be
allowed to travel to distant parts of the world;
where they should do their utmost to bring the
inhabitants to a knowledge of the truth as con-

tained in the Bible. Every means should be
furnished to these Missionaries, to enable them
to form similar societies in all parts of the
world. The Bible should be printed and distributed gratuitously over the whole earth.
That love towards man, which would be so
deeply implanted in every breast under the new
system, should be allowed to operate everywhere, so that no dangers might deter, nor
any obstacle prevent, the endeavours of the
Missionaries, to bring about the desired effect:
but Missionary upon Missionary should go
forth, to teach mankind where true happiness
might be found, and to prove to all the world
that co-operation, love to one another, the utter
abolition of money, and a firm reliance upon
God and his promises, are the only means that
will produce permanent enjoyment in this life :
that if these means were employed, all earthly
honors as well as all wretchedness, misery,
slavery both mental and bodily, war, and those
innumerable other evils, which now exist,
would soon vanish from the earth ; and that,
upon the ruins of the old world, a new one
would arise, superior in all its parts. The

mind of man, which is ever grasping at new attainments, would (under such instructors) become more refined; the power of truth would aid their persuasive eloquence, and nations might then be said to be "born in a day."

Thus, if money capital was discontinued, and extreme love to God and our neighbours, deeply impressed upon every heart; would all men be constrained to believe in the Scriptures. God, beholding from his high abode, the efforts of man, to shake off the yoke with which he has been galled these six thousand years, would surely smile upon those efforts, and, in mercy, pour out his spirit upon all flesh; encouraging man to wait in humble preparation for the coming of the Saviour's kingdom.

And, O my reader! what a blissful period would burst upon the wondering gaze of a delighted world! All flesh would behold, with astonishment and gratitude, the stupendous power and goodness of God. The soul of man would be lost in extacy and surprise—Hosannas would fill every tongue—while unalloyed praise and thanksgiving would come from every lip.

Think not, my christian readers, that times
of toil and trials would be always necessary.
I know full well, that they are now required
to fit us for eternal glory ; for if God was not
pleased thereby to loose us from that heavy
shining metal, it would weigh us down to
eternal misery. Such is its worldly nature,
that it would fetter and defile our souls, and
totally unfit us for a blissful eternity. Oh!
open your eyes, and see the chain by which
Satan has bound you; and when you see it,
burst it asunder by one vigorous effort,
trusting upon your Saviour ; and though it be
like the seven green withes, with which Delilah
bound Samson, yet you, like Samson, shall
then " break it, as a thread of tow is broken,
when it toucheth the fire. "   Let your
ministers and preachers proclaim this to the
world.—Let them shew to all, that, by a simple
act of man, trials and toil may be driven away,
leaving behind them a sabbath of rest. Then
will those petty differences, that now exist, be
buried in oblivion : then will the different sects
of Religion shake hands, and exclaim,—
"Behold the day of the Lord !"   Then will the

Mahometan, the Papist, and the Pagan, be swept away by the besom of truth ; the Jews brought in with the feelings of the Gentiles, and all the world become one Brotherhood.

CONCLUSION.

HAVING now brought the Development of my system to a conclusion, it remains for me to point out the way in which that system might be most easily reduced to practice. This I shall presently shew : but in order to induce men more readily to come forward, and lay the foundation of a change so desirable, allow me first to recapitulate the blessings which would follow its accomplishment; and, with that view, I will ask you to join me for a moment, in contemplating the sentiments which would rise in the breast of a stranger, on entering a community, regulated according to the principles laid down in this work.

Behold him, then, on entering the town, met by a courteous youth, who, with a modest grace, the result of that superior mode of education which has been described, conducts him from place to place, and answers all his eager enquiries in the most ingenuous manner.

First, he takes him to the manufactories, or the workshops; where he sees man labouring hard at some employment, which he knows to be requisite for the general good; or, beholds him straining every nerve, to perfect some grand discovery: with happiness sparkling in his eyes, and joy beaming in his countenance, at the delightful conviction, that he is exerting himself for the benefit of his fellow-creatures. Next, he accompanies his conductor, in his hours of amusement, to the Garden of Pleasure. If he is a youth of gay habits, he leads him to the Dancing Hall; where he invites him to join in the dance, while the joyous strains of music enliven his heart. If the youth is sedate, he takes him to the Reading Rooms; where his mind can range over the events of past ages, or delight in the regions of prose and poetry. If the stranger delight in music, or eloquence, he leads him to the Amphitheatre; where his mind is lost in ecstacy, amidst the softest and sublimest strains

K

of music, or raised to admiration, at the matchless powers of the poet and the orator. In the Gardens, the sublimity of nature calls forth praises to his Creator, and the beautiful effects of Art strike him dumb with admiration. If he loves to behold the diversified and enlivening charms of rural scenery, the youth leads him to yonder summit; where, on the terrace, that overlooks the surrounding country, he beholds rural walks, adorned with splendid edifices, and numberless mansions. If he asks, " To whom do all these belong? " The youth tells him, " To the society, "—that they are as much his property as another's, and whenever he feels inclined to make use of them, he is at liberty to do so.

Leaving his interesting guide, the stranger seeks the elders of the society. If he prefers conversation, he goes with them to the Conversation Hall, where he is surprised to see the tables spread out with wines, and delicacies of every kind. Looking around, he views with admiration, the elegant simplicity with which the building is decorated. He finds the conversation refined, animated, and delightful. No boist-

CONCLUSION. 67

erous mirth, no irreverent jest prevails, but
from the lips of all around him flow instruction, and delight; while the bright sallies of
the imagination are conducted with harmony
and moderation. Here he is waited on by youths
between ten and fourteen years of age; whose
graceful modesty and attention delight him,
while he is astonished at the filial reverence
and ready obedience evinced by them toward
their seniors.

He next attends the Garden of Praise, on
the sabbath. Hark! What delightful strains
are those that steal upon his ear? They are the
Hosannas of children, chaunting the sabbath
morning hymn. See that old man on the right
hand; who, appreciating the blessings that
surround him, is openly praising his Creator!
Mark that youth sitting in yonder alcove, at
the foot of the fountain, on the left; who is
raising his voice in the sweetest melody, while
he strikes the instrument in his hand with the
touch of a master of harmony. Now the
stranger enters the Temple. The solemn peal
of the organ, as it rolls across the edifice,
strikes his heart with awe: the gentle and sil-

very voices of the singers, pierce into his soul, and raise it to the Deity. Suddenly, every voice is hushed : one of the seniors rises, and opens the service by solemn prayer. Now they form themselves into parties, and partake of the sacrament, with feelings of joy not to be described ; while music's sweetest strains gently carry the soul, in imagination, far beyond this earth.

In the afternoon, he beholds the eager youth, leading the willing maid to the Hymeneal Altar. No dark prospects of futurity cloud their day of happiness, or dim their view of enlarged, uninterrupted felicity. At length evening arrives; and, while music once more fills the air with melody, he sees all return to their houses, with hearts filled with thanksgiving, and mouths with praise.

On the morrow he attends the Government Hall. The elders are debating an affair of great consequence. What is it that demands such deep deliberation? It is a deputation from a neighbouring community, with proposals to the young men, inviting them to join a party of Missionaries, in attempting to establish communities in Africa. The task is arduous, but listen to the animated language employed on the subject.—" Who can be so selfish, as to refuse his aid, to procure for others, those blessings, which he so lavishly enjoys; and which are in his power to bestow?—" None," "none!" resounds from every side ; "We give our united and cordial assent to the proposition, let the invitation be printed, and sent to the inhabitants!" Now our stranger walks through the Town. Mark that fine manly youth, with what pleasure he reads the announcement! Notice that group of young men, with what eagerness they prepare to obey the mandate ! "We go," say they, "to conquer the evil passions of men ; and we will achieve the victory, for it is the noblest field in which fame can be won!"

He now visits the Schools, and sees the children all joyous and happy, delighted with the instruction they are receiving. Then, entering the dwellings of several of the inhabitants, in different parts of the town, he is charmed with the cleanliness and order that prevail throughout: he views the tastefully decorated rooms, and is delighted with the possessors of them. There the mother is seen, gracefully occupying herself, in whatever will give pleasure and happiness to her husband and children. Her eldest daughter is assisting her, while strong and healthy infants are playing about the room.

And now he walks to the Temple of Happiness. There he beholds the cheerful old man, employing his thoughts on " another and a better world. " Mark, how perfect are his intellects ! how upright his form ! and though his locks are bleached by time, still a serene smile of happiness and content plays on his countenance. See, how attentively the youth on his left observes him, anticipates every wish, and listens with respect to his heavenly discourse, which contains lessons never to be forgotten ! they speak of universal love here, and eternal bliss hereafter.

Here let me close the picture, and ask the rich and titled man, If riches, or power, ever purchased such happiness as this ? no : they envelope him in a cloud, which he must chase away, before he can become wise or happy.

He is enslaved and tantalized by a power, which he must know, ere he can resist it. It is the want of this knowledge that is the barrier to the attainment of perfect freedom, consummate wisdom, and true happiness. Ye rich and mighty of the earth, ignorance is the cloud that envelopes, and gold is the power that enslaves and tantalizes you! Do you ask proof of this? Is it not true, that you spend your time in the trifles of an hour, and waste it in silly pageantries and mockeries? Your wisdom is turned into foolishness: your speeches uttered in the senate, night after night, for what you term the good of the nation, tend not to secure the country's weal; for your ideas, your actions, and your time, are all taken up in the pursuit of that which is your bane : so much are you enslaved by gold. Divest yourselves of this worthless dross, and let the grand truth, that our own real happiness consists in bestowing happiness on the greatest number of our fellow creatures, be deeply impressed on your mind; and at once exert your powers to let every action evince the depth of that impression. Let every

object, but the vast one of abolishing Individual
Property and the accumulation of money, and
promoting Brotherly Love in their stead, be laid
aside. Form communities, build schools, and
let cheap knowledge go forth among all classes
of the people. Then will thousands in your
time, and millions yet unborn, bless you for
the joy they will experience through your
means; and proclaim aloud, the names of
their benefactors; while distant lands shall
echo to the sound, and future ages repeat them
with admiration.

I have now to answer the question, Which
are the quickest and best means that may be
employed, to bring such a superior system into
active operation?   They are these : First, let
men of benevolent, and philanthropic principles,
who, although they possess property, are also
blessed with noble minds, (for some such there
are even in the present depraved times) and
would gladly soar above the mean, grovelling
passion for gold, the sordid covetousness of the
age; in whose breasts, feelings of humanity, and
sympathy for their fellow men, abound.   Let
such men, I say, view with unprejudiced eye

the existing system, through all its ramifications, and compare it with the one now laid
before them; then, let them turn and behold
the beautiful harmony in which all inanimate
nature exists,—the blessings ever offered
to man. Again, let their thoughts pierce
through the skies, into the heaven of heavens;
and behold, with reverential awe, the King of
Kings, the great Omniscient, watching for the
least indication of man's endeavouring to free
himself from the errors by which he is enslaved; and, through the mediation of the
Saviour of mankind, pouring out his spirit
upon him, and bringing him out of darkness into
his marvellous light. And when they are thus
convinced of the extent of the blessings with-
held from them, by the present demoralizing
constitution of society; let them come forward
boldly, as the benefactors of mankind: for if
two hundred such men were to unite, and give
their money, time, and talents, how soon we
should see that happiness which I have already
described, diffused on all around us. Methinks
I see many of my readers start back at the
proposal, their minds still clinging to their

darling gold, like a dying man to life ; they cannot break the spell. "What! live without
money? it is impossible !" says one: "Human
nature is too bad to be so changed, " says another : "It never has been, and never can be ,"
says a third. And is it a small thing for you
to be the chosen few, that shall give, not only
earthly, but heavenly happiness, to millions in
future ages, that you bring forward such weak
and futile reasons as these, for the support of
your sordid dust? Away, away with them,
and let your better feelings operate, while I
open to you the simple means required to bring
about the desired object.

The before described individuals should, in
order to commence a society, each give, either
raw or wrought materials, or money, to the
amount of £500. Those donors, who besides
their money or goods, also gave their time and
talents to forward the cause, should be considered governors for life. The amount of the
capital thus raised would be £100,000. ; part
of which should be appropriated to purchase
land, and build houses, with a warehouse,
assembly room, school, and chapel. The gov-

ernors should select 400 persons of different trades, choosing such only as are really requisite for the support of each other; as tailors, hatters, shoemakers, butchers, bakers, cabinetmakers, smiths, bricklayers, carpenters, engineers, about 50 husbandmen, 20 instructors of youth, with men of literary talents, and printers; adding others as they were able. They might also accomplish much by their own exertions· Thus men of literary and oratorical talent should give lectures upon the new system, in the different towns in England, and endeavour to form corresponding societies, for the enlargement of the capital; and their lectures should be printed and circulated gratuitously over the whole Kingdom. Tradesmen should superintend the materials, which might be laid up in temporary warehouses: medical men should lend their aid to preserve health: and so on. The governors should, above all, see that youth were educated in strict accordance with my plan; and, in the infancy of the society, adopt the amusements, &c. planned out in the preceding pages, as extensively as their means would permit; regulate the hours of work;

issue strict rules for the due preservation of
morality; and commission persons to travel, for
the purpose of exchanging the surplus productions of the society, for raw and wrought materials.   In the course of a few months,
factories might be erected, and machinery
constructed, so that raw· materials only would
be required : and, in a short time, the surplus
produce would be so much increased, that ships
might be hired to carry it to foreign lands; and
thus a new source of wealth would be opened,
to enable the governors to purchase land and
bring more persons into the community.   Thus
would the society progressively improve, until
they were enabled to build a town, according to
the plan herein given.   Meanwhile, other communities would be gradually forming in different
parts : and soon, very soon, would the new and
superior system unite the world in one vast
family; reigning in the undisturbed possession
of perfect freedom, and unalloyed happiness.

BARNET:
PRINTED BY W. BALDOCK.

TO

ARTISANS AND WORKMEN.

RULES AND REGULATIONS

OF THE ASSOCIATION FOR THE

INTERNAL COLONISATION OF ARTISANS AND THE POOR,

BY MEANS OF

A NEW SYSTEM OF MUTUAL LABOUR.

WITH

A PLAN

OF THE

ORGANIZATION AND COLONISATION

OF THE

SETTLEMENTS.

PRICE TWO PENCE.

London:

GEO. NICHOLS, PRINTER, EARL'S CT. CRANBOURN STREET,
LEICESTER SQUARE.

1837.

SUBSTITUTE

FOR

POOR LAWS.

~~~~~~~~~~~~~~~~~~~~

A society was formed in the month of March, and designated, " An association for the internal colonisation of artisans and the poor, by means of a new system of mutual labour." The constitutional act, statutes, and plan, are as follow :—

I.—CONSTITUTIONAL ACT.

Having duly considered Mr. John Miller's plan, to provide for, within the space of five years, the poor of Great Britain and Ireland, and having appointed the statutes, deeming—

That the condition of the working classes is capable of a thorough amelioration.

That the disabled poor are entitled to a full subsistence, which by the present constitution they do not possess.

That the subsistence of a number of persons, to be employed as artisans, labourers, &c., is absolutely secured by this association.

That this association will provide for twenty disabled poor, and employ thirty able poor as labourers for every sixty artisans who may join it.

That, by means of this association, in a few years a provision will be made for all the poor in the kingdom, and thus poor rates be totally abolished.

That expediency and philanthropy require the providing for the poor—which provision is to be a leading feature in the formation of the association.

That even an inconsiderable number of artisans may lay the foundation of the association.

WE, THE UNDERSIGNED, HAVE RESOLVED,

1. That a society shall be formed, consisting of persons of all classes, and that it shall be denominated—" An association for internal colonisation for artisans and the poor, by means of a new system of mutual labour."

2. That the statutes of the association be printed.

3. That an account of the nature and objects of the society be drawn up, by Mr. John Miller; and that the said account be printed in a pamphlet, to be sold, or distributed gratis, as the committee may direct.

London, March 21st, 1837.

(SIGNATURES.)

II.—RULES AND REGULATIONS OF THE SOCIETY.

1. *Rules and Regulations relating to the objects and plan of this Institution.*

1. The object of this association is, to provide for the welfare of its members, and to give employment to the poor of the united kingdom

2. The means for obtaining this double object consist in uniting artisans and labourers in settlements, to be formed within the united kingdom, so that they may benefit each other by mutual labour.

3. The settlers to be under no other engagement than to work in his proper vocation for such a limited number of hours as may be agreed upon; and his freedom is to be in no way restricted for the fulfilment of his engagement.

4. The remedy against the abuse of this freedom and its consequent degenerating into drunkenness, idleness, quarrelling, &c., consists in the power of expelling all guilty members.

5. For the legal working hours, the committee supply the settlers with all things needful, (and, in time, with a house and garden likewise.)

6. Besides the legal hours, every settler is to be allowed to work OVER HOURS, and thus to procure for himself NONEY to spend for his own convenience or luxury.

2. *Rules and Regulations relative to the Organization of the Association.*

7. The association is to consist of—

A. Ordinary or working members :—Persons belonging to any of the settlements.

B. Honorary members giving a donation or annual subscription.

8. The association to be divided into sections, each containing neither more than 150 nor less than 25 ordinary members.

9. Each section to choose exclusively from honorary members, who either have subscribed £1 1s. annually,

or presented a donation of £10 10s. at least, the following officers :—

A. PRESIDENT.
B. VICE PRESIDENTS. (As many as may be deemed necessary.)
C. SECRETARY.
D. CASHIER.

10. The entire association to be under the control of a central committee; to consist of a president, several vice presidents, sixteen directors, (four English, four Scotch, four Irish, and four Foreigners,) four trustees, a treasurer, and principal secretary.—The directory to comprise four divisions.—1st. for agriculture,—2nd, for building,—3rd, for trade,—4th, for finances.

11. The principal secretary brings into effect the orders of the committee.

12. The central committee to be held in London, and to meet for business once a week

13. Twice a year, viz.—on the 21st January and the 21st June, three deputies, two working, and one honorary member, from every section, are to be sent to London, in order to form with the central committee a congress. This congress is to take into consideration the affairs of the association, and the revision of the rules, regulations, by-laws, organizations, &c., whenever necessary. The deputies at this congress have legislative votes.

3. *Rules and Regulations relative to Elections.*

14. Every reputable person has a right to become a member of this association.

15. Every person has likewise the right, at any moment, to quit the association.

16. To become a member, it is only necessary to state to the principal secretary, or to the secretary of any of the sections, name, family, profession, age, country, and religion.

17. In every town of the united kingdom sections of this association are to be formed; each section to choose its officers as soon as the number of its members amounts to twenty-five; of which due notice is to be forwarded to the principal secretary,

18. To form a new section three persons are sufficient. These are to choose a fourth to act as deputy secretary, in order to superintend the affairs of the section until the proper officer be chosen.

19. As soon as 20 or more sections shall be formed within the united kingdom, they shall forthwith proceed to choose the central committee, by deputations of one honorary and two working members from each section.

20. The directors to be elected for three years, and one third of the number to go out of office every year. Those who go out not to be eligible for re-election for twelve months. Those who have attended the fewest meetings of the board to retire after the first two years; after which to go out by rotation.

21. All other officers to be elected on the 21st June, every year.

22. The only paid officer to be the principal secretary, who shall be elected for life ; and to whom, on account of the numerous and difficult duties attached to the office requiring his constant attendance, a fixed and moderate salary shall be paid quarterly,—21st March, June, September, and December.

4. *Rules and Regulations relative to the Funds.*

23. The funds will consist of—
    A. The subscriptions of the honorary members.
    B. Donations, legacies, &c.
    c. Shares.

24. The disbursements of the funds may be thus arranged :—
    A. The costs for enrolment of the association.
    B. The necessary expenses for establishing the various settlements.

25. There shall be a general fund for all the associates, and for each section a separate fund.

26. The cashiers of the various sections to deduct their expenditure from their receipts, and to pay over the surplus into the general fund.

27. Honorary members pay their contributions to the cashiers of the different sections   All other revenues are only to be collected by the central committee and treasurer of the general fund.

5. *Additional Rules and Regulations.*

28. A separate statement shall be drawn up detailing the duties of the various officers, the manner of their election, the functions of the committee, &c. &c.

29. The reports of the association, detailing its proceedings to be published every week in one of the weekly newspapers, as the means of general information for the members.

30. The provisional principal secretary of the association to be vested with the functions of the central committee till its nomination.

I.—SYSTEM.

Three things are required :—1. Land—2. Money—3. Men. The founder of the association has considered the acquisition of men the only difficulty, and has, in consequence, commenced the execution of his plan, by forming the association. The system of political economy upon which this society is founded, is the system of compensation, which provides for the existing wants of an individual, or settlement, by means of the affluence existing in some other settlement, without having recourse either to exchanges (as it has been proposed by Mr. Owen) or to buying and selling.

Supposing that 100 settlements should already exist, each containing—20 agriculturists, 60 or 70 artisans, 10 servants, and 20 disabled persons ; it will be easily understood, that some will produce more iron, wood, stone, &c., than they require ; others, more manufactured goods, &c. &c. It is, therefore evident, that, under such circumstances, the surplus of each settlement may be applied to cover the deficiency of the other, without requiring a formal exchange of produce. Suppose, also, that inns were established on the roads from one settlement to another, and warehouses in towns ; the conveyance of goods would not cost any money, as waggoners would find accommodation gratis there.—By such means the circulation of money becomes entirely useless. In the settlements, every active man may live comfortably *without* money, and every unfortunate individual find an asylum

This system of compensation is calculated entirely for *moral* people ; and requires modifications to render it practicable under given circumstances. In consequence of the moderate proportion of labour required of each settler, the settlement can bestow upon him only the necessaries of life; but as men are accustomed to certain luxuries, it is necessary to give to each settler the opportunity of earning *ready money*, by his labour during the time not devoted to the commonwealth; and with these earnings he may supply articles necessary for his own comfort. This arrangement must continue till the debts of the settlement are repaid : this result obtained, the revenues will be divided annually among the settlers.

The secret of uniting and keeping together men of such various professions, inclinations, passions, and even vices, consists in not only providing for their wants, but in also allowing them the greatest possible *freedom*, so as to render them as independent as they now are.

Three causes have produced the failure of all attempts at internal colonisation :—1st, some sort of exchange taking place ; 2nd, the nonexistence of intimate connection between agriculture and trade ; 3rd, the limitation of the freedom of the settlers in some way or other : as, for instance, in dress, in food, in labour, in religion, in manners and customs, &c —Respecting this important matter the settlers will have but *one* obligation, viz : to furnish on an average six or seven hours' labour daily : in all other respects they are entirely unrestrained by any regulation ; as the very plain and natural guarantee against abuse of every sort (idleness, drunkenness, &c.) will be, the right of the community to expel (at any time or for ever) an unworthy member

In opposition to the various systems, attempts, and settlements of Owen, Fourrier, St. Simon, Rapp, Baeumler, &c., the distinguishing features of the colonial system of compensation are the following :—

1. Intimate connection of agriculture, trade and manufactures.

2. Absolute independence of the settlers.

3. The possibility of each settler earning ready money, and thereby attaining to affluence,

4. Suppression of all exchange of articles.

5. Noninterference of the association in politics, religion, laws, manners, and customs of the country,

6. Such inconsiderable capital that the interest thereof may be easily paid and the capital returned within a few years—as the following organizations will show.

IV.—PLAN OF THE ORGANIZATION.
1. *Of the Buildings.*

1. In the beginning of September, a wooden block-house is to be erected on the lands of the association, containing workshops for two weavers; one carpenter, with assistant; one cabinet maker, one locksmith, one tool-smith, one brick maker, with two assistants; a kitchen, a dining room, and a stable for two working oxen; (ten artisans, a woman for cooking and washing, and a director—in all twelve persons.)

2. The ten artisans immediately set to work to prepare beds for 100 persons, and linen for them, with furniture and utensils for the various trades, as far as practicable; bricks and tiles for the walls, roof, &c. of a large building, into which all the settlers are to enter next March; beams for the roof, excavations for the foundation, build the kitchen, a baking oven; and prepare all the utensils necessary for a larger brick field.

3. In the beginning of March the ten above-mentioned artisans enter the new building with the following, viz.:—one brick maker, two weavers, one smith, one lock-smith, one tool-smith, two carpenters, six masons, two joiners, two tailors, two shoe makers, one baker, one butcher, one gardener, one *steward*, one glazier, two tin men, one pin maker, three saddlers, four coach makers, two coopers, two turners, two iron turners, two furriers, one brewer (who is also to be inn-keeper), besides which fifty poor, viz. :— ten assistants, carriers, &c. eighteen agriculturists, five female domestics, and seventeen disabled persons; altogether forty-four artisans and fifty poor—nearly 100 persons.

4. These 100 persons are to sleep in the beds already prepared in the wooden block house, until the brick house has been finished by their common efforts.

5. The wood work of the block house will serve to

make the partitions in the new building into workshops, bed rooms, &c.

6. A brick field, and an inn for strangers must be established as soon as the building is entirely finished.

7. Public buildings are next to be erected, viz. ;—1st, a small school ; second, a mill ; third, a warehouse, in which the director will also live ; fourth, the farm house, consisting of the cow house, the sheepfold, the pig stye, the hen house, the barn, the cart and manure, sheds, the hay, straw and corn lofts. All these various buildings must be finished before the harvest.

8. Two millers, two cloth weavers, two dyers, &c. may enter the settlement after the harvest, and by and by from ten to twenty artisans more, such as potters, curriers, &c. until the population amounts to about 150.

9. When the harvest is over, private dwellings will be built ; first of all for those who first entered the settlement, and laboured during the winter, and then for the remaining artisans in rotation, or by lot.

10. The private dwellings are to be sufficient for two families, and each to have two stories ; from twenty-six to thirty such houses will be required. With the view of affording, as soon as possible, a home to the settlers, it will be expedient first to construct the lower story only, in which the settler must endeavour to manage until the second story is erected.

11. The poor will be divided into families, consisting of man, wife, and children—or young men, seven persons ; and a house will be built afterwards for each family.

2. *Concerning Agriculture.*

12. No more land will be taken than just sufficient for 150 persons—it may be partly heath.

13 The land will be divided into portions, and will be cultivated according to the most approved principles.

14. Artificial manure will be used the first spring.

15. The land shall be worked with the spade only, and the plough be excluded for ever.

16. After the harvest—fourteen cows, one bull, fifty-six sheep, three rams, fourteen pigs, and sufficient fowls will be bought. The cows will be used during harvest as draught cattle, as in Switzerland.

3. *Respecting Employment.*

17 Each settlement will contain artisans conservative and productive; agriculturists, assistants, carriers, servants, officers, as the director, schoolmaster, &c. and strangers who are either passing through, or settle in the colony without wishing to belong to the association.

18. The conservative artisans, such as the baker, butcher, &c. are unable, by their profession, to produce any profit in money. The productive artisans ensure the continuance of the colony, by the production of saleable goods, viz. ;—carriages, waggons, machinery, and muskets, and other articles of luxury.

19. The artisans will be employed in their respective professions, at any time suitable to themselves, with this only restriction, that they furnish thirty-six hours' labour weekly, consequently only six hours daily on an average.

20. Should it be found requisite, nine hours' labour per day instead of six, on the average, may be enforced the first year of settlement.

21. The agriculturists (labourers in the field) and assistants are under the immediate control of the steward. They have to furnish the same number of hours' labour as the artisans ; but they will also be bound to a certain work daily, in consequence of the nature of agriculture; and if they work more than the fixed hours daily, the surplus will be accounted for. At all events they will not be bound to work more than nine hours daily. They will be bound, however, to follow the instructions given with respect to the *manner* of field labour and the place.

22. The carriers and assistants, servants, &c. are bound by the same regulations

23. The time of employment for the officers will be seven hours, whenever it is possible to fix the time.

24. With respect to strangers, there will be a scale of prices for every thing.

25. Labour will be divided,—1st, into that for the association—2nd, private—3rd, into producing works of genius, corresponding to the necessaries, the comforts, and the luxuries of life.

26. Respecting private labour, each settler will be allowed to procure customers, wherever and whenever,

and however he can; and he may use in his private la
bour the tools which he possesses.

27. As some professions, viz.; the baker, butcher, &c.
are unable to earn money out of the settlement, a factory will be established, where every one may work
during his leisure hours, and the produce of such labour
will be paid in cash, at such a rate as that the establishment will not make any profit.

28. The productions of genius consist of inventions,
&c. and will be remunerated by premiums, to be determined by the central committee.

4. *With respect to the Warehouse and the Sale of Goods.*

29. In the warehouse in which the director resides,
and which is confided to *his care,* all raw products of the
land, and manufactured goods of the settlement will be
kept—from this all the wants of the settlers will be supplied, and all goods will be sent and exported therefrom.

30. In all the towns near the settlement, similar warehouses will be erected, where clerks will reside, and sell
the goods at fixed prices.

31. On the high roads, at suitable distances, inns are
to be erected, to be kept by settlers belonging to the
association, in which the carriers may find accommodation without payment in cash.

5. *On the Food, Clothing, Beds, &c. of the Settlers.*

32. As soon as one of the settlers has received a residence of his own, he will be entirely at liberty with regard
to food, and may get any quantity he needs of meat,
bread, vegetables, beer, &c., in the warehouse, if he prefers living by himself.

33. As long as the settlers live in the common dwelling house, and take their meals together, each receives
daily, upon an average, one pound of meat, two cups of
coffee or tea in the morning, a glass of rum in the evening, four pints of beer, and as much bread and vegetables as he requires.

34. Each settler will receive a new suit of Sunday
clothes every two years, and as much wearing apparel
and linen as he may require.

35. The necessary utensils will be immediately delivered to each settler, and furniture will be supplied as
soon as possible.

36. Considering the high price of beds, the settlers must be satisfied at first with mattresses, filled with moss or maize, and the administration will take care to have them changed when they begin to harden.

6. *On Property, Justice, Instruction, Religion, Marriage, &c.*

37. Only the goods brought into the colony by the settler; the money, and what is produced by that money, and his clothing is the property of the settler.

38. Every thing else is held by the colonist, only in *possession*, but from this possession he cannot be removed, except by a voluntary secession from the colony, or general association, or by an authorized ejectment.

39. Whatever is purposely injured, alienated, or destroyed, by a settler, must be made good by himself.

40. A jury of twelve persons, a judge, and a public accuser, shall be appointed yearly by the inhabitants of the whole settlement, who are of the requisite age.

41. The public accuser has the right to call to account every individual member, not excepting the members of the directory, for all such transgressions as are not looked upon or punished by the state as crimes, viz. ; idleness, drunkenness, quarrelling, &c. The jury decides guilty or not guilty, by a majority of votes ; and the judge pronounces, in every case, the expulsion of the individual from the settlement, for a fixed period or for life, according to established regulations.

42. All crimes, properly so called, will naturally fall under the cognizance and laws of the state.

43. With regard to education, establishments will be appointed, in which the children of both sexes may receive the benefit of school instruction; and in time teachers will be appointed to give, every day, an hours' lecture, on the most essential parts of knowledge, to the adults.

44. Religion will be absolutely free, and protected—all making of proselytes will be strictly forbidden; and care will be taken that every settler may follow up his religious duties.

45. With respect to marriage, each colonist as soon as he shall have his own house built and prepared, may immediately contract an alliance. To marry sooner will not be permitted.

46. Besides Sundays, the settlers will have, every month, three days holidays. This time, amounting to thirty-six days in the year, may be employed in travelling abroad.

47. The time during which a settler may travel abroad, or remain in any town in the interior, will not depend upon the choice of the settler himself, but on the permission of the administration.

48. For these thirty-six days (in case of absence) the settler will receive a sum of money equivalent to what his wants would require in the settlement.

49. For any time over and above these 36 days, the association will give no provision, except in cases of *necessity*, and then only during three years consecutively.

50. Children will not be allowed to undergo any real or difficult labour.

7. *On the extension of the Settlements.*

51. In the first year, if the funds permit, four experimental settlements shall be established : one English, one Scotch, one Irish, and one German.

52. In the second year, about 100 settlements, and in the third and fourth years, as many as may be necessary will be established, in order to provide for all the poor of the united kingdom.

53. The union of the colonies by means of depots and magazines shall be arranged as soon as possible.

54. In establishing the colonies in the third year, all trades will be admitted, without distinction, so that there will be settlements which furnish only articles of luxury, and again, some that will consist only of shepherds, or woodcutters, or fishermen, or miners, &c.

55. In order to establish in the second year 100, and in the third, 1000 settlements, 100 and 1000 directories will be respectively necessary. To obtain these, young men who are willing to devote themselves to this philanthropic design will be invited to take up their abode in the four colonies, in order to obtain upon the spot a practical acquaintance with all the details requisite for founding and managing a settlement. For this purpose ten such men are necessary.

56. These ten persons become in the following year

directors, and each will have to visit and inspect ten colonies.

57. Moreover, the directors of the first four colonies will publish daily bulletins, which will serve as guides to the sub-directors in establishing other settlements, (and particularly in regard to the management of the people.)

58. In the next 100 colonies, 100 directors may be trained for the 1000 colonies of the 3rd year.

59. All directors will be appointed by the central committee, but may be removed by the settlers.

60. The duties of these directors will be prescribed in the regulations.

Of the Funds, Expenses, and Treasury.

61. The sum required for founding a setttlement will be, according to a calculation of the several particular expenses, £2,000, at the utmost.

62. These expenses, which the central committee will raise by shares, will be taken as a loan from the treasury.

63. No interest will be paid upon these loans either by the colonies to the association or by this to the shareholders, but the whole profits arising from the undertaking, during 25 years from the foundation of the association, will be equally divided between the shareholders and settlers As the directors may introduce into the settlements as many productive labourers as they may deem necessary, and thus produce a surplus of profit, so are the shareholders thereby assured of an immense gain.

64. Whether these future revenues of the settlers shall go into a general treasury, or whether each settlement shall have its own treasury, also, when and in what manner the said revenues shall be shared among the settlers, will be decided upon and settled by law at one of the next meetings.

65. From the day that the foundation of a settlement shall be determined upon by the association, the treasury becomes chargeable with all the necessary expenses, and for the costs of the journey to the place selected.

66. All officers of the colony who are removable, (except in case of expulsion), that is, the directors, will have an appointed salary.

Printed by Geo. Nichols, Earl's Court, Cranbourn Street, Soho.

A PROSPECTUS

FOR THE ESTABLISHMENT OF A

CONCORDIUM;

OR AN

INDUSTRY HARMONY COLLEGE.

" The great END in human DESTINY requires as the first scientific measure, the proper organization of the outward resources at man's disposal : and as the first moral effort the awakening in man of a renewed confidence in spirit, that it shall supply him with all the pre-requisite powers."

PRICE, ONE PENNY.

LONDON :

PUBLISHED BY STRANGE, PATERNOSTER ROW.

Sold by all Booksellers and News Dealers.

————

1841.

THE CONCORDIUM.

ITS ESSENTIAL BEING AND PRACTICAL WORKING IDEALLY SET FORTH

PART I.

" Abstinence from low pleasures is the only means of obtaining and enjoying the higher."—Demosthenes.

Man requires for his harmonious developement free and harmonizing conditions; not only does he for the physical nature need pure physical conditions, and for the psychical nature uncontaminated psychic associations, but needs that both be furnished before either nature can be harmoniously developed. The great aim in all societarian arrangements should be to furnish simultaneously to the creative spirit the best means for man's growth in each sphere—physical, intellectual, and moral; for in order to a right result in either nature the entire series of elements must be constantly presented.

That the present modes of individual and social life have led to unsatisfactory results, and hold out little prospect of permanent elevation, are conclusions generally admitted by right-thinking minds; and it is not difficult for any to perceive that the conditions gathered around mankind are not such as the harmony-law demands. Hence the continued call for reform. There is a love-instinct-law struggling perpetually in every mind for freedom, and which from time to time generates many scientific schemes for the reform or melioration of the old oppressive conditions.

But these reforms being isolated, partial, and contracted, are not calculated to meet the entire wants of man; while for the same reason they do not in any one point develope a complete result. Each project leaves something both in man and in his outward associations which still needs reform, and thus only a lame and impotent conclusion is exhibited, to the discredit of all attempts.

It becomes therefore most urgent to produce plans for reformation as extensive as man's deformation, and founded on a basis as universal as the love-instinct-nature, whose perfect freedom is essential to man's harmonious and happy progress in the love existence.

A division of the subject into two parts may be made according as the plans have relation to men personally, or the circumstances in which they are placed; for, though intimately and inseparably connected, these two branches of reform are quite distinct.

Our reforms hitherto have not only been confined to a mere modification of circumstances, but the bases in the new modes have been entirely connected with old principles: whereas it is necessary both that men should be themselves reformed, and that institutions should be remodelled in connexion with new principles, and this in harmony with the love-instinct-nature. Both may proceed together, with relation to the great mass of mankind ; but as it is obvious that, in the commencement, reformed men can alone produce reformed principles and reformed institutions, the preponderance in effort will judiciously be given at present towards fortifying, awakening, and increasing the good in man.

It is now generally admitted that our evils are not *political* but *social :* it remains to be seen that they are less *social* than *personal.* A reform in which man should be personally reclaimed to a more perfect union with the love-instinct-law, would be one in which he would be placed in such a position as easily and briefly to command all social and political reforms. On the other hand, political reforms however rigid, or social reforms however scientific, can never attain to man's personal renewal ; they can only lead to a state of things less obstructive to man's highest developement, and as such they should alone be considered and thankfully accepted.

Attention is called therefore to the following detail of a Concordium, or Primitive Home, which is about to be commenced by united individuals who are desirous, under industrial and progressive education, with simplicity in diet, dress, lodging, &c. to retain the means for the harmonic developement of their physical, intellectual, and moral natures.

The detail is submitted for the purpose of inviting concurrence and co-action in an attempt to realize, in a progressive and secure manner, the necessary double reform essential to human happiness.

The Concordium is a lodge as much as possible adapted for the associated residence of human beings in concert.

It is designed to afford conditions for that physical and mental harmony which the spirit-law-nature requires in order to establish itself in every individual, and become a nature sufficiently strong to surmount every obstacle, whether of personal habit or social usuage. Such means are not at present afforded. Singly, the aspiring mind finds itself weak and inefficient : and, as the excellent approaches in us we discover ourselves to be ever slow and faltering. In the absence of true constitutional relationship with the universe-being-law we are impelled to seek the companionship and co-operation of our fellow men. But with the antecedent relationship realized we should be enabled to find within the content and happiness our natures require, and should triumph over every obstruction presented by the incoherent principles and forms of present society. It will be found that from spirit relationship, through combined exertions, in social union, an accelerated progress is obtained.

No human association can be the progress cause ! though when founded on the spirit-progress-law, it may represent the cause in harmonious consequences. In such a union all that is selfish will be superseded ; a self-denying process with respect to the inferior natures will be commenced, and persevered in, until the new love-nature shall have fully established itself and subordinated all the inferior passions.

One of the first steps on the part of the union will be to withdraw itself from the external discordance and disagreement of actual society, and to place itself in more immediate connection with the universe harmonizer, in those simple conditions which it demands for the exhibition of true harmony.

The Concordium will be in the country. It will unite the desirable intelligent vivacity of urban intercourse and rural quiet; of which love will be the ruler through the representative agency of the concordist father.

Having retired from the mass of outward deteriorating circumstances with their depressing false sympathies, the new love-nature in its operations will proceed with more facility, and every individual may receive more freely of the Spirit and its gifts.

The unitary members seeking to become participants of the highest nature, their relationship with each other will also be of a higher character. The uniting unity bond is love.

They inwardly submit to the universe-love-nature as the central-union-power; and outwardly govern themselves by a paternal head. The union is a family; its executive a pater and mater.

There are no bonds nor contracts after the selfish or worldly order between the different members of the family, or between them individually or collectively and its head. In the pater or father are vested all power and authority. A loveful confidence is the ruling law in the Concordium.

A suitable quantity of land will be appendaged to it, on which the members will be co-operative materially, and communitive spiritually.

A dry and airy domicile in a salubrious climate with plenty of fresh water in its vicinage for bathing, &c. with other natural advantages will be regarded in fixing its site.

Custom having burthened us with a multitude of artificial wants, it will be the business of the members to divest themselves of all those to which they may have been subject.

As economy, no less than the conditions for the developement of man's highest natures, calls for the utmost simplicity in food, raiment, furniture, dwellings, and other outward means, the inmates on all occasions endeavour assiduously to reduce the number of these adventitious wants. Their drink will be water and their food vegetables and fruits, and they will eat their food chiefly uncooked by fire; often it may be prepared and combined novelly, and in a superior way with reference to its homogeneous qualities.

Their clothing will be that best adapted to man, without reference to fashion or caprice; of one common texture, according to variety in unity, however they may be different in shape and colour for age and sex.

They will sleep on mattresses, without down or feathers, and they will rise and retire early. Daily ablutions, or bathing, will be observed by all as far as possible. For convenience and usefulness the Concordium may be situated not far distant from a considerable town in an agricultural county.

All will labour on the soil of their domain for the production of their simple food, and the market or the shop resorted to as seldom as possible : it being the desire of every one to find a contenting sufficiency in the produce of the land they themselves cultivate.

Every member will consider that educational as well as industrial duties devolve upon him, and will therefore seek to be natured for exercising an elevating influence upon the young. A combination of scientific and moral knowledge, and of love, light, and life-being are essential requisites to the teacher.

The educational arrangements of the Concordium being intended as better conditions, both for the adult and infant, for the operation of the universal laws, they will have reference to the triune human being, and include gymnastics, industrial manipulation in agriculture, horticulture, and mechanics; perceptive science, moral philosophy, and spirit relationship.

The Concordium will be a preparatory practical school for the Community, the phalanstery, the republic, and the universal commonwealth.

Accommodation will be made, from time to time, to receive as many children of both sexes as may be offered to their charge, at ages chiefly from two to eight years. The terms to be as low as possible, consistent with the circumstances of the family.

As excessive physical labour will not be required there will be abundant leisure at the disposal of the members, which will be used for the highest end in the developement of love, faith, and knowledge, health and strength; by meditation, conversation, reading, writing, lecturing, study, and gymnastics.

Each candidate may make a short probationary residence in the Concordium previous to being admitted a member of it; during which time a moderate weekly sum must be paid in addition to his personal services.

The accepted probationers will become members. The terms of their admission will, in ordinary cases, be according to a graduated scale of charges prepared for the purpose. In extraordinary cases, the admission terms will be determined by the father.

Every probationer and member recognizing in the Concordist father an entire undivided authority in all matters whatsoever, without limitation of time, or other circumstance, submits to his fatherly guidance, as well when he shall require them to leave the establishment as during their stay in it.

The pater or father of the Concordium should be the highest manifestation of active intelligent love among the residents. The preferability would be with the married man whose unioned partner would have the capability of being the mater or mother in the establishment.

The general function of the pater and mater will be the diffusion of concentrated love sentiment, truthful intelligence, and communitive practice.

PART II.

The Concordium is proposed as the first coherent step in the transition from the present incoherent to the future harmonic state of humanity.

In order to its actualization, the first duty is the association of a moderate number of individuals who see and feel the necessity, utility, and beauty of real progress in their own being, both for their own happiness and the elevation of society at large.

Such of these as are really determined towards the attainment of true human destiny, that is to say, of the universe-love-developement, through the highest practicable intelligence, and the best regulated physical existence, will form the actual centre or core of the Concordium. Around these are to be collated other persons who, though less consciously awakened to the advantages of such communitory conditions, yet, being sincere inquirers and investigators, are desirous of testing the adequacy of new modes, as well as their own capabilities for progressive life.

Children of either sex, whose parents are wishful to have them reared in harmony with the universe-life-law, in physical health and vigour, intellectual clearness and vivacity, moral purity and love, form another human circle in carrying out this design.

By means of the best organized beings who may be presented, both with respect to affection and intelligence, as well as the physical nature, the highest results can be manifested in the shortest time, such principles will therefore influence the admission of candidates.

According to the numbers who may thus be united, buildings and land will be duly provided, and apportioned in the manner most conducive to the end proposed.

In harmony with the progressive principle the buildings will be chosen of the simplest construction possible, so as to ensure every personal convenience and every needful defence in an unfavourable climate. Divided into apartments suitable for study, reflection, bathing, exercise, employment, conversation, sleeping, public communion, &c. warmed, ventilated, and furnished in the most appropriate manner, combining elegance, convenience, and economy.

The land will be, on the same principle, apportioned to the purposes of recreation, exercise, study, the raising of food, fuel, and, as far as possible, all articles for dress, so that all the produce required may be obtained from the estate. At every favourable season as much time as possible should be occupied in the open air.

Operations on the land are to be conducted in the most skilful manner, and the food raised will be of the best quality ; constant attention being paid to agricultural and horticultural improvements.

With an aim so comprehensive as that of the Concordium the constant controul and supervision of a watchful government being necessary, the daily management is confided to three persons. One called the father or patriarch, and two inspectors, one male and one female.

Together these three form a council, whose orders are binding on the whole community ; and, one of them being always in the executive position, the advantages of unity are constantly presented. There is always a definite authority to appeal to : while the council, by frequent meetings, preserve to themselves all discussions which would distract the inmates; at the same time they study the wishes and tastes of the latter and gladly accept any suggestions or advice.

All initiative proceedings issue from this council, which consists of those on whom the money responsibility rests, or of individuals appointed by them.

In the Concordium, occupation, education, and instruction are so intimately blended that it is almost impossible to be engaged in either without progressing also in both the others. As, however, scarcely any experience in true life has yet been made, it is not easy to depict the course of events in which this threefold operation will be manifested. As such experience is effected, daily modifications in practice will be required of an ever watchful council, aided by every one who feels an adequate interest in the undertaking.

No fixed routine can therefore be adopted, but, by a general outline of a day's procedure, some idea may be suggested of the superior means thus offered for the attainment of the end. It is essential to the just developement of the human character that means should be adopted for the separation of the sexes as well as their continuance in their natural position. There are seasons for isolation as well as for communion.

The domestic arrangements are therefore necessarily divided into two departments for sleeping, bathing, &c. The one placed under the controul of the male superintendent, the other under that of the female superintendent, each being responsible in the respective branches, and looking to the class leaders appointed by them for the fulfilment of the duties in detail.

Assuming that seven or eight hours of the twenty-four are requisite for sleep, the remaining sixteen hours should be appropriated equally to universal and individual progress ; that is to say, about eight hours are to be given to each member's own improvement, and eight hours to productive industry for the needful support of the Concordium.

The inmates rise at the earliest convenient hour according to the season. The first moments are given to personal ablutions, which should be done completely, healthfully, and joyously, by means of a shower or plunging bath direct from a pure spring ; an operation, which with dressing, shoe cleaning, &c. will occupy the first hour of the day. The lively free re-action from such bath will render an hour's work (out of doors when possible) a most delightful duty. This exercise will be succeeded by breakfast, which will complete the two first hours of the day. This meal, being simple, leaves the intellect clear, and the energies renewed for the various mental and physical employments which will follow in succession for the next four hours. Each member's taste, powers, and organization being left free, will be exercised with the greatest pleasure to the individual, and the best productive results to the whole family : they will be varied as frequently as agreeable, so that every faculty may in succession be harmoniously developed, and the soul preserved in a cheerful equable temper. The next hour is devoted to individual improvement in study and preparation for the afternoon lessons.

The second repast then succeeds, consisting of such varieties of food as each season affords, in agreement with the health law. One hour is given to this mid-day eating and its profitable suggestions carried out in appropriate conversations, &c. Then will follow two successive hours for individual progress, by means of education and instruction. Teachers being provided who are themselves associated with the universe-love-spirit by which they are altogether actuated, there will be secured for every individual in the various classes, the means of moral, intellectual, and manipulative progress, such as the most costly colleges may in vain attempt under the system of paid instructors. After these pursuits for personal advancement the succeeding two hours will be given to various employments for the Community. After the intervention of an hour for the last eating, another hour when requisite is given to the lighter employments, and the remainder of the evening, until bed time, is occupied in social communion, by all means that can contribute to the elevation, beauty, and gratification of the moral sympathies.

This is the general outline or order of the day as it respects the adults. The eating times will be the same for all, so that at one board, spread with due regard to simplicity and purity, every inmate, young and old, may be assembled in the true family spirit. The children will throughout the day be employed in processes for their own developement, education, and instruction ; while the elders are employed in providing for the family sustenance, the children are being prepared to contribute in their turn to the general harmony. In personal education, literary studies, gymnastics, with gardening, rural excursions, and those light labours which accord with their highest advancement, the juvenile portion of the Concordium will pass profitable and blissful dnys. The frequent transitions from one position to another, will take place with as little disturbance as possible, a mere knowledge of the time being sufficient in most cases to call each one to his new engagement. As cleanliness in person is one indication of personal progress, so cleanliness in all domestic management will be assiduously preserved to the highest possible degree. In like manner an unsophisticated behaviour in social communion will characterize the Concordian family. A kindly and courteous deportment will be practiced, which is the more necessary, as many of the adult beings who can now be associated, may still retain some of the old results of previous neglect or ill training. As soon as individuals have grown up and passed their whole educative career in concordance with the universe law, they will not from mere instruction or consideration, but, from being, spontaneously manifest in triune harmony, the love-wisdom-power, from which their being is derived.

With respect to individual property it is proposed that every one shall retain what he thinks proper of his present possessions, and that whatever shall accrue while in the Concordium shall be common property. It will be quite incompatible with true progress in the Concordium for any one to have engagements which should remain a pecuniary burden; these must be all disposed of in such a manner previous to entrance as to leave the mind free to follow with undivided attention its upward tendencies.

While better conditions are provided for the human being, it is obvious that in order to be regenerated in the new life, the human being must at the same time become a better condition for the creative spirit. The primitive purpose of the Concordium, as an external establishment, is to enfranchise the individual from the lower and degrading pursuits and trammels now prevalent, so that as a creature still in novitiate he may be more directly presented to the Creator.

There is an apparent improvement in social conditions which must be distinguished from true elevation. Riches, honours, indulgencies, though still sought by great numbers of mankind, are yet acknowledged to conduce little towards man's permanent happiness. All such good, and indeed all lower good, even of the purest kind, unless accepted and used with relation to the highest good, is really an obstruction, for by detaining the mind in a lower happiness, the human being is effectively degraded. While present principles prevail, if the whole human race had at command a superabundance of earthly good, it would in fact be a depressing circumstance, and such must ever be the case, until man, by a close relation with the Highest Good, knows how to use the lower good. Hence in the Concordium the Highest Good is the basis in all operations, and the end in all pursuits.

Persons desirous of joining such Establishment are requested to apply by letter addressed to " the Superintendent of the first Concordium" at the Publisher's.

CHELTENHAM :
PRINTED BY W. PAINE, IMPERIAL OFFICES, HIGH STREET.

ELEMENTS OF PRINCIPLES

CALCULATED TO

HEAL THE WOES OF MANKIND:

PUBLISHED BY

THE CHRISTIAN

Co-operative Community Society,

WHO HOLD A PUBLIC MEETING

AT THEIR

EMPORIUM, 69, ST. GEORGE'S PLACE,

CHELTENHAM,

Every Monday Evening, at Eight o'Clock.

☞ They recommend every one to read this tract twice through, as they consider the subject important to all people.

PRICE THREE HALF-PENCE.

CHELTENHAM:
PRINTED BY T. WILLEY, OXFORD PASSAGE.

TEST.

I believe that I am a responsible being and accountable to God for my conduct; and that it is my duty to practice the precepts of the Gospel of Jesus Christ; as revealed in the New Testament.

ELEMENTS OF PRINCIPLES,

&c.

MAN is essentially a rational and moral being, destined to
draw his chief happiness from the pursuit of objects directly
related to his moral and intellectual faculties, the propensities
he has in common with other animals, acting merely as the servants of the sentiments, to maintain and assist them while pursuing their high and beneficent objects. History represents
man, in past ages, as ever, either openly pursuing the gratification of the propensities, as the avowed and only object of life,
or merely curbing them so far as to enable him to obtain higher
satisfaction from them, but never directly pursuing moral ends
as the chief object of his existence. This is also our present
condition.

Even in civilised communities, each individual who is not
born to hereditary fortune, enters into a vivid competition for
wealth, power and distinction, with all who move in his own
sphere. Life is spent in one incessant struggle. We initiate
our children into the system at the very dawn of their intelligence. We place them in classes at school, and offer them
marks of merit, and prizes to stimulate their ambition, not
according to the extent of useful knowledge which they have
gained, but according to the place which they hold in relation
to their fellows.

Viewed on the principle that the object of life is self-aggran-
dizement, all this order of proceeding appears proper and profitable. But if you trace out the moral effects of it, they will be
found extremely questionable.

The tendency of the system is to throw an accumulating
burden of mere labour on the industrious classes. In some of
the great machine manufactories in the west of Scotland, men
labour for sixteen hours a-day, stimulated by additions to their
wages in proportion to the quantity of work which they produce.
Masters, who push trade on a great scale, exact the most energetic
and long-continued exertion from all the artizans whom they
employ. In such circumstances, man becomes a mere labouring animal. Excessive muscular exertion drains off nervous

B

energy from the brain; and when labour ceases sleep ensues, unless the artificial stimulus of intoxicating liquors be applied, as it generally is in such instances, to rouse the dormant mental organs, and confer a temporary enjoyment. To call a man, who passes his life in such a routine of occupation; eating, sleeping, labouring, and drinking; a Christian, an immortal being, preparing, by his exertions here, for an eternity hereafter, to be passed in the society of pure, intelligent, and blessed spirits; is a complete mockery. He is preparing for himself a premature grave, in which he shall be laid, exhausted with toil and benumbed in all the higher attributes of his nature, more like a jaded and ill-treated horse than a human being. Yet this system pervades every department of practical life in these islands. If a farm be advertised to be let, tenants compete with each other in bidding high rents, which when carried to excess, can be paid only by their converting themselves and their servants into labouring animals, bestowing on the land the last effort of their strength and skill, and resting satisfied with very little enjoyment from it in return.

By the competition of individual interests, directed to the acquisition of property, and the attainment of distinction, the practical members of society are not only stimulated to exertion, but actually forced to submit to a most jading, laborious, and endless course of toil; in which neither time, opportunity, nor inclination, is left for the cultivation and enjoyment of the higher powers of the mind.

The whole order and institutions of society are framed in harmony with this principle. The law prohibits men from using force and fraud in order to acquire property, but sets no limits to their employment of all other means. Our education and mode of transacting mercantile business, support the same system of selfishness. It is an approved maxim, that secrecy is the soul of trade; and each manufacturer and merchant pursues his speculations secretly, so that his rivals may know as little as possible of the kind and quantity of goods he is manufacturing, of the sources whence he draws his materials, or the channels by which he disposes of his produce. The direct advantage of this system is, that it confers a superiority on the man of acute and extensive observation and profound sagacity. He contrives to penetrate many of the secrets which are attempted, though not very successfully, to be kept; and he directs his own trade and manufacture, not always according to the current in which his neighbours are floating, but rather according to the results which he foresees will take place from the course they are adopting ; and then the days of their adversity become those of his prosperity. The general effect of the system, however, is, that each trader stretches his capital, his credit, his skill, and his industry, to produce the utmost possible quantity of goods, under the idea, that the more he manufactures and sells, the more profit he will reap. But as all his neighbours are animated by the same spirit, *they* manufacture as much as possible also ; and none of them know certainly how much the other traders in their own line are producing, or how much of the commodity in which they deal the public will really want, pay for and consume, within any specific time. The consequence is, that a superfluity of goods is produced, the market is glutted, prices fall ruinously low ; and all the manufacturers who have proceeded on credit, or who have limited capital, become bankrupt and the effects of their rash speculations fall upon their creditors. They are, however, excluded from trade for a season ; the other manufacturers restrict their operations, the operatives are thrown idle, or their wages are greatly reduced. The surplus commodities are at length consumed, demand revives, prices rise, and the rush towards production again takes place ; and thus in all trades the pendulum oscillates, generation after generations, first towards prosperity, then to the equal balance, then towards adversity ; back again to equality, and once more to prosperity.

The ordinary observer perceives in this system what he conceives to be the natural, the healthy, and the inevitable play of the constituent elements of human nature. He discovers many advantages attending it, and some evils : but these he regards as inseparable from all that belongs to mortal man. The competition of individual interests, for example, he assures us, keeps the human energies alive, and stimulates all to the highest exercise of the bodily and mental powers ; and the result is, that abundance of every article that man needs, is poured into the general treasury of civilized life, even to superfluity. We are all interested, he continues, in cheap production ; and though we apparently suffer in the excessive reduction of the prices of our own commodities, the evil is transitory, and the ultimate effect is unmixed good, for all our neighbours are running the same career of over-production with ourselves. While we are reducing our shoes to a ruinously low price, the stocking maker is doing the same with his stockings, and the hat maker with his hats ; and after we all shall have exchanged article for article, we shall still obtain as many pairs of stockings, and as many hats, for any given quantity of shoes as ever ; so that the real effect of competition is to render the nation richer, and to enable it to maintain more inhabitants, or to provide for those it posseses more abundantly, without rendering any individuals poorer. The evils attending the rise and fall of fortune, the heartbreaking scenes of bankruptcy, and the occasional degradation of one family and elevation of another, they regard as storms in the moral, corresponding to those in the physical, world; which, although inconvenient to the individuals whom they overtake, are, on the whole, beneficial, by stirring and purifying the atmosphere; and, regarding this life as a mere pilgrimage to a better, they view these incidental misfortunes as means of preparation for a higher sphere.

This representation has so much of actual truth in it, and such an infinite plausibility, that it is almost adventurous in us to question its soundness, yet we are forced to do so, or to give up our best and brightest hope of human nature and its destinies. In making these remarks, of course, we blame no individuals ; it is the system which we condemn. Individuals are as much controlled by the social system in which they live; as a raft is by the current in which it floats.

In all the systems we have described, you will discover no motives, higher than those furnished by the propensities regulated by justice, animating the competing members of society in their evolutions. The grand object of each is to gain as much wealth, and, as its consequence, as much power and distinction to himself, as possible ; he pursues this object without any direct regard to his neighbour's interest or welfare ; and no high religious, moral, or intellectual aim elevates, ennobles, or adorns his career. The first effect is, that he dedicates his whole powers and energies to the production of the mere *means of living*, and he forces all his fellows to devote their lives to precisely the same pursuits. If leisure for moral and intellectual cultivation be necessary to the enjoyment of a rational, a moral, and a religious being, this is excluded ; for the labour is incessant during six days of the week, and the effect of this is to benumb his faculties on the seventh. If the soft play of the affections ; if the enjoyment of the splendid loveliness of nature and the beauties of art ; if the expansion of the intellect in the pursuits of science ; if refinement of manners ; if strengthening and improving the tone and forms of our physical frames ; and if the adoration, with minds full of knowledge and souls melted with love, of our most bounteous Creator, constitute the real objects of human life in this world, the end for which we live ; and if the fulfilment of this end be the only rational idea of preparation for a higher state of existence; then the system of action which we have contemplated, when viewed as the leading object of human life, appears stale, barren, and unprofitable. It no doubt supports the activity of our minds and bodies, but its benefits end here. It affords an example of the independence of the several natural laws. The system is one in which the mind and body are devoted for ten or twelve hours a day, on six days in the week, to the production of those useful and ornamental articles which constitute wealth; and in this end we are eminently successful. Verily we have our reward; for no nation in the world possesses so much wealth as Britain; none displays such vast property in the possession of individuals of every rank; none approaches her in the general splendour of living; and none in the multitude of inhabitants who live in idleness and luxury on the accumulated fruits of industry. But still, with all the dazzling advantages which Britain derives from her wealth, she is very far from being happy. Her large towns are overrun with heathenism and pauperism; and in many English counties, even the agricultural population has lately been engaged in burning corn stacks and farm offices, out of sheer misery and discontent. The overwrought manufacturers are too frequently degraded by intemperance, licentiousness, and other forms of vice. In the classes distinguished by industry and morality, the keen competition for employment and profit imposes excessive labour and anxiety on nearly all; while the higher classes are often the victims of idleness, vanity, ambition, vice, ennui, and a thousand attendant sufferings of body and mind. The pure, calm, dignified, and lasting felicity which our higher feelings pant for, and which reason whispers ought to be our aim, is seldom or never attained.

The present condition of society, therefore, does not seem to be the most perfect which human nature is capable of reaching; hitherto man has been progressive, and there is no reason to believe that he has yet reached the goal.

The evils of the selfish system have the tendency to prolong and extend themselves indefinitely. We have seen, for example, that the institution of different employments is natural, springing from differences in native talent and inclination. This leads to the division of labour, by which every person has it in his power to confine his exertions to that species of art for which he has the greatest aptitude and liking; while, by interchanging commodities, all become richer. But under the present system, this institution is attended with considerable disadvantages. Workmen are trained to perform the minutest portions of labour on a particular article, and to do nothing else : one man can point a pin, and do no more ; another can make a pin's head, but finish no other part of it ; one can make the eye of a needle, but can neither fashion the body nor point it. In preparing steam engines, there are now even different branches of trade, and different workshops for the different parts. One person makes boilers, another casts the frame-work and heavy iron beams, a third makes cylinders, a fourth pistons, and so on ; and the persons who furnish steam engines to the public, merely goes to the different workshops, buys the different parts of the skeleton, and his own trade consists in fitting them together, and selling the engine entire.

This system rears an immense number of industrious men, who are utterly ignorant, except of the minute details of their own small department of art, and who are altogether useless and helpless, except when combined under one employer. If not counteracted in its effects by an extensive education, it renders the workmen incapable of properly discharging their duties as parents, or members of society, by leaving them ignorant of everything except their own narrow department of trade. It leaves them also exposed, by ignorance, to become the dupes of political agitators and fanatics, and renders them dependent on the capitalist. Trained from infancy to a minute operation, their mental culture neglected, and destitute of capital, they are incapable of exercising sound judgment on any subject, and of combining their labour and their skill for the promotion of their own advantage. They are, therefore, the mere implements of trade in the hands of men of more enlarged minds and more extensive property ; and as these men also compete, keenly, talent against talent, and capital against capital, each of them is compelled to throw back a part of the burden on his artisans, demanding more labour, and giving less wages, to enable him to maintain his own position.

Nor does the capitalist escape the evils of the system. In consequence of manufacturer competing with manufacturer, and merchant with merchant, who will execute most work, and sell his goods cheapest, profits fall extremely low, and the rate of interest, which is just the proportion of profit corresponding to the capital employed in trade, becomes depressed. The result is, that the artisan's wages are lowered to the verge of a decent subsistence, earned by his utmost exertions; the manufacturer and merchant are exposed to incessant toil and risk, and are moderately recompensed ; and the capitalist, who desires to retire from active business, and live on the produce of his previous industry, in the form of interest, participates in their depression, and starves on the smallest pittance of annual return. Thus selfish competition presents the anomaly of universal abundance co-existing with individual want, and a ceaseless struggle to obtain objects fitted chiefly to gratify our inferior powers.

The attainment of power and distinction in politics, in rank, or in fashion, is the Alpha and Omega of the machinery of the present social system; yet it does not produce general happiness. Every moral, and religious advantage, is incidental to, and not a part of the system itself. There are laws to compel us to pay taxes, for the maintenance of officers of justice, whose duty it is to punish crime after it is committed; but there are no general laws to prevent crime by means of penitentiaries and of abundant and instructive schools. There are laws which tax us to support armies and navies for the purpose of fighting our neighbours; but no law to compel us to pay taxes for the purpose of providing, in our great cities, the humblest luxury, nay, almost necessaries, for the poor, such as baths to preserve their health, reading rooms, or places of instruction and amusement, in which their rational faculties may be cultivated and their comfort promoted, after their days of toil are finished. There are taxes to maintain the utterly destitute and miserably poor after they have fallen into that condition; but none to provide means for arresting them in their downward progress towards it. In short, the system, as one of self-interest, is wonderfully perfect. From the beginning to the end of it, prizes are held out to the laborious. intelligent, and moral, who choose to dedicate their lives, out and out, honestly and fairly, to the general scramble for property and distinction; but equal facilities are presented to all who are incapable of maintaining this struggle, to fall down, and sink to the lowest depths of wretchedness and degradation. When they have reached the bottom, and are helpless and completely undone, the hand of a meagre charity is stretched forth to support life, till disappointment, penury, and old age, consign them to the grave. The taxes occasioned by our national and immoral wars render us unable to support imposts for moral objects,

Now it is worthy of remark, that if the system of individual aggrandizement be the necessary, unalterable, and highest result of the human faculties, as constituted by nature, it altogether precludes the possibility of Christianity ever becoming practical in this world. The leading and distinguishing moral precepts of

Christianity, are those which command us to do to others as we would wish that they should do unto us; to love our neighbours as ourselves; and not to permit our minds to become engrossed in the pursuit of wealth, or infatuated by the vanity and ambition of the world. But if a constant struggle for supremacy in wealth and station be unavoidable among men, it is clearly impossible for us to obey such precepts, which must therefore be as little adapted to our nature and condition, as the command to love and protect poultry, but never to eat them, would be to the fox.

Man's ignorance of himself and of external nature, and his consequent inexperience of the attainments which he is capable of reaching, appear to have been the chief causes of his past errors; and the following, among other reasons, authorize us to hope for better things hereafter. His propensities although strong, are felt by all to be the inferior powers in dignity and authority. There is, therefore in man a natural longing for the realization of a more perfect social condition than any hitherto exhibited, in which justice and benevolence shall prevail. Plato's Republic, is the most ancient recorded example of this desire of a perfect social state. Josephus describes the sect of the Essenes, among the Jews, as aiming at the same object. "The Essenes" says he, "despise riches, and are so liberal as to excite our admiration. Nor can any be found amongst them who is more wealthy than the rest; for it is a law with them, that those who join their order should distribute their possessions among the members, the property of each being added to that of all the rest, as being all brethren." The Essenes laboured in agriculture and in various trades, and maintained their principles in active operation, for a considerable period of time.

The Harmonites, now flourishing in America, are stated to have been a colony of Moravians, united under one or more religious leaders. They emigrated from Germany with a little property, purchased a considerable territory in Indiana, and proceeded to realize the scheme of common property, and christian brotherhood. They sustained many privations at first; but in time they built a commodious and handsome village, including a church, a school-house, a library, and baths. They cultivate the ground, and carry on various manufactures; but all labour for the common good, and are fed and clothed by the community. They live as families in distinct dwellings, and enjoy all the pleasures of the domestic affections; but their minds are not agitated by ambition, nor racked by anxiety about providing for their children. The children are early trained to industry, co-operation, and religion; and if their parents die, they are at once adopted by the community. The Harmonites are not distracted with cares about their old age or sickness, because they are then abundantly provided for. There is division of labour, but no exhausting fatigue : a fertile soil favourable climate, and moral habits, renders moderate exertion amply sufficient to provide for every want. **J. S. Buckingham, Esq.** thus describes them in 1840. I visited the co-operative community of the Rappites, in this we were delighted with the patriarchal character of the venerable founder, now healthy and vigorous, though past his eightieth year; and with the health, competency, contentment, and morality, of this cheerful community, who have completely proved, by their success, the soundness of the principle, that co-operation in society ensures the most equitable mode of distribution, and largest share of enjoyment for all.

CHAPTER II.

Of all the relations of life there is none more endearing than that of a brother. In sickness and health, in joy and sorrow, in prosperity and adversity, this relationship is a balm for every wound. A family is the place where we are to look for the purest and happiest feelings which man is permitted to enjoy upon earth. A family is a community, as far as it goes. All are fed from the same stock. All sit at the same table and drink of the same cup. All have a common lot, either of prosperity or adversity. All hold the same rank in society. If one should happen to be more fortunate than the rests in the world, and rise to wealth or honour, he imparts a portion of his prosperity to the others. He soothes the old age of his parents, or he makes them happy by his public honours, and by his kind and filial attention to their wishes. He lends his hand to those who are of his own age, and helps them on their journey; or he superintends, directs, and patronizes those who are younger than himself, in their studies, their pursuits, and their professions. Thus, by a feeling of grateful and laudable ambition, he becomes the father of his household ; and every one, at his approach, " rise up and calls him blessed."

This family affection ought to extend itself from private to public life ; from the family to the world. It ought to be the model upon which every one should endeavour to form his own

character. The reward of such a character is sweet in the extreme. It exists in the sympathy of every bosom; it makes
a family of the world; it sees a brother in every human being,
and rejoices in every opportunity of doing him good. Man was
evidently intended to be brought to this lovely state by nature
and by providence. Man was never intended to live by the
misery or the ruin of his neighbour, but by his prosperity and
happiness. That portion of evil which unavoidably befalls
some people in the present state of the world, was intended to
be mitigated, if not obviated, by the general prosperity and happiness, As one individual bears but a trifling proportion to the
whole race, so the misfortunes or unhappiness of one may be
abundantly compensated by the overwhelming prosperity of the
great mass of mankind.

"There is a friend," says the wise man, that "sticketh faster
than a brother!" However strong the affection and interest
of a family may be, man is so formed as to contract indissoluble
attachments to some one or more of his fellow-creatures. Two
minds may have the same pursuits and studies, the same views
and objects; they may delight in the same species of knowledge,
and may join together in the same career of improvement and
science. The common object may be sufficient to bind them
together in friendship, and they may follow the common pursuit
with double ardour and double relish.

It is from the heart that every valuable feeling springs, and
every source of pleasure and happiness. No kind of pursuit or
knowledge becomes a source of happiness to a man till it takes
fast hold of the heart and affections. When we love a science,
then we appreciate its value and beauties. And thus in religion: it is not till a person is brought to love the Lord Jesus
Christ that he feels the obedience required is a burden not
grievous but joyous. They grow and expand every day, and
the more we examine them, the more inexhaustible do we find
them. We see that the objects of our love are infinite—our
hearts dilate with a feeling of the same infinity—we ourselves
experience a kind of growth within us—our very nature seems to
change, to enlarge, to purify, to be exalted; and we are led,
continually, to wonder at the vast and improving character of the
powers we possess.

The feeling of friendship is so peculiar and delightful, that it
has been the subject of some of the most beautiful compositions
which have ever been written. This, however, is not of so much
importance in our view, as the fact that, friendship of some kind
and in some degree, is absolutely necessary to every man's com-

fort in the common intercourse of life. No man would wish to say, and no man can say, that he has not a friend in the world. It is considered a most forlorn estate for a man not to know to whom to turn for an act of kindness; and when we meet with so extreme a case, we instantly forget all the common forms of society and of rank, and, by an instinctive impulse, we become that friend ourselves; as if to prevent the world from being loaded with the disgrace of bearing on its face a friendless man.

It is oppressive to contemplate the picture of a man in this state, approaching to friendless destitution. The heart mourns over it, and seeks relief in imagining the possibility of a state of things in which we may extend the delightful feeling, of friendship from one to many—in which we may open our bosom and receive into our arms, all who wear the fair form and features of man. Such is the state which co-operation holds out, and co-operation alone. Co-operation removes the almost insurmountable obstacle to friendship; namely, self-interest, rivalry, jealousy, and envy. When two persons have an inclination to cultivate a friencship for each other, they seldom proceed far without finding their interests clash. The delicate feeling of mutual esteem, which at first is small and weak, and requires time for its growth, and a variety of kind offices for its strength, receives a check in its very onset. Mutual suspicions and jealousies arise, and the tender plant is nipped in the bud. Men must have different pursuits, and be wholly independent of each other, in order to stand any chance of a real and sincere friendship.

But, if persons were so situated that their interests were, in all respects, the same; if the prosperity of the one insured the prosperity of the other, and the happiness of the one the happiness of the other; then, instead of suspicion and jealousy, they could only feel towards each other, love, esteem, and affeetion. If one were cleverer than another, or more indefatigable; if he had more genius, knowledge, or energy than another, or were more zealous, industrious, and persevering than another, while that other reaped an equal share of all this superiority, surely that other could not but entertain for his kind friend, a high degree of respect, esteem, and admiration, in proportion to his superior merits. The weak is now beaten down by the strong; the ignorant man by the man of genius: but were they to find in the strength and wisdom of others, their own protection and safeguard, they would feel no longer unhappy and discontented in their own moderate powers, while they would look with pleasure and approbation, on the greater powers of their neighbour.

Such is the state of things which co-operation holds out. Every man, on entering such a society, immediately becomes surrounded by a host of friends. All the abilities and labour of all those friends are pledged to him, to protect him against the common evils of life; and to ensure to him its comforts and enjoyments. While he presents the Society with the labour, skill, and knowledge of one single individual, the Society presents him with those of many. He gives little, he receives much. In himself he is subject to all the uncertainties, the ups and downs of life, to anxiety and care, to laborious days and sleepless nights; but in the Society, he has insured himself against all these things; he cannot be ruined unless the Society be so too: and the ruin of a society of labourers is an impossibility; because, as every labourer produces about four times as much as he consumes, a society of one hundred labourers must produce four hundred times more than they consume; which is amply sufficient to provide against all the chances and accidents of life.

Suppose a workman, a member of such a society, to form a friendship for another member, how delightful would it be for them to live under the same roof, to work at the same employment, to eat at the same table, to spend the hours of rest and recreation in mutual conversation or improvement? They would never be separated by change of masters, want of work, sickness or old age. One would never look down upon the other because he was rising more in the world, nor feel contempt for him as belonging to a different trade. They would continually be striving to oblige each other, by little acts of kindness and attention. They would lighten each other's labour as opportunity offered, and they would unite in this labour with the greatest cordiality and zeal, in order to insure a common independence.

Another pleasing occupation of such friendship would be, to assist in explaining and enforcing the great principles of the Society; to instruct the ignorant: to encourage the timid; to help the weak; to be patterns to the other members; to be foremost in exertion, in zeal, in activity; to be always ready to meet difficulties, and to bear the heat and burden of the day. Such objects would be worthy of the warmest friendship and the highest energies; and would be a fit employment for those exalted faculties which God has given to man.

We do not mean to assert that each member of a society or community would possess that high degree of feeling, which is called friendship, towards every other member. We only argue

on the general truth, that friendship, in some degree, is common
and necessary to all men; that the circumstances of ordinary
life are very unfavourable to it; and that those of a co-operative community are essentially favourable: and when such
friendship does exist, between two or more members, their circumstances enable them to reap from it the highest possible
enjoyment. But this friendly feeling, among the members
generally, must not be left to chance and accident. It must not
only be recommended as an advantage; it must be enforced as
an imperative and paramount duty and obligation. When a
man enters a co-operative society, he enters upon a new relation
with his fellow-men; and that relation immediately becomes
the subject of every sanction, both moral and religious. Mutual regard, friendship and affection, become then as binding
upon a member as the duties of common honesty and sobriety.
Religion will step in here, as into other relations, and will hold
forth her promises of future reward and punishment, in proportion as men are good or bad members of the community to
which they belong. Zeal, energy and fidelity, will draw after
them the glorious rewards of a future life: whilst indolence, indifference and unfaithfulness, will naturally anticipate the gloomy
sentence of disapprobation and punishment. Though the profession of a common creed will not be one of the objects of a
community, yet, every member will be glad to unite in that view
of religion which will give additional force and sanction to all
their regulations for the common good.

However we cannot withhold our opinion, that the delightful
feelings of friendship will pervade the whole society to a considerable extent. The common yearnings of our nature, and the
common ties of the society, will necessarily open the hearts of
the members. While nothing opposes them, many things will
favour them; and when many rivers run in one direction, without opposing currents, they must at last unite in one common
ocean.

The common capital is the great bond of union. Each member is nothing in his individual capacity; but every thing in
his social capacity. If he separates himself from the society and
the common capital, he is ruined. While he is united with them
his fortune is made. The importance of each member, and the
value of his labour, as a single individual, are nothing; so small
is the proportion they bear to the whole Society, and the common capital. The older the Society grows, and the larger the
capital, the more insignificant is each member as an individual.
These, and similar reflections, must make him look to the Society

and its common capital, so as to entertain for them the utmost regard and love.

But if a number of persons are continually admiring and loving the same object; if that object possesses many beauties and excellences; if it be the great and unfailing source of their happiness; they must, necessarily, by continually loving the same interesting object, draw towards each other in the bonds of love. It would be the height of absurdity to suppose that mankind should be prone, even to a fault, to a common sympathy, under the present course of things, and dead to this sympathy, when united in a common society, with a common capital. It is much more reasonable to suppose, and to prophecy, that this sympathy would act in co-operation with new energies, and rise occasionally, even to enthusiasm. If men are now to be found, so full of public spirit as to sacrifice their ease and peace, their prosperity and happiness, and even life itself, for the public good, when the reward is but an empty name, or a monument, when they are no longer sensible to the honour—or, perhaps the mistaken execration of an ungrateful world—what efforts will they not be capable of, when, to the certainty of posthumous fame, is added the present prosperity and happiness of all around them!

Yes; enough has now been done to justify us in anticipating the happiest results: and we are convinced that our motto,—"Sirs, ye are brethren,"—will be the talisman which every co-operator will wear next his heart. It will be the rosary on which every member will tell his morning and evening aspirations, to the great Fountain of all love; to impart the principles more and more widely and deeply to his own breast, and to those of his friends and brethren. The spirit of co-operation is the spirit of friendship and brotherly love, which, though small at first, in the infancy of the Society, will gather strength and stature as it goes; will at length lift its head sublimely to the skies, and *enfold in its parental and everlasting embrace,* all the children of the happy community.

The changes proposed consist of new arrangements derived from science.

1st. *To erect comfortable residences* for the *Members, better and cheaper* than can be accomplished in any other way; so that they may have the advantage of town and country.

2nd. *To feed them better and cheaper.*

3rd. *To clothe them better and cheaper.*

4th. *To train and educate them better and cheaper.*

5th. *To secure to them* BETTER HEALTH *than they now enjoy,*

6th. *To apply their labour to Agriculture, Manufactures, and all the purposes of society, with science better directed than heretofore.*

And lastly, *To make them in all respects better members of society.*

Every one must acknowledge that these will be important improvements, if they can be obtained,

It is uow to be shown that they are easily attainable, and that all the means necessary to give them permanence, superabound.

The most difficult problem to solve was, " to ascertain what number of persons could be associated together, so as to give to each the most advantage, with the least inconvenience.

The second, " to discover on what principle this new association could be formed, in order to avoid the evils which have hitherto kept society in a state of poverty, degradation, imbecility and misery."

The third, " to find out how all their wants could be permanently and amply supplied, without a collition of individual interests, and at the same time to secure a progressive improvement in all knowledge, so as to give a continued zest and enjoyment to human existence."

The arrangements best adapted for the improvement and happiness of the members, and which must at the same time render their labour to, and cheaper than, that of all other labourers, are as follows :—From about 500 to 1,500 individuals, or (supposing four to a family) about 300 families are to reside in habitations in the country, on which much foresight has been exercised in devising their erection and combination, so as to secure every possible domestic comfort. They comprise convenient detached dwelling houses, public kitchen and dining rooms, place for Divine worship, library and lecture room, schools, baths, &c., with suitable play and pleasure grounds. The estimated cost of which will be as under :—

	£.	s.	d.
Houses, manufactory, and alteration of buildings	8,000	0	0
Stock for 800 acres of land : viz. 60 cows, 100 sheep, 20 pigs, horses, carts, farming implements, &c.	870	0	0
Seed	180	0	0
First year's rent of 800 acres of land	1,600	0	0
Rates and taxes, first year	400	0	0
Maintenance of 150 families, first year	4,680	0	0
Contingencies	270	0	0
	£16,000	0	0

Now, in a population of 1,200 persons, there appears, from the most accurate data that can be obtained, an average of 248 individuals, male and female, under 10 years, First Class 178 ditto, ditto, from 10 to 15, Second Class 719 ditto, ditto, from 15 to 60, Third Class 55 ditto, ditto, 60 and upwards, Fourth Class The labour of the Children in the first is not taken to account, although the occasional employment of those, from seven to ten, in weeding the gardens, and other light occupations, will be of value to the Establishment. Deducting 67 who would be engaged in domestic concerns, or indisposed; we may say the labour of both sexes, with the aid of machinery, will certainly produce at least as under; at a very moderate calculation :—

ANNUAL INCOME.

	£.	s.	d.
165 individuals, at four shillings per week, is	1,716	0	0
680 ditto, of third class, 10s. ditto	17,680	0	0
40 ditto of fourth class, at 5s..........	520	0	0
	£19,916	0	0

EXPENDITURE.

Food and clothing for 300
    families, per annum ..£9,360
Interest of £10,000 borrowed   500
Rent................... 1,600———11,460 0 0
          Annual surplus £8,456 0 0

Thus, in return for their services, estimated at the common prices of manual labour, will the members obtain more substantial comforts than can be now procured by many of the middle classes, at an expenditure of several hundreds per annum.

The surplus of £8,456, after it shall have repaid the capital expended in forming the establishment, will be an excess of wealth perpetually accumulating to form new establishments as the population increases.

Thus will terminate the present commercial system of profit upon price; since by these simple, yet truly scientific arrangements, this profit will be rendered not only unnecessary and disadvantageous to all parties, but utterly impracticable.

From the preceding calculations, it is evident that the inhabitants of these establishments will be in full possession, even at the commencement of their exertions, of far more substantial advantages than are now acquired by the favoured few, after a

life of great exertion, and what is called success. It is evident
that the members of such communities will be able, with facility,
to create a considerable surplus beyond their own consumption;
this surplus produce they will exchange for the surplus produce
of other similar communities, by estimating the value of such
surplus produce in labour, and not in money, as at present.

By this arrangement they will receive all their external supply, and thereby render money, and all money transactions
(except with present society) wholly unnecessarv; their labour
by these arrangements, will require no other representative
than notes or vouchers, to be given when the articles are delivered at the appointed depot; these notes or vouchers will
designate the exact amount of labour contained in such articles,
which amount will be estimated upon equitable principles,
ascertained and fixed by the Communities. Thus all bargain-
ing, and its degrading effects on the human character, will be
obviated.

But even this stage of society will be but temporary; for,
by the most simple arrangements, which will be beneficial to
all, supply may be made so far to exceed any possible demand,
that it will be discovered in a comparatively short time, that all
may use whatever they desire, without the necessity existing
for the intervention of any immediate or direct equivalent.

The advantages of these new arrangements to the physical, moral, and intellectual character of the members are so
great, that when they can be once fairly comprehended by the
public, they will plainly show the extravagance, loss, and gross
absurdity of the present occupation and expenditure of the
producing classes.

The general advantage of these new arrangements are, (to
state them in few words) that they clearly discover to us the
only true solution of that hitherto most difficult problem in
Political Economy, viz.—The true distribution of that immense
amount of production which manufactures and agriculture,
aided by machinery and other scientific improvements, can
now create.

Under these arrangements, an abundant harvest, and a liberal
supply of all useful and agreeable commodities by machinery,
will not produce, (as under the existing system) distress and
ruin; on the contrary, these arrangements will eventually prevent the rising generation from being subject to poverty, or the
fear of poverty; will preserve them from ignorance; from acquiring any bad habits or dispositions; from all cause of anger
or malevolence towards their fellow-creatures, or from being in

any degree intolerant to them, in consequence of any opinions, habits, or disposition, which they may have been taught.

The particular advantages are, that they and their children, and their children's children, to the most remote posterity, will, to the ends of their lives, exist amidst a superfluity of whatever can be necessary to their well being and happiness; until the whole surface of the habitual parts of the earth shall be cultivated like a garden; that they will be made active and intelligent, be trained to possess the most charitable, kind, and benevolent sentiments and dispositions; and that, through their example, all classes, sects, and parties, will be induced to adopt whatever experience shall prove to be beneficial, wise, and good in these establishments.

It has been frequently asserted, by theoretical political economists and others, that this system has a tendency to degrade and enslave the human race, and place it under unnatural restraints. No conclusion, however, can be more unfounded and fallacious, and it must proceed entirely from an ignorance of human nature and society. On the contrary, every part of this system has been purposely and carefully devised, after a calm and attentive consideration of ancient and modern history and existing facts, with a view to impart to man the utmost freedom and independence of which he *is* susceptible, under a social system of order and happiness.

And it can never be too much impressed on the public mind, that the only solid foundation of public liberty is to be found in the full supply of the wants, in the virtuous habits, in the intelligence and consequent happiness of the whole population.

Let us suppose that a community, consisting of about 1,200 persons, of both sexes and all ages, that is to say, made up of the average proportion of children, adults, aged and infirm members, were about to form a colony on one of the unoccupied spots in this kingdom, and that it was their determination, as far as possible to possess every requisite within themselves. Their first object would, doubtless, be to secure to themselves such an extent of land as should be capable of yielding a quantity of alimentary produce, more than sufficient for their subsistence; their next object would be to erect commodious dwellings, and to supply themselves with the other necessaries, conveniences, and comforts, to which they had been more of less accustomed in the society whence they emigrated They would be aware that a regard to their own true interests required that they should, as far as praticable, without trenching on individual liberty, carry on every operation conjointly, and economise to the utmost both their materials and labour. They would, according to the practice of the most experienced agriculturists, erect their dwellings as nearly as possible in the centre of the estate; and in the construction of them, a regard to economy would require that one contrivance should answer numerous purposes. Hence they would see the advantage of making one convenient kitchen. The females would also divide among themselves many of the domestic duties; and by doing so, those duties would be performed with more skill and in a tenth of the time. The children of such a community would be sufficiently numerous to admit of the introduction of the best system of education. For the purpose of manufacturing the several articles of clothing and furniture, machinery would be resorted to; and as each member would have a common interest, on equitable principles, in the whole produce of the land and manufactures, it is obvious, that the more extensively and efficiently mechanical inventions were introduced and applied, the more would the wealth of each individual be increased. There could then arise no collision of interests between the Manufacturers and Agriculturists, for those interests would be identified. Abundant harvests, and plenty of provisions, could not be regarded, as with us, an evil; what constituted the joy of one could not be a source of sorrow to another; all would rejoice together, and receive with gratitude the gifts of Providence.

The grand desideratum of society, is to carry the principles of union and combination, as far as practicable, into effect. The only limit that should be assigned to the operation of these principles, is that point where they would invade the right of privacy and freedom of action. Under the proposed arrangements, provision is made for the enjoyment of privacy, each family having a separate dwelling house, the size and convenience of which might be increased as the association advanced in wealth; and freedom of action is insured, by the right of each member having an equal portion of influence with every other member in the choice of managers and passing rules; also, by any member having a right to withdraw, if so disposed; and by the inalienable right of the society to expel an individual that disturbed its peace.

Though a strict equality prevails with respect to all the associated members of each community, it by no means extends to the public at large, nor even to all the persons connected with each concern. It is, in fact, nothing more than the equality of partners, all of whom have an equal interest in their joint concern, but whose relation to the community at large remains unchanged. Thus, each society will remain in the same relation as exists at present with respect to all individuals with the Government of the country, as to the payment of taxes, and subjection to the laws of the state.

We are convinced that, eventually, the advantages of the system will be so apparent, and the happiness to be derived from acting upon it so great and so obvious, that after the effects have been for some time exhibited in practice, all men will be eager to associate every where in communities upon the same principles; and that the power of producing wealth will become so unlimited, as to render the possession of superfluous riches as little desirable then, as the possession of a superfluous quantity of water is at present; and that by this means, if not by any other, the plan will eventually resolve itself into an *universal community of goods!*

If this plan may one day result in equality, because it will render men so wise, so wealthy and so happy, that distinctions in property and in rank will no longer be deemed desirable; so may the progress of Christianity result in equality, when Christianity shall have rendered all men so humble, so benevolent, and so virtuous, that they shall esteem all earthly distinctions as unreal vanities, if not as sinful presumptions! An universal equality, produced by means such as these, is indeed a consummation every Christian will most devoutly wish for, and will most joyfully and gratefully receive.

Our scheme proposes to begin with the acquisition of good; with the attainment of happiness, with the cultivation of the moral and intellectual powers, from the earliest childhood, and continued to the latest period of existence; and with the abolition of no *distinctions*, but such as all men would desire to see removed, the wretched distinctions afforded by gradations in *vice, poverty* and *misery!*

Our scheme *begins* with the *end* which others only purpose eventually to accomplish; and our scheme is utterly regardless of further results, let those results be what they may, in the firm assurance that, to whatever state men shall be led by the guidance of Christian principle, of reason, and of virtue, that state must be the more favourable to their felicity.

Even as respects each society, the object sought to be obtained is not equality in rank or possessions; is not community of goods; but full, complete, unrestrained co-operation, on the part of all the members, for every purpose of social life, whether as regards the means of subsistence, or promoting the intellectual and moral improvement and happiness of the whole body.

This is the true and only secret of the system; the natural course of action, under which alone social beings, possessing powers of combination derived from natural instincts, and improved by scientific principles, can derive all the advantages which are within their reach, and by which alone they can be bound together in society, without the agency of force and sanguinary laws, which have always, hitherto, been found necessary to keep them together. Even Christianity, because its professors have omitted to obey the injunctions of the Author of their Faith on this point; because they have excluded from their societies the true and natural principle on which alone society can be permanently and securely founded; even Christianity has, hitherto, on this account, failed to unite men in the bonds of love and fellowship; and it is found as necessary to employ force in Christian countries, for the preservation of the existing system, as in those parts of the world to which Christianity has not yet been communicated!

This is one amongst the numberless facts, which ought at once to satisfy all, unprejudiced, not only of the great imperfection of the present system of society: but of the fact, that the fundamental error of society is the opposition of interests, the artificial obstacles thus created to prevent cordial co-operation; and the ruinous checks thus entailed upon the production and distribution of wealth, as well as upon the spread of true prinples.

Even a religion, enjoining all men to be of "one heart and of one soul," teaching a pure morality; and, offering the most consolatory doctrines and brilliant hopes and expectations to mankind, has for upwards of eighteen centuries exerted its influence in vain, because its influence has necessarily been counteracted by the nature of society, fruitful only in counteractions; and it might continue to exert its influence for many centuries more, with the same success, if the form of society remain unchanged. Indeed the earthly triumph of Christianity would be the establishment of the new system of society. Its successful progress would result in such an extension of the benevolent principle, as to induce every individual to merge his individual interest and happiness in the general good, and in the promotion of the general welfare. Either then, we must wait for the earthly felicity promised by Christianity, until Christianity itself shall have slowly and impercetibly removed the obstacle which opposes its full and complete action; or, aided by science and benevolent feelings, and under the guidance of Christian principles, we must so far as is at present possible, remove the obstacle, now that it has at length been discovered ; induce men, by interesting even their selfishness, to enter into that state of society which is most favourable to virtue and to happiness, and which presents the greatest facilities for the universal diffusion of knowledge, and for the early formation of good habits and amiable character ; and thus facilitate the arrival of that felicitous state which Christianity has foretold, and which it has promised to establish.

When that period shall at length arrive, then indeed all men will be of one heart and one soul ; will have but one interest, and will enjoy a perfect equality of rank and an unlimited community of goods.

The new system proposes to unite, in each community, only two or three hundred families, by the bond of their mutual interests, and their sense of the great advantage which may be derived by each from the cordial co-operation of all.

The individuals forming an association may possess various portions of wealth at the moment the association is formed. One member is worth nothing ; another has a hundred, a third a thousand pounds, and so on ; but each member may lodge his personal property where he thinks proper. He may employ it as he thinks proper, and spend it as he thinks proper. The distinguishing feature is *unity of physical and intellectual power ;* the instrument, or agency, *unrestrained co-operation ;* the object, the unlimited and uncontrolled production and distribution of *wealth ;* in which term we include every thing that is desirable to man, or that is necessary to his true well-being and happiness.

We cannot dismiss this subject, without pointing to a few of the evils of competition ; which now afflict society, and we believe will rapidly increase in the poignancy of their afflicting power. Competition limits the income of every individual, and consequently of the whole community. And each obtains the *least* that his *labour,* his *services,* or the use of his property, can possibly be obtained for. It is competition that limits the quantity of wealth obtained by *individuals ;* the quantity obtained by *individuals,* collectively, composes the aggregate quantity obtained by the *whole community ;* this aggregate quantity forms the demand, and demand limits production. When this subject is clearly understood, it will be seen by all, that the exhaustion of our productive powers, and the satisfaction of our wants, are the *only natural limits* to the production of wealth ; that so long as capital shall continue to be employed in *competition* with capital, instead of in conjunction with it, we shall never be able either to exhaust our productive powers, or to satisfy our wants; because production must ever be limited to the quantity which the labour, the services, and the property of the community will command.

We are for ever told, that we have more articles of wealth, *more produce*, than we want. Strange and foolish error! Let those who entertain such a thought understand their own words. They *say*, we have more produce than we want. They *mean*, there is more produce than there is a *demand for*. When every human being has everything his heart can wish, then, and not till then, we shall have as much produce as we want. But dreadful is the contrast to this in society as it now is. Go, see your wretched fellow creatures, of which there are thousands in this country, hungry, houseless, and in rags, and inquire of them, whether thy have a superabundance of wealth? Go to your manufacturing towns, and see the wretched producers of your wealth, ye who roll in luxurious profusion. Ask of them whether they have more than they have need of, and blush when ye tell us of superabundance? We have frequently more produce than we have a *demand for* a great deal more; but *demand is limited by competition*: abolish *this*, and demand shall be equal to production, though it be increased a thousand-fold.

It is competition, then, and nothing but competition, which limits the annual income of the country. And as competition necessarily arises from the division, and opposition, or conflict of the interests of men, in the distribution of the produce of labour, it is certain that nothing less than an *entire change* in the commercial arrangements of society, can be productive of any essential benefit to mankind.

As men are instinctively led to unite in societies, we may rest assured, that if their associations were maintained on the true principles of their nature, the further any society advanced in knowledge, and in the invention and exercise of mechanical productive powers, their increse of happiness would be in proportion to the progress of intellect, and to the increase in their means of production and of comfort. In fact, their sense of the great advantages which may be derived from the combination of their powers; not to a portion of their members only, but to the whole community, would become continually stronger and stronger, until, so far from the principle becoming continually weaker and weaker, SELF-LOVE would ultimately be lost in UNIVERSAL BENEVOLENCE.

In proportion as nations have become great and powerful,

and have made advances in wealth and acquirements, the mass of misery corrupting and rankling at their base, has also continued progressively to be enlarged, until it may be truly said, that the foundations of society are laid in wretchedness, and that there is no addition made to the superstructure of luxury and wealth, without a more than corresponding enlargement of the sphere of misery below.

The surplus wealth, created by useful inventions and the skilful combinations of labour, has. never been equitably distributed. The inventions of machinery, to assist or supersede human labour, *has never been the mean's of abating one hour's labour to the labourer.* The discovery of productive powers which are capable of producing more wealth than the world can consume, *has not afforded one ounce of additional plenty to the poor.* The very increase of knowledge, and of intellectual elevation, among some classes, has been accompanied by corresponding degradation and debasement to others. Even the progress of virtue has been accompanied by an increase of vice ; and this country itself presents the appalling spectacle of the rapidly increasing demoralization and misery of one portion of its people, at the very moment that active beneficence, and the principles of universal philanthropy, are more than ever conspicuous amongst another.

The degree and kind of exertion which are to be given to the productive powers of a nation, are never regulated by the real interests of the whole nation, but by the supposed interest of individuals. The landholders regulate the quantity of the produce, not by the *wants of the people,* but by the amount of *pecuniary* advantage which can be derived to *themselves.* Whilst there are hundreds of thousands of unemployed labourers, and myriads of uncultivated acres, the land is suffered to lie waste, and the pauper labourers continue to be but half fed ; because the plough must not touch the forbidden soil until its cultivation shall be deemed advantageous, not only to society, but to its possessors ; not only to a famishing multitude, but to individuals already in possession of a superabundance.

Though we do not wish it to be inferred from this, that the landholders act otherwise than the existing nature of things compel them. The form which society has assumed renders it indispensable that each individual should disregard the interests of the whole, when his own immediate interests are concerned ; and from this imperative necessity no one can escape. If mechanics, manufacturers, &c. were to create all the goods which the real wants and necessities of society require, the money price of the commodities would sink below the level, which as society is now constituted, is advantageous to the manufacturer. A million of men may be destitute of comfortable woollen apparel ; and a single great manufacturer may possess the requisite machinery and other powers for producing the necessary articles with facility ; but the quantity of his product is determined, not by the necessities of the people, but by the money-price which his commodities can command in the market.

We earnestly invite every one who would wish to realize such a state of society as have been here propounded, (and it cannot be prevented as soon as a sufficient number of persons feel its importance) to attend our meetings as before announced, or leave their address at the Emporium, 69, St. George's Place.

28

INVITATION.

Awake, ye sons of Adam's race,
And sweet community embrace,
The door is open wide to those
Who wish a happy life to choose.

Come to the paradise on earth,
And change your sorrow into mirth;
Where, by the labour of your hand,
You'll reap the first fruits of the land.

Parents and children here will find
A tranquil home and peaceful mind;
Secure from base and selfish ways,
To spend the remnant of their days.

Beneath its fruitful shelt'ring tree,
Will be procured the widow's fee ;
And helpless orphans, too, will share
A father's love, a mother's care.

Children, like Samuel, in their youth,
Will here be taught God's sacred truth ;
And when mature each one will see,
The goodness of community.

The wealthy lord the wretched poor,
Will not be known within our door;
In this sweet vineyard all will be
Content with an equality.

Here we may sing our cheerful rhyme,
Under the fig-tree and the vine;
'Till Christ shall call us by his love,
To join in nobler strains above.

BY A MEMBER.

Willey, Printer, Cheltenham.

[The following Letter is reprinted for general circulation, from the Morning Chronicle of Tuesday, December 13, 1842.]

NOTES FROM THE FARMING DISTRICTS.

No. XVII.

A JOURNEY TO HARMONY HALL, IN HAMPSHIRE, WITH SOME PARTICULARS OF THE SOCIALIST COMMUNITY, TO WHICH THE ATTENTION OF THE NOBILITY, GENTRY, AND CLERGY, IS EARNESTLY REQUESTED.

HAVING heard a remark made at the inn where I was staying for a few days in Salisbury, that two travellers, who had left behind them two cloaks and two walking-sticks while they attended to some business in the market, were supposed to belong to the Socialist community at Tytherly, in Hampshire, from the circumstance of their walking-sticks having engraved on the heads the resemblance of a beehive, and the words, " the working bees," I was induced to make some inquiry about the distance to and situation of their *Beehive.* The correct information to be gathered in Salisbury was extremely scanty, and accordingly, on being told that the distance was only twelve miles to the village of Broughton, and that the community were located near that village, I procured a conveyance, and, in company of another gentleman, set off for Hampshire.

This was two or three days after the visit of the two members of the Beehive to Salisbury. It was a lovely day. If a country with so good a soil, and so poorly cultivated, could have afforded pleasure to a traveller at any time, it would have done so on such a day as this. But the road lay through a section of that bare country formerly described as visible from Old Sarum, and there was nothing to be satisfied with but the excellent roads, which, being of flint on a hard bottom, are maintained at little expense. Leaving Salisbury, we had the seat of W. Wyndham, Esq., one of the members of Parliament for the borough, on our left ; and, for the next twelve miles, the entire distance, I saw nothing worth mentioning, save that a field of good turnips, and another of beautiful young wheat, would be seen as spots on a wide uncultivated common, much of the soil of which was quite as good as that sending up the young wheat and the respectable turnips ; which turnips again might have been of a much better quality but for the neglect which characterized their cultivation. I have said nothing more was seen worth mentioning. But, at an inn called the Winterslow Hut, I received information that the wages of labouring men had been reduced to seven shillings a week by the largest farmer in that district, and that the other farmers were expected to follow immediately with a similar reduction ; and the common expression of those who were present, some of whom were tradesmen from Salisbury, and one the respectable landlady of the house, was to this effect: " God above only knows how the poor creatures are to be fed ! What matters it to them that flour and bread be cheaper this year than last ? They could buy little of either last year, and they can buy as little this. They must buy potatoes, not bread, and potatoes are but a middling crop this year; they are good, but small."

This place, Winterslow Hut, was the scene of a singular incident six-and-twenty years ago. On the night of Sunday, the 20th of October, 1816, the Exeter mail-coach was changing horses at the door when an attack was made on the leading horses by a lioness, which had broken loose from a travelling menagerie. There is a coloured print of the scene hung up in the parlour, which purports to have been executed from the description given by Mr. Joseph Pike, guard of the mail, the said Mr. Joseph Pike being himself, next to the lioness, the most conspicuous figure of the group. The ferocious beast is worrying the off-side leader, having seized it by the throat, and the courageous Joseph is standing on his seat with a levelled carbine, as if about to fire. A dog, which, as the hostess informed me, was the most efficient assistant in getting the lioness secured, is shown in the foreground, in very small dimensions, perhaps to set off the enraged assailant as larger and more formidable than she really was. At all events the scene is a startling one; what with the terrified faces at the upper windows of the inn, and in the inside of the coach; what with the blue, and the red, and the yellow which paints the faces and the waistcoats of the outside passengers; what with each seizing his umbrella or luggage as if determined not to die without a struggle; and what with the likelihood of the whole being devoured by such tusks as have already destroyed a horse, the spectator, not of the reality but of the coloured print, is excited to call, even at this day, to Joseph Pike and the carbine, "Why don't you fire?" However, there is no sign of fire, nor is there any record. One horse was killed, and by some means, not fully explained, the lioness was secured in her caravan.

We arrived at the village of Broughton about one o'clock, and having put up our horse at the inn, we proceeded on foot to *Harmony Hall.* Broughton is but a poor looking village, irregularly built, and surrounded by farms which indicated that the Working Bee community would have no difficult task to compete with them. The soil all around is quite deep enough for common cultivation. It is deeper than many of those parts in the Lothians, or Roxburgh or Berwick shires, where a rent of from £2 10s. to £3 10s. an acre is paid for a middling soil. The sub-soil is chalk; and I believe that wherever there is a sufficient depth of soil above chalk, that soil is, generally speaking, fertile. It might be shallow on some of the higher districts; but all that I saw, and I examined it in several situations, varied from twelve to twenty-seven inches in depth. The chalk was a variety well adapted for lime, but, saving by the Socialist community, little advantage was derived from it; *their* lime-kiln was the only one I saw during the day's journey. The rent of the land about Broughton is from ten to fifteen shillings an acre. With other burdens, not borne by the Scotch farmers, it would amount to 20s. or 25s. an acre. But while the tenants of the Marquess of Tweeddale, the Earl of Wemyss, the Earl of Haddington, Sir George Clark, the Duke of Roxburgh, and other landlords, whose land I happen to be acquainted with, would pay from £2 10s. to £3 10s. for such soils, and make a profit, the farmers of that part of Hampshire find they have a hard bargain with the moderate rents they now pay. When I saw their style of farming, their wastefulness of fertilizing agencies, their insufficiency of manual labour, their want of economy in horse power, and the unconquered foulness of weeds, which seemed to wage perpetual war with their crops and prove victorious, I was not surprised to hear them murmur and tell of hard times.

Leaving the village, we proceeded southward. For nearly a mile the lane in which we walked, hedged by coarse bushes, gradually ascended, and the soil on each side seemed wearing thinner and thinner. Having fortunately met a woman who directed us through a field towards the left, we followed a waggon's track, and in five minutes I was standing in a field of turnips which grew in drills, showing a bulk of crop and robustness of health quite refreshing to the eye, after the poor specimens of turnip culture I had seen in that and adjoining counties. I observed to my companion that if these were "Socialist turnips" they promise well.

But before going further, I should remark that I knew nothing of the Socialist property, nor of any individual connected with it. I had, like others, been reading wandering paragraphs in the newspapers about this community, some of which had not long before stated that the whole establishment was broken up, that the members were dispersed, the property seized by creditors, and so on. My companion knew nothing of them but by hearsay. In fact, though living within twelve miles, he knew as much of China as he did of Harmony Hall, and that was not much. He was one of those jolly countrymen well to do in the world, who believe the British army and navy can, and ought to, thrash all the world, if the world needs a thrashing; who grumble when the tax-gatherer comes round, who take in a paper which they seldom read, but who still grumble at the government—no matter what party is in power; who think no times are so hard as the present times; but who forget all grievances when the next hot joint comes on the table. Such was my companion. Little as I knew of the Socialists, I had been able to inform him that they did not wear claws, nor horns, nor wings, nor tails; that though they were human in shape they were not cannibals; neither did they steal little children and put them in boiling cauldrons just for the love of the thing. But though able to tell him all this, I was not able to obliterate the opinion which he had imbibed from the hearsay common in Salisbury, that the Socialists were an assemblage of the greatest vagabonds that a too lenient law had left upon the face of the earth. In short, some of the stories I heard in Salisbury are too ridiculous, I might say criminally libellous, to be mentioned. Yet by many they were believed. My companion had never read for himself on any subject, and I was much amused with his account of what he had heard of the Socialists. He had a friend in Broughton, on whom we called, and who gave us the first information of their property and personal reputation : it surprised both of us considerably. "Their pro-perty," said he, "consists at present of one thousand acres of land, and they are now in treaty for the purchase of another estate; they have paid down £500 of a deposit on it, and it will be theirs next year." To this I rejoined, that I was completely astonished ; that I had never dreamed of their having such a property ; and begged to know how it was cultivated, compared with the farms I had seen in the neighbourhood. To this the gentleman replied (and I may state he is a man of property and respectability in the village), that, so far as he could judge, they were cultivating it very well. "But," inquired my companion somewhat eagerly, "What sort of people are they? We have heard such strange tales about them, over our way, that I have been quite at a loss what to think of such people being allowed to live among you." "Why," replied the other, "all that I have seen of them, or have heard, amounts to this, that it would be a high honour to this parish if one half our inhabitants were as decent in their behaviour as they are—it would indeed. And more, it would be a credit to our gentry if they would employ people in as great numbers and to as much advantage on the land as they do."

"Lord bless me! you don't say so!" exclaimed my friend from Salisbury, "and such stories as we have heard of them! Do you say all this of them in sober earnest?"

"I do," replied the Broughton gentleman. "As for their peculiar notions about property, I don't agree with them; but, so far as saying they are well behaved people, setting a good example to this neighbourhood, I say it most sincerely."

"But," interrogated my companion, "are they not all *Deists* that believe there is neither a God nor a devil?"

"If I understand the term *Deist*," replied the other, "it means a believer in God. As to their belief in religion I suppose they are like other people, of different opinions. One thing I know is that they come to our church, and some to the chapel. They sit and hear the sermons, and go away again as others do. They never introduce religion nor politics into any conversation with us in the village, but I once talked to two of them on the subject of religion, of my own accord, and they told me they had the same opinions of religion now as formerly; that there was no peculiar opinions among the Socialists, save that each man might enjoy his own opinion without molestation; that they, the two, being believers in the Christian doctrine of salvation through Jesus Christ, attended a place of worship, and that no attempt was made by any member of the community to dissuade them from going to church."

"Lord bless me!" exclaimed my companion;" you don't say so in earnest, do you?"

"But," I inquired, for I had not been prepared to hear this favourable account of their tolerance, "what do the clergy say of them, *they* don't like them, I should suppose?"

"The Methodists and Baptists, and such like, make an outcry against them," replied the gentleman, "but our clergyman of the parish church says nothing about them. All of us hereabouts were much alarmed when we heard of their coming at first; but we look on them now as very good neighbours; and as they set a good moral example to our population, and employ a good many of our poor, and as they never attempt to impose any opinion on us, we have no reason to dislike them. One of them married the daughter of a farmer in this neighbourhood, a short while ago; the banns were put up in the parish church, and our parson married them. Oh, depend upon it, they are doing good here in a moral point of view."

"Lord bless me!" exclaimed my Salisbury friend once more, on hearing this; "did the father of the young woman give his daughter to a Socialist?"

"Certainly," returned the other, "Why should he not?"

"Because," said my companion, "they have a new wife whenever they tire of the old one."

"Nonsense!" returned the Broughton gentleman; "ridiculous nonsense. They have no such practices, and, so far as I ever heard, no such doctrines in theory. They propose, when they can get an act of Parliament for the purpose, to simplify the law of divorce, by allowing married persons to separate by mutual consent after several repeated notices, and repeated trials enjoined on them to try once more, and once more again, for certain periods of time, for some months each period, to agree; if after those trials they are still desirous of being parted they may be divorced. As for any other laxity of principle I know none. The most delicate and well-bred conduct characterizes them so far as I know; and nobody hereabout, however opposed to them, attempts to say a word against their moral character; *that*, as I said before, might be an example worthy of imitation to many in this parish. In short, the Socialists are very well but on one point, which concerns themselves more than anybody else; on that point I believe them to be fatally in error; and more, that sooner or later they will split and fall to pieces on it—I mean the community of property. There will always be idle men willing to talk and to live at the expense of the industrious. Your talking men are not commonly the best workmen, and seldomer still are they willing workmen. In fact, those of them that are really the industrious men are pretty well tired of the numbers who come visiting and living idly from distant parts of the country. Besides that, if they were all willing alike, they are not able alike, nor used alike to such works as cultivating a farm; and I have heard that several of their carpenters bricklayers, and such like, are but indifferent workmen when put to a job. In fact, the ignorance of most of those who came here at first of practical matters has led them into extravagant expenses. They have been imposed upon on every hand. Then, again, consider the folly of expending thirty thousand pounds, and upwards, on a building before improving their land. Instead of beginning, like working bees, they have done quite the reverse. The bees begin by making honey, using any place for a retreat that may fall most readily in their way. There we have the working bees and the drones living alike on the common store, building and building, and leaving the honey-making to the last."

Such was the account I received of the Socialist community in the village of Broughton, and it is given at full length, because of the opinions of others in the neighbourhood, who spoke to the same effect. When we reached the turnip field, as already said, I remarked to my friend that if these were "Socialist turnips" they promised well. They were Socialist turnips, and we soon after found seven hundred Socialist sheep, which made my friend exclaim, "Lord bless me! who would have thought it!"

Winding down a gentle declivity, we saw a red three-storied brick building near some large forest trees. These trees seemed the commencement of a wooded district, which contrasted pleasantly with the naked country we had travelled over from Salisbury. As we approached the red brick house we could observe that its outward form was tasteful and all its proportions substantial. It stood at about fifty yards to our right, while on the left was a farm-yard, old and uncomfortable looking, with some ricks of wheat, waggons, pigs, and cattle. Adjoining the farm-yard was a new house, which might have been taken at first view for the respectable residence of a substantial farmer. This we found was built as a temporary residence for those members who arrived previous to the large house being built.

On every side of us we saw unfinished work; heaps of bricks, piles of mortar, logs of timber, half-built walls, and broken ground as if in process of being laid out into gardens. No person being visible, we looked around us for some time; at last I saw three dogs approaching, which I proceeded to meet, supposing that, as it was Harmony Hall, there could be no harm in meeting the dogs. They did not deceive me; but one of them belied the reputation of the place by snarling at the other two. They growled in concert, and then departed on some errand of their own to a dust-heap, where one of them finding a bone, produced a contention much in the same way as dogs do in the old world.

We advanced to the open door, which showed a spacious lobby, from which stairs went down, and stairs went up. I met a middle-aged female who politely told me some one would speak with us presently. Following her were three younger women, plainly, but tidily and respectably, dressed. My eye was following them up stairs, when I perceived a man before me. He wore a cloth cap, and a respectable suit of clothes. After the preliminary courtesies, I told him that we had come to see the establishment, and any information he choose to give us would be received as a kindness. We were then conducted into an office, where two men were sitting, one as if posting a ledger, the other writing a letter. All the London daily papers, and several others, were on the table. A book lay open, in which we were requested to write our names, which done, our guide, whose name I afterwards understood to be Atkins, or Atkinson, told us to walk " this way."

We descended to the basement floor, which, on the other side of the house, looked out on a level with a lawn partly in process of formation. On this floor there were several large apartments ; one of them a dining-room. Dinner was just over, and as a finale to it, the members were singing a beautiful piece of solemn music. We were not asked to go into their presence, but we went to the kitchen, after examining an excellent piece of machinery, which, through a tunnel, conveyed the dishes and the dinner from the kitchen to the door of the dining hall. A boy, who was passing, showed us how it worked, and presently several other boys appeared. All of them were so clean and neat in their clothes, so healthy in their appearance, and at the same time so respectful in their manners to us and to each other, that I could not help staying behind to talk with and look at them.

In the kitchen there were three or four women, with a very large assortment of dishes to wash. I did not know what the dinner had been, but judging from the refuse of bits and scraps, which seemed to me to tell more of abundance than economy, I supposed they had all got enough of it. The women in the kitchen were like all the others, tidy and respectable in appearance. The only thing that puzzled me was, how they should be so well as they were, with such prodigious piles of plates, washed and unwashed, around them : I can say nothing adequately descriptive of the fittings of this kitchen. At Broughton I was told that the London architect who superintended the erection of the whole, said that there were very few kitchens so completely and expensively fitted up as it in London. I am sorry to say that such is to all appearance, and by all accounts, the case.

Outside the kitchen there were commodious wash-houses, cellarage, baths, and a well-arranged place for each member to wash himself as he comes from his work before going to meals.

Ascending again to the next floor we entered a ball room, and going up stairs we saw the sleeping rooms, all as conveniently arranged as can be under one roof. Upon the whole the house is commodious, but I was much disappointed at seeing such a house. A village of cottages, each with a garden, would have surely been more appropriate for a working community, and much cheaper ; the sum expended on this building, not yet half furnished, is said to exceed £30,000. Such extravagance previous to cultivating the land would stagger most people on the question of the sagacity of the working bees.

Mr. Atkinson conducted us to the new garden, which contains twenty-seven acres. I was then introduced to a Mr. Scott, the chief gardener, whom I found to be an intelligent and thoroughly practical man. His operations of trenching and planting, and indeed gardening in every department, were extensive. Brickmakers were making bricks ; builders were building, lime-burners were burning lime ; road makers were making roads ; the shepherds were with the sheep ; nine ploughs were at work ; a hundred acres of wheat were already sown, and more wheat land was being prepared. A reservoir was being constructed to save all the liquid manure ; and in short, everything was being done to improve the land which industry and capital could accomplish, and skill direct.

Mr. Scott was having portions of some of the fields trenched with the spade. He paid the labourers £5 per acre for it, and expected them to work so as to make two shillings a day. I remarked that this was more wages than common. He said it was ; they only gave the ploughmen and other day labourers nine shillings a week ; but as it was scarcely possible to get a good workman in that part of the country, he allowed a higher rate of wages to get them to work with some spirit. In answer to a remark I made about proselytizing their workmen to Socialism, he replied that they never made any attempt ; but if they did attempt it, he believed anything might be accomplished, any change might be effected, but a change in the old slovenly style of working : on that point he believed the present generation of Hampshire labourers to be incurable.

It will be perceived by this that the members of the community do not themselves cultivate the land. Some of them work in the garden, but few of them I suspect, are fitted for rough out-door work. Their number was at the time I was there sixty, thirty more were expected soon after. The quantity of land is 1,000 acres, held on a lease of ninety-nine years, at a rent of fifteen shillings an acre. They have the power of purchasing it within that time at a certain price ; and they have paid down a deposit on a neighbouring estate of three hundred acres. Their landlord is Sir Isaac Lyon Goldsmid. There is some fine wood on the ground, and an avenue of fine old yews, which for beauty and extent is perhaps not equalled in any other part of England. The community intend converting a portion of that avenue into a summer ball-room. Adjoining, are large numbers of full grown trees, resembling the size and shape of the main-mast of a man-of-war.

I saw in several parts of the woodlands that the vegetable mould was gathered into heaps to be carried and used as manure. On almost every estate in the kingdom there is a rich soil of this kind that might be collected and carried away without any injury to the trees. Mixed with lime it forms an excellent compost.

I did not see the agriculturist, but Mr. Scott, the gardener, was conducting several experiments in the fields with the spade on alternate ridges with the plough. His manner of trenching was this :—the earth was lifted two spadesful in width, and to the depth of about a foot. This was taken in wheel-barrows to the place where trenching was to cease, there to fill up the last opening. A pick was taken, and the bottom of the trench loosened to the depth of eight or ten inches. This loosened subsoil was allowed to remain. The adjoining soil, two spadesful in breadth, was then turned over, taking care to bury the weeds in the bottom. A second working with the spade in the same trench, turned up a fresh soil to form the surface of the new seed soil. The bottom of this second trench was lossened with the pick as that of the first, and the next was begun by again burying the top mould. They had a subsoil plough on its way from Smith, of Deanstone's factory, in Scotland. They were gradually introducing improved implements, but the greatest difficulty they found was to get the Hampshire labourers to work with them. They had thirty of these labourers at work.

I was told at Broughton that about one-half of the members ate no butcher-meat, but lived entirely on vegetable diet. They at first brewed beer, but now they have curtailed that expense. One shilling a week is allowed for pocket money, but few of them are ever seen to spend even that in the neighbourhood.

To conclude, I may remark that I believe their land to be well worth £3 per acre of rent, and they only pay 15s. They have an excellent bargain, if they manage it well ; and whatever may be said of their Social crotchets, it must be said of them that their style of farming is of a superior kind. Those noblemen, gentlemen, clergy and others who dislike the Socialists would do well to show the working population that good farming is not necessarily an adjunct of Socialism ; else, perhaps, the working population will think the doctrines of those who pay best, employ most, and produce the greatest abundance of crops, are the best doctrines. This is no light subject. Missionaries of all religions in all parts of the world, in all ages, have succeeded in proselytising more by introducing arts and sciences, by teaching new means of acquiring wealth, than by preaching abstract theories. We have an eminent instance of this in New Zealand, at the present time ; and unless the landed gentry take a step in advance, or at least side by side in the same road with the Socialists, they will find the labourers of Hampshire voluntarily converted to the new doctrine. Again I say this is no light subject. Let the gentry and clergy look to it.

ONE WHO HAS WHISTLED AT THE PLOUGH.

[NOTE.—In giving circulation to this paper, the Governor of Harmony wishes it to be understood that the writer is not correct in all his statements. Firstly : the regulations of the establishment do not permit of persons coming " visiting and living idly from all parts of the country." Secondly : a very large sum was expended in farm-stock and improvements of various kinds ere any buildings were erected. These latter have not cost more than half the sum stated ; and it must be understood that a large proportion of them are intended for the accommodation of pupils in infant, elementary, and polytechnic schools, which are now forming. Thirdly : very many of the members are at present occupied on the land, and it is intended that all shall be partially so occupied. There are other inaccuracies of a minor kind, which it is not deemed necessary to notice. On the whole, however, the account is the most correct and impartial yet given to the world by a stranger.—Harmony Hall, near Stockbridge, Hants, December 17, 1842.]

LONDON : PRINTED BY WILLIAM OSTELL, HART STREET, BLOOMSBURY

A VISIT

TO

HARMONY HALL!

(Reprinted from the " Movement ")

𝔚𝔦𝔱𝔥 𝔈𝔪𝔢𝔫𝔡𝔞𝔱𝔦𝔬𝔫𝔰, 𝔞𝔫𝔡 𝔞 𝔑𝔢𝔴 𝔞𝔫𝔡 𝔆𝔲𝔯𝔦𝔬𝔲𝔰

VINDICATORY CHAPTER.

DEDICATED TO THE SOCIALISTS OF ENGLAND AND SCOTLAND.

By G. J. H.

In thy halls
Let faction so convolve her serpent councils
That art may ne'er untwist them : let them in
Perplexed entanglement, unravelled rot,
And so be buried in forgetfulness.
Leagued friendship clip thy people in one bond
Of compact guard, for very lack of cunning
To plot a mischievous division—so farewell.
                                    Pemberton's Podesta.

London:

H. HETHERINGTON, 40, HOLYWELL STREET, STRAND.

1844.

A VISIT TO HARMONY HALL.

Chap. I.

It is a perfect pilgrimage to visit Harmony, so remotely is it situated from any of the Socialist Branches. Really, those who have the hardihood to make the journey ought to be enabled thereby to ensure their social salvation. Catholic redemption has often been purchased on easier terms.

Reader, if you set out from the provinces, and your road to Harmony Hall lies through London, ask before you leave home where the Nine Elms Terminus is situated. Nobody in London knows it. I asked twenty people before I found one who had the slightest notion of its whereabouts. The *New Moral World* says, go to the *Nine* Elms Terminus, at *nine* o'clock in the morning, and book yourself for the *nine* mile water—but there are *nine* chances to one against a stranger doing this.

On Monday morning, October 14, I " wended my way," as the novelists have it, down by Parliament House and over Vauxhall Bridge, on my visit to Harmony Hall. At nine o'clock, to a minute, at the Nine Elms Terminus, I demanded a ticket for Nine mile water, Harmony Hall. " Oh " said the official in the railway office, " you must take a ticket to Farnboro' ! that's the station." Taking it for granted that he knew all about it, in five minutes I was on my way to Farnboro'—the rain pelting down as though it was half an hour too late, and the wind blowing as though they were trying a new pair of bellows up above. In about an hour I alighted at Farnboro' station, and thought— " well, after all, Harmony is not so far off as people have said," and I looked about for friend Buxton and one of the Harmony vehicles. But I found myself surrounded by a crowd of Frenchmen, gabbling like mad, and I thought surely these people can't belong to Harmony Hall, unless they are the " hired labourers" of the old Executive. I enquired at once for Queenwood, " Queenwood ?" said the marvelling superintendent, " there was a gentleman who once before came here asking for that place. It is forty or fifty miles below. You had better take the next train to Winchester, and then enquire again." I gave up all ideas of seeing Harmony that day, and expected only to find my way there in the course of the week. I had nothing to do but to turn myself to the fire and the Frenchmen, in the hopes of finding either warmth or amusement. In a few minutes I found that the Frenchmen were king's attendants, waiting for the arrival of Louis Philippe and the Queen, who were expected from Windsor at one o'clock. Before long I observed some strange looking men darting off at all angles, without any apparent reason, and

A 2

pushing people about I could not tell why. But soon I discovered their movements followed on the nod and beck of a marble eyed elderly gentleman, who was, if I mistake not, one of Sir James Graham's special commissioners, whom I saw at Gloucester Gaol, and I knew I was surrounded by the famous A Division of Police, from Scotland Yard, who darted about at every roll of the official orbs, before mentioned. I immediately called in all external signs of curiosity, and looked as much like nobody as possible, by which means I noticed everybody in security. When the royal party arrived from Windsor, even the gaping gentry of the neighbourhood were thrust to the back of the building—at every avenue policemen brandished their batons—a poor Frenchman looking over a gate was rudely thrust back and given in charge of the police, and none but officials, and the Editor of the *Movement* stood in the narrow passage made for their majesties to pass. I inserted myself in the midst of the police, deeming that the best place for not being seen by them—and I was right. Guizot first interested me. His half military dress detracted from his philosophical character, but his well moulded head and firm features, resting upon his iron looking shoulders, gave him, though rather a short man, an appearance of majesty, which none of their Majesties possessed. He looked one of the princes of what the Chambers style, the "intellectual aristocracy." Many a Frenchman will envy me. Louis Philippe I could have shot half a dozen times, had I been so disposed. There is nothing inviting about him. His cheeks hang like collapsed pudding bags. His frontispiece struck me as resembling Jupiter's with the brains out. His head baffled all my phrenology—it is something between facetiæ and mathematics—half comical and half conical. The only thing to which I can compare it is an inverted humming-top.* Perhaps his conduct had prejudiced me, for I gladly turned away from the odious restrictor of the French press.

Prince Albert had a right princely appearance. His large German eyes are singularly full and glaring. He looks as though he was very well fed, and never thought where it came from. None of these I had seen before. The Queen I had not seen since she was a girl, and I wondered how the cooped up, swaddled thing I saw in Birmingham, had become so nice a young woman— I was agreeably surprised at her. The breezes of Blair Athol have left her quite blooming, and her pretty Saxon face beaming both with maternal affection and thought,† quite prepossessed me

---

* The people of France, I have since learned, nick-named him *Louis le poire* —or the pear-headed, from the resemblance they discovered in his face and head to an inverted pear. And Paris—till he interfered—used to be placarded with pictures of pears, bearing his face, with the words annexed, " When the pear is rotten it will fall." An event not deemed unlikely to happen.

† The people of Belgium, during the Queen's visit there, thought her affected with the malady of her grandfather, George III., from the vacancy of

in her favour. I don't think that she means us any harm—though she does us no good. The royal party passed on to Gosport, for Louis Philippe was going home.

By three o'clook I was again on the line, making another violent attempt to get to Harmony Hall. O! Æolus, how the wind blows on the Southampton railway! Those who travel there this weather, should tie caps on their heads, and to ligature their heads on their shoulders will be found no superfluous precaution. My cap, which had seen some service—having had six months' imprisonment, was almost blown into its original fleece, and was near taking up its old abode on the backs of the neighbouring sheep.

At last I reached Winchester, having paid 12s. for my ride in the 2nd class. It was half-past four, and Stockbridge was nine miles off. No conveyance being procurable, and the rain abating, I walked the distance.

The *New Moral World* directs that persons visiting Harmony should " book themselves at Noyce's coach office, to go by the nine o'clock morning train." Those who do so are taken by the second class to Winchester, and then on Noyce's coach to nine mile water, thirteen miles farther on, for 10s. But not being able to understand what booking at a coach office had to do with the morning railway train, I took my ticket in the railway instead of the coach office. The railway people have an arrangement whereby those who only travel to Winchester pay 12s., but if they go thirteen miles farther on, they pay only 10s. The farther you go the less they charge.

The road from Winchester to Stockbridge lies over bleak hills and barren dales. Here and there a solitary tree or bush raises its disconsolate head, and looks half alarmed at its own temerity in getting out of the earth in that bald district. Before I reached Stockbridge

> The gloomy night was gathering fast,
> Loud roar'd the wild inconstant blast,
> The murky clouds were big with rain,
> I saw them driving o'er the plain.

At last, regular Egyptian darkness—such as could be felt—set in, but where Stockbridge lay, whether near or far, on hill or in hollow, I knew not. At last, poking my way with my umbrella, I ran against something that proved to be a ploughman, from whom I learned that I was on the verge of the village, that I must turn by the "Ship," ask for the "Queen's Head," and tell " Stone " that I was one of the " *Zozialites*," and I should be all right. There I found a pretty kind creature of a landlady, and in due time (by half-past seven) I was munching toast, and listening to one of those organised funguses, which seem to vegetate about

---

her laugh, and it is said that her repeated visitings are ordered by her physicians, to keep away a melancholy with which she is threatened. At times she sobs and cries much. If so, I should say she is improving now.

tockbridge in the shape of farmers' labourers, singing for the amusement of his companions—

> If I had a wife wot blow'd me up,
> I'd get a gal and make her jealous.

For supper, bed, and song, having paid 1s. 6d., next morning found me on my way to Harmony Hall. It rained then as it did when Noah took the fish into the ark to prevent them being drowned.

My directions were to pass through the village, and at a mile and half onwards, to turn off to the left, by a gentleman's house, which would lead me (somehow) to Broughton. I was now fairly in the land of flint and chalk. Everywhere lay flanks of earth, dressed in nature's shabbiest attire—not unlike a man in thread-bare hose, and the mounds of white chalk, peeping up here and there, presented the picture of nature out at the elbows. While the hills presenting their raw noses around, with only an old dark brown coat on their backs, flabbing in rags over their slough covered feet, looked like vegetable swells out of luck.

When high on the road that "lay by the gentleman's house," I asked my way of an old villager, who, unfortunately for me, "knew the road well." He sent me along this field, over that, by a stile, "which I should be sure to see," (but be sure not to know), and after turning here, and turning there, I should come out (somewhere) in Broughton.

Reader! let me entreat you to take warning by my fate. Men who "know the way" have nearly been the ruin of me. In every town they have been by greatest bores and most dreaded perse-cutors. If I was going to be hanged, the first thing I should warn young persons against would be all those "people who know the way." If all the misfortunes of my life, from other causes, were gathered together, they would fall far short of the miseries heaped upon me by these officious tormentors. Every week of my life I have walked five times farther than the real way, through following the directions of people who sent me "the nearest way." When a stranger asks his road, instead of being directed straight forward, through high-ways, or well known streets, which he could not miss—somebody who knows all the lanes and bye-ways, courts and alleys, will direct him through them. The moment a stranger enters the first of these, he knows not where he is, and has to spend more time in making enquiries than would take him ten times the actual distance. Some plain person, who knows little about a place, is the man to seek as a guide. In Bristol, I had the good luck on my entrance, to be taken to Bristol Bridge. This became my centre—everywhere I went I started from Bristol Bridge. I was never so happy in any town. In London, through always being directed "the nearest way," I am sure I have walked 1000 unnecessary miles. After travelling until I thought it was dinner time, I happily discovered the road I had left, and soon came in sight of Broughton, which is scarcely four miles from Stockbridge. But what with the weather and bad guides, I shall hardly be able to reach Harmony Hall in this chapter.

Broughton is a pleasant village to look at, but all its pleasantness is outside—it is plain and dull enough within. But as it is the first relief from barrenness and stones, one is glad to see it. About a mile through it, over a chalk hill, is the next road to be taken, and as the traveller descends the hill's brow, he comes suddenly upon Harmony Hall. It is a very respectable looking building—imbedded in a mountain—half red, half blue—a compound of brick and slate, of no conceivable shape, with two spires in front, and two glass chimneys, apparently intended to let people see the smoke come up, but farther examination tells you they are skylights over the corridors, leading to the dormitories. C.M. 1841, are observable at one end of the building, which informed me, for the first time, that the Millenium had commenced *three years* ago.

Verdure and beauty first make their appearance in the neighbourhood of the Hall. Around, pleasant prospects arise. But it was a place to look at rather than to live on. The soil has *now* been made productive, at great expence, but the flints which cover the land, point out the place as one intended by nature, not for a colony of Socialists, but for a colony of gunsmiths, who, before percussion caps came up, might have made their fortunes by gathering the flints. The more a stranger gazes on that estate, the more he wonders at the sagacity which first selected it, and he comes to the conclusion that it was chosen with an eye to insolvency, under the impression that the chalk pits in the neighbourhood would be convenient for " white washing."

CHAP. II.

YES, reader! in a remote part of Britain, down in Hampshire's very heart, as far as possible from any seat of manufacture or commerce, and out of the way of every body concerned, is situated the famous Socialist experiment. Had it been near Manchester, or Birmingham, it would have commanded, in its own friends, without expense of conveyance, a ready and unfailing market for all its produce. Had it been near some coal district, and contiguous to some river, manufactures might have formed, as was always intended, a part of its operations. But it has neither natural nor artificial advantages as a trading community. As an agricultural colony only can it, for a long time, succeed, and for this species of success nature has done little, and its directors less. Their first care was to erect normal schools when they wanted farmsteads.

Among the inmates of Harmony Hall and its dependencies, I found numerous old friends and acquaintances, from all parts of the country. The Hall itself more resembles Drayton Manor, the residence of Sir Robert Peel, than the home of pioneers. Every thing has been provided in the most expensive way. Economy appears to have been laughed at in its erection. During that panic of pride, a pretty infants' school, erected under Mr. Joseph Smith's superintendence, was contemptuously termed a "shed." The cellar of the Hall, now used as a dining room, has a costly range of windows, tastefully pannelled, the sides of the whole room ribbed with mahogany, and all the tables, neither few nor small, of the same costly material. Of the kitchen, it has been reported, that there are few in London so completely and expensively fitted up, and with "one who has whistled at the plough, I am sorry to say, that such is to all appearance the case." No objection can be held against having every thing that is really useful and of good quality. It is the profusion of contrivances and vessels that strike the observer as being only necessary in the higher stage of epicureanism. The ball room and class rooms, on the basement story, have ceilings richly finished, and every where are elegance and splendour, The Hall is a monument of *ill-timed* magnificence. At first, nothing was wanted but utility, convenience, and economy. The Hall was not intended for a community, but for a normal school, and in this the Directors appear to have departed from the Socialist's original, most necessary, and most cherished intention. They aimed at a conquest of the world, when they should have been achieving the independence of the young community, and giving, in the words of Mr. Hunt, "a practical demonstration to the working classes, that any given number of them possess the means within themselves, to effect a similar change in their own condition."

Under the strange ideas entertained by Messrs. Owen and Galpin, and so readily swallowed by their coadjutors, that Sir Robert Peel and the Queen's Cabinet were coming to embrace them, the oddest things were done. Instead of colonization, it appears to have been squanderization. Books of Mr. Owen were reprinted which nobody read—and *New Moral Worlds* amassed which nobody bought, and prospectuses issued to which nobody attended. To ask for less than a million of money was thought mean and beggarly. When the garden was laid out, Mr. Owen instructed Mr. Scott to make arrangements for two thousand people, before two hundred had a chance of coming. Walks were laid out when the land wanted sowing, and such walks they promised to be! The old Roman roads, made for two thousand years, were not more deeply trenched, nor more wastefully bedded with flints—and thus, from six to seven hundred pounds were expended. The Late Acting Governor continued walk making, while the landlord's rent was accumulating in arrears. They talked of "experience," indeed, but talk was all. The *New Moral World* rang with their sagacity, but the visitor to Harmony Hall will seek in vain for proofs of it. They went on until their coffers were exhausted—till debts were thicker than their crops—and their walks and fountains still unfinished, corroborate the truth of the Spaniard's proverb, that "knowledge will become folly unless good sense take care of it." The intensely sublimated imaginations of those Directors told them of capital half crazy to be spent by them, and continually crying "Come, use me." Public opinion they deemed absolutely impatient to be theirs. Really, these strange expectations make one think there cannot be a breathing man who knows so little of human nature as Robert Owen. No objections can be urged to speculations, even the wildest, when the speculators spend their own money—but in this case the money of others went in expensive schemes, and security and self-support were forgotten in the dreams of grandeur. They seemed to believe that the more they asked the more they would have. On capital, instead of on the land, these Home Colonization people fixed their precious eyes. With them a prime mind meant a full purse. Their policy was that of a spendthrift—their wisdom that of a gamester. A long vine wall was erected, which probably cost a guinea a yard. When Mr. Southwell was there with a friend, it was debated with them, whether the wall was erected to support the vine or the vine planted to support the wall. It scarcely need be added, that be this as it may, the grapes at present are mortal few. I do not doubt or insinuate that the Directors of this community did not intend the best of things, but carried away by Mr. Owen, they fancied all the world was coming to their arms, while, in fact, they were coming fast to the Gazette. Some of them, like Mr. Ironside, were not really blinded, but were determined to carry out the spirit of the paternal form of government, and in doing so they carried themselves, and nearly the society, out along with it. Had not the last Congress made the present changes, the experiment would ere this have passed for ever from the dreams of hope. "What has all this to do with the present state of the establishment?" some will ask. It has this: heavy debts were accumulated, which the present Executive have had to pay, by which their efforts have been crippled, and the thousands of pounds untimely expended on the building, not only now lie producing nothing—but are heaping up unpaid interest which presses like an incubus on the young energies of the household—and, though it may not be demanded, it is *expected*—if it is not asked for, it is owing—and the capitalists are rendered nervous, angry, fretful, and often threatening, till the wheels of the Executive government roll on through untold obstacles and unknown anxieties. "Why rake up old grievances—better bury the past," will cry some sapient soul, whose chief wisdom consists in crying peace, peace, when there is no peace. I tell the past as a warning for the future. It is not good to blunder in vain. Let failure tell its tale and teach its lesson. Let us have the means of judging principles by their product. The more is known of the truth of the case, the less surprise we shall feel at the declaration of Mr. Southwell, at the public breakfast to Mr. Buxton, at Branch A 1,—"The old Executive are dead and buried, and may they [their policy he meant] never suffer a resurrection." If the true position of the present Executive is not told, at next Congress, their failure, should they fail, will be ascribed to their policy, when it will have resulted from their position, and a position made for them by the very men who will then so blandly blame the results.

It will be said, but do not railway and canal companies expend immense sums of money, and erect their termini and arches in elegant and durable forms—in what respect did these old Directors differ from railway and such like people? But do railway people lay out their lines, or do canal companies commence expensively to erect their works before they know where the capital is to come from to finish the whole with? More than this, they neither attempt to cut line nor dig river, until they have seen their boats swim and their carriages run. It should be so with communities. With us communities are but experiments, and we can't too cheaply try whether co-operative life can be made to accord with the genius of the English people, and the communities at the same time be self-supporting establishments. When this has been proved it will be time enough for Socialists to engage the architect of the Birmingham Town Hall to erect their farm houses.

I was surprised at the estate's extent. A day is insufficient to walk round it. Stretching far over hill, dale, and entangled woodland, lie the Great and Little Bentley farms, with their rosy orchards, venerable homesteads, and antique wainscotted rooms. But, reader, I could never forget for a single moment that the rent was unpaid.

As I walked over that estate, and its glorious undulations of hill and dale, through its broad expanse, and woodland relief, and down its gorgeous yew tree avenue, with its long aisles of vernal glory, colonnades of venerable firs, and gothic ceiling of fretted trellis work, and bright sky bursting in at the bottom, like a silver lamp lighting the whole, making a palace scene which no picture has exaggerated and no language done justice—I could not do as some have done, bound along, exclaiming, brethren, " *This is ours,*"—I could not, like the *New Moral World,* of last week, talk of " breathing the air of freedom—listening to the melody of *our own* birds in *our own* woods." I could not forget the madness which had perilled to us that splendid place—the unpaid rent gave its beauty the air of desolation. I could not even stand upright under its gothic arches, where a bailiff might next walk. Those men who favoured us with their paternal wisdom could have had no love of nature left amid their vast dreamings or they would have clung with a lover's fondness to those sunny scenes, and by economy, foresight, and care, have secured that place from every liability. So soon as the welcome day arrives when that experiment shall be declared free, and standing on its own pillars of support, no longer be dependent on casual bounty, on accidental subscription, or the tremblingly lent loan of the timid capitalist, then could I walk from England's remotest bound to mingle again with those devoted communists, and stroll once more up that glorious avenue—when no claim is unmet, and every capitalist has deep down in his pocket the last cent. of stipulated interest, then could I exult with any one—but not till then. Till then the very blades of grass would reproach me; nor could I reciprocate the dasies' smile or the buttercups' glow.

When the last congress met, hopeless were the prospects, and when it separated matters were, in its immediate neighbourhood, worse. The news spread like wildfire that the establishment would be broken up. £1000 of debts were owing, exchequers were empty, confidence was low, capitalists looked iron things, the late Acting Governor demanded his loan, and professed friends were cold as ice. Under such circumstances Mr. Buxton took office, and deep is the debt of gratitude due to him for the responsibility he assumed, and the sacrifices he has made. Persons who had let their debts stand over for years then threatened legal proceedings unless instant payment was made, and for weeks after taking office, sleepless nights were passed by the Governor—and well it might be so—a man might rather " coin his heart for drachmas " than live so besought.

An agreeable fiction has been received of Mr. Owen being on visiting terms with Sir Isaac Lyon Goldsmid, and some dreamed of favours to flow, or that thence have flowed. Those that have flowed, so far as I can learn, belong to the region of dreams. Aristocratic friendship is not worth much when rent is unpaid. Socialists, don't forget that your landlord would as soon lay his hands on your broad acres as on any one else's,—and rather, as they are of more worth—if you leave them in his power. You are not safe, you ought not to be safe while under obligation. If I lived at Harmony, I am sure I should sleep, as Cooke declared the Bristol people do, with one eye open, that I might miss no chance until every stiver of rent was paid.

To remedy this state of things Mr. Buxton, and his excellent coadjutor, Mr. Simpson, have done everything economy and self-denial could do. During his short term of office he has paid £800 of bad debts. All useless expenditure is nipped in the bud. All salaries abolished. The land is being made productive. Every soul is usefully employed, and the experiment is at last on the high road to be self-supporting.

In the hall, contentment and equality reign. The fare is wholesome, good and sufficient. All eat and drink alike. The Governor sits at the same table as the members, and Mrs. Buxton does the same share of labour as any other woman. No private tables are spread. No lady in velvet frowns for the benefit of good order, and no friend Galpin prohibits laughing in the name of propriety.

The family meetings are family parliaments. There are no

secrets, no mysteries, no private carousings of heads of departments, no listening at office doors. Every member knows every
thing. Upon everything all deliberate, all advise. All seem to
feel that the experiment depends upon each. The result is that
they make all conceivable sacrifices; they toil early and late—the
ls. a week, allowed them, they leave in the Governor's hands
until the exchequer can better spare it. Knowing the difficulties of the establishment, they work like heroines and heroes, and
endure like devotees.

Those who join the family, are with few exceptions, at first disappointed. The duty of a pioneer is no sinecure, and the new habits are hard to put on. Those who were well to do seem sooner to
conform to the new associations than those who have been less
happily placed. The reason is, the comfortable expect to make
personal sacrifices while the others anticipate immediate advantages. Had I space for details, I have many to tell, but I must
hasten to treat of the hinges on which success or failure hangs. It
was easy to see in this new and improved state of the family
feeling, the reason of the anticipated failure of the democratic
form of government by the old executive. They said it would
not do because they never tried it. They could not descend to the
same equality—they had few feelings, few sympathies in common.
How could there be democracy where the rulers had a contempt
for the ruled ? The old executive said the mere members could
not understand their views—this was the secret, they could not
trust them to them, as many a tale could tell.

Rude may be the endeavours, many may be the mistakes made,
slow may be the progress of a democratic society, but without such
principle and practice only negative will be the progress made.
Working men must work out their own freedom ere they can have
it. I have never known a poor man's institution that was began
to be conducted on respectable principles that was not at once
seized with the agonies of death, and that did not expire in the most
polished torments. *Cæteris paribus*, the vulgarest democracy is
preferable to the paternal presidency of an almighty god. Democracy may be vulgar but its frankness is to be cherished. It is the
only government of equality—and its perpetual demand on individual perfection, makes it the only government of true progression.

Marvellous was the wisdom employed in building up the paternal form of government, in insisting on the wholesale subjugation
of the understanding, and the long exploded doctrines of despotism were to be for ever popularised among us—but most signal
has been the failure of these principles in practice. Mr. Owen
must have "heads of departments," by which means he lost all
head over his own. If anything was wanted, "Oh," he would
say, "you must ask Mr. So-and-so, it belongs to his department."
But when you reached Mr. So-and-so he did not think so, and
another and another Mr. So-and-so had to be found, until the unhappy applicant had at last to sit down very "so so" himself,

without what he wanted being done. Then these heads of departments (at Ham Common there were more departments than heads) were little demi-gods in their several districts, and a thing was right in Mr. Owen's eyes, not because of its fitness, for about that he never troubled himself, but because the heads of departments ordered it. Now the Governor superintends and judges all.

To generalise was another point of the new philosophy—and how they did generalise! Mr. Reid said at the London Mechanics' Institution, with some truth, that Mr. Owen was so anxious for the good of the whole community that when one member had a fever, to especially attend to him would be contrary to his principles, he could not conscientiously trouble himself unless they *all* had a fever.

Talk of men of business —shade of Walkingame, what specimens those prime minds were! Congress after congress owned, as Dr. Reid did of Clarke's " A priori argument," that their book-keeping might be very sublime, but they could not understand it. What was borrowed they did not know, what was spent they could not tell. When the late Acting Governor made his claim of £500, voucher, receipt, or entry could not by him be produced, nor any where be found. At last the Central Board made their Minute Book serve for a Ledger, and ordered an entry of the loan there, *twelve months* after it was received.

To ask what they were doing was deemed proof positive that the questioner was beside himself. Friend Rigby, or Galpin, or Fleming, or Jones, would shake his head, and ask how a localised inexperienced mind could understand such magnificent operations, as digging the precious earth and keeping an account of what was got by it. Simple as it was, they might well ask who could understand it, for I don't believe they could themselves. Sometimes our government seizes the documents of a society and discovers all its secrets, but often have I prayed that the government might seize ours, for could they discover the state of affairs they would do more than we could.

At Harmony I lighted on one or two remnants of the old wisdom, who said that twelve months would be too little to understand what was going on there, until I had the impression that that mysticism which had crept into their morality pervaded their works, and that Harmony resembled nothing so much as theology, where all we know is that nothing can be known. But being accustomed to such repulses, I contented myself with humbly hoping that I might at least be able to discover that nothing could be discovered.

But luckily, there is a clear headed man at the secretary's desk now. In Mr. Simpson's hands I saw books that by next congress will tell many a tale. Take one book as a specimen. On one side of a folio, every field is entered, its acres, yards, and inches; its present condition and value. With every day and hour's labour upon it, whether of man or horse, with whatever of seed and compost

B

14

are laid upon it, that field is *debited*. On the opposite folio it is *credited* with all the produce it is found to yield. Side by side stands the gain or loss upon that field during the year. So plain is all this that a child can understand it. Thus in every department mystery is disssipated, and if the executive are enabled to continue their labours, by next congress they will have matters in such genuine business like order, that a plain man may tell in an hour what will become of his money if he invest it there.

CHAP. III.

THE tendency to diminish expenditure is in every department of Harmony Community observable. Twenty-five shillings a-week were paid for hired labour in the laundry two or three weeks ago —now all is done by the wives of the members. Hired labour on the farm is being rapidly dispensed with. The well furnished orchard, the property everywhere exposed, naturally, to an unknown extent, fall a prey to people having no common interest in its preservation. While I was there, twenty-four yards of new cloth, which lay out bleaching, walked off. Not even a policeman was spoken to, lest some poor devil should have his hard lot made hopelessly harder. So much as £21 were paid to hired labourers, as wages, the week prior to my visit. Much more economical, besides much more consistent and agreeable, would be the employment of our own members. In proof of this it may be stated, that Mr. Buxton has been able to increase the number of hands on the estate and decrease the expenditure. Yet Mr. Finch protests against the dismissal of a certain functionary, and Mr. B. exclaims, " my property will be ruined if members are brought down "—but what says facts. Mr. Thompson of Manchester was three times nominated by his Branch, and three times objected to by the Central Board, on account of his family. Mr. Buxton had him brought down, and this is the result. He displaces 18s. per week, Mrs. T. 9s., one son 14s., and another 11s. Thus, this one family saves the establishment 52s. weekly in wages, probably not costing themselves more than a third of the sum. I do not desire to obscure the fact that the labourer is to be regarded as indigenous to the soil—that he may justly expect to live on the land on which he was found living— that if he is not retained as a labourer, he may become chargeable as a pauper, and that the estate must either pay wages or poor's rates—these points may be admitted, and it may still be true that the Community's best servants are its own members.

Take an example of how much a little cash is needed at this juncture. Sixty sheep are feeding in the fields, worth about £75. During the next six weeks they will eat up produce without being worth more. But if £20 could be expended on them in linseed oil cake, they would, at the end of the same six weeks, be worth some £130, and the fields on which they pastured be worth £20 more, through their being fed on the oil cake. Moreover, the land not being thus manured, will prevent ten acres of wheat from being sown, the produce of which would yield some thirty quarters, worth about £70 or £75. Who that had £20 to spare would not send it down ?

In telling how Communists live in Community, I must not omit to add how strangers live there, which is by paying 2s. per day—less than half the former charge, which 2s. entitles them to three meals, wholesome, excellent, varied, and substantial, and a capital snoose at night in a nice room, a wide bed, and friend Cotterell's trumpet to wake them with in the morning.

One reason why the accounts of the society are not farther on the way to intelligibility is. that too many people are doing one work. To wit, the Central Board receive Community funds and school fees, which, as they belong to Harmony, ought to be sent there direct. As it is, double accounts have to be kept, and sundry official transmissions of money have weekly to be made, by which confusion sometimes, jealousy often, unavoidably spring up. Whether the Community fund is not being appropriated as Mr. Newall appropriated it—to the support of Missionaries, nobody certainly knows—there may or may not be large arrears of school fees, but as some are paid at Harmony and others in London—until those two accounts can be compared, it remains a mystery, and it is with book-keeping as with bipeds in general—whoever or whatever sits on two stools, has a seat somewhere on the ground. Thus, the society is pretty much in the condition of Elwes, the miser, who, when he had one servant he had his work always done, when he had two, it was only half done, and when he had three, he had to do it himself. The duties of the Central Board would be best restricted to the management of the General Fund and propagandism in general, and Harmony should be suffered to take its own affairs into its own hands.

Of the schools at Harmony I am the most puzzled to speak. The class rooms are fine, the conveniences of education are many, and the children are rubicund and happy. Staying but for a short time, and having many things to see, it was impossible to make that examination that a school requires. The children keep no register of their acquisitions, because it is thought likely to deceive parents—but such indexes never deceive teachers, and had such a record been in existence, I could have satisfied myself respecting them. As a principal is just now wanting, no general system can be expected to prevail. From all I heard, the future may be promising. The past career of the schools has left few indications of that wisdom that belongs to our philosophy, and is expected from our professions. The former appointments were unhappy ones. Mr. Reid publicly established, in London, his utter inefficiency for his office, and Mr. Oestreicher, in my

16

opinion, did pretty much the same thing in the *New Moral World.* Mr. R. failing in morals, and Mr. O. through mysticism. It appears not to have been known at Harmony that the grand problem of Education has been solved by Phiquepal d'Arusmont, namely—"that instruction may be so judiciously calculated as to develope, simultaneously, the moral, intellectual, physical, and industrial faculties of children, and cover all its own expences, together with those of the preceding state of infancy." An experiment of this kind, under the intelligent management named, was found fully adequate to its own support in *six months.* But it is impossible that the Harmony schools, with their vast advantages, will not share in the common impetus, and some day revive the spirit of the ancient academies, and rival the best efforts of Heldenmaier.

When I set out for Harmony, I had no confidence whatever in the success of the experiment. I did not doubt the industry of the members, but I much questioned the fertility of their soil. I had no fears for the judgment or integrity of the new Executive, but I expected the difficulties in which they were placed would be too great for them. Some persons holding back their money for fear the experiment should not answer, and some for fear it should, some because the new Executive had taken office, and some through fear they would not be kept there, had made funds a very scarce article. But finding the land better than expectation, witnessing the devotion of the Communists there, the prudence and economy of the Governor, and the efforts made to get out of debt, quite satisfied me that they will succeed if they meet with support during their year of office, and that by next Congress the experiment will be on safer and more satisfactory grounds than it ever yet was, and nearly, if not quite, self-supporting.

The true predicament, at this time, of the Harmony experiment deserves investigation, because all sorts of persons will judge, by its success or failure, the ability of the working classes to manage their own affairs. Even Mr. Owen, the last thing he said was, "I doubt the power of the working classes (from their necessarily contracted knowledge of things) to manage beneficially their own affairs, or to carry on the Harmony experiment successfully." Now it will be to libel the working classes to ascribe the failure of Harmony to them. If fail it should, it will not be through the "contracted knowledge of the working classes" so much as through the distracted condition in which the capitalists have left it, who not only expended, in a nearly useless manner, all the money the working classes subscribed, but mortgaged all they can now raise in the shape of debts, they, the capitalists, left unpaid. The reproaches of the President of Branch A 1, addressed to the Northern Branches, have no application, because those Branches have contributed what would have amply carried on one of their own experiments, but as it is, they have to extricate a capitalist's experiment from difficulty. Strenuously have Mr. Owen and his coadjutors inculcated the sad doctrine of the absolute dependence of the working classes on capitalists. Behold, Socialists! in your hour of need, what assistance you get from them ! The letter just addressed by your Central Board to all members and friends, respecting the day's wages to be presented to Harmony, has this passage.

"We are informed there are monied parties watching our proceedings, who believe Harmony cannot be carried on in accordance with the resolutions of Congress, and *therefore will not assist us with their capital.*"

Precious men to depend on are these capitalists! When you are safe through all your difficulties they will run to your assistance, and credit themselves with all the wisdom and all the success. Miserable imitators of God Almighty! who helps only those who can help themselves, and takes all the glory.

The governing party of Socialists have erred chiefly in extremes. At first they were all talk, and at last they were all bustle. Those who would coolly enquire into what they intended at the beginning, and what they were at in the end, met with no little contempt. The only reply would be, "we are past that point now, we can't stop to dispute. We have had enough of talking, we must be *doing*." Forgetful that *doing* without the talking, which explains our intention and informs our friends, is but the blind thumping of ignorance, without a plan and without an advantage.

To very different causes than those usually assigned, will the judicious commentator on Socialism ascribe the apathy of friends and the disorganization of Branches. Mr. Lloyd Jones lately declared to the people of Edinburgh that their paralyzed state is owing to their having engaged an heterodox lecturer. Although it is a fact, that hardly a year since, when the old Executive were in power, the President of the Edinburgh Branch came to London, and handed over to the Central Board £60, saying, that had the people of Edinburgh confidence in that Board's proceedings, of which Board Mr. Jones was one, he should have had £130 to pay into their hands—thus proving that it was not to heterodoxy so much as to orthodoxy that the Edinburgh Branch owes its inactivity. When Mr. Owen was last in Birmingham, some two years ago, he wrote in the *New Moral World*, March 18, 1842, that theological discussions had ruined that Branch. Passing through Birmingham at that time, I made enquiries respecting this statement, and found that the very two lectures which followed his, and which were upon Atheism, proved far more attractive than his own—aided as his were by large placards and the popularity of his name. And it is conceded that Mr. Southwell always drew better audiences than the preacher of the most sedate namby pambyism the society ever patronized. It was what is now tolerably well known as "back-

bone Owenism" that ruined the Birmingham Branch. They
grew respectable and they grew dead, and the finest set of fellows,
in the finest town in the kingdom, shrunk into utter inanity.

The great difficulty under which the present managers at Harmony have lain—a difficulty not to be overlooked in any just estimate to be formed of the value of their policy and exertions, as it
is a difficulty under which no former executive laboured—the want
of an organ at their command, in which themselves and friends
could be heard. The paper of the society has not been the paper
of the executive—the *New Moral World* has been notoriously in the
interests of the old party. In my reply to the late Acting Governor, in No. 32 of the *Movement*, I drew attention to this fact,
and it will not be invidious in me to notice it again. Mr. Buxton,
from a desire to conciliate, was anxious to retain all the officers he
found appointed. But in my opinion, his chief error has been in
not taking the *New Moral World* into his own hands. It was of
immense importance that the organ of the society should express
the opinions and represent the wishes of the society. To its not
doing so may be ascribed the inefficient assistance yet rendered to
the new Executive. In other repects the results have been disas-
trous. Letters like those of Mr. Vines and the late Acting Governor, have appeared, and the friends of the new Executive
denied the chance of reply. Indeed Mr. Buxton himself has not
enjoyed the privilege always conceded to the humblest correspondent of the *Movement*, that of being heard in his own words
and in his own way. Whole paragraphs of great importance have
been struck out of his letters. His communications have been
carried to the Central Board by the Editor, and they induced (Mr.
Buxton being absent) to consent to their suppression, until he has
ceased to write at all, or only on general unimportant topics. Who
can learn the true situation of the new Executive, with the hands
of the old Executive on its mouth?

The old Executive, with all their faults, would not have committed the mistake of not securing the *New Moral World*. They
would have dismissed Mr. Fleming again, as they did before. Mr.
Galpin, with all his extravagancies, was brave. Why, Mr. Fleming would have dismissed any man who was half as much an
obstacle as himself. When I published the "Spirit of Bonner,"
in defence of Mr. Southwell, Mr. Fleming came down to Sheffield,
and told the Branch that I was an obstacle in the Society's way,
and as such, would be removed. Then Mr. Jones came, and while
I was sent to Bradford, delivered a lecture, in which he recommended the Branch to dismiss me. To all this I made no objection then, nor since, nor now. At any time that my exertions in
favour of free discussion, or any other cause, shall render me an
obstacle in the progress of my own chosen party, I say with
Atrides—

Let me be deem'd the hateful cause of all,
And suffer, rather than my people fall.

In these reflections, the most malevolent will hardly ascribe to

19

me envious motives, or suppose that I personally disparage the
parties to whom I have referred. Mr. Fleming and Mr. Jones
may be conceded to be able men, without at the same time being
exactly suited to advance a cause, with which they have little
sympathy, and that has become a cause in spite of them. At Congress they declined to act on the Central Board, and how can they
advocate what they could not advise? How can they recommend
that to which they are conscientiously opposed? They cannot
even wish success, much less promote the new policy. It is not
in human nature—it would be building up an imputation on their
own wisdom. Let readers of the *New Moral World* think even
better of present doings than that paper may pourtray. It can be
but negatively favourable. It rather tolerates the present Executive than supports it, and seems to write in its favour rather
from a sense of decency than a feeling of enthusiasm. The Editor
resembles an old servant, who has been taken to among the other
fixtures of a forfeited estate, and who is rather respectful than
affectionate to his new masters, who renders his services—not his
heart, and who has sworn never to say anything in favour of his
new protectors that will be likely to compromise his old ones.

As I have neither time nor space to detail elaborately all I saw
and learned during my visit to Harmony Hall, it may be that my
recitals will want something of fullness, but brief as the picture is,
it wants nothing of truth, and the fact that all discussion of the
conduct of the late Executive has been purposely suppressed in
the *New Moral World*, is presumptive evidence in favour of this
opinion. There must have been a reason for such conduct. No
man avoids discussion when his cause will bear it. Reflecting men
will not hesitate a moment in coming to the conclusion that a case
to which no reference is to be made is a case condemned.

Some will suspect my criticism as being vastly too free—

Where I must speak what wisdom would conceal,
And truths, invidious to the great, reveal—

but I stay not to weigh the scruples of Calchas. I value private
friendship much, but public duty more. Then I cannot attack as
is the socialists' fashion—speak of an opponent as "an unfavourable circumstance,"—conceal a sting under charitable regards,
and stab while I pity. I do not shelter myself under bland gene-
ralities, but step out, tap the men I mean on the shoulder, call
them by their names, tell them who strikes, and leave them free
to do their mightiest.

Charity, that bastard child of justice, in the person of some piece
of neutrality whose sole virtue consists in doing nothing and avert-
ing nothing, will admonish me that I had better not moot the topics
of this chapter—"they only irritate," or "at least they had better be delayed to the next congress." Reader, if you can endure
such a formal proceedure, permit me to tell an anecdote on this
point.

When confined in Gloucester Gaol, I commenced to address applications and memorials to the authorities there for an amelioration

of my treatment. Upon this, Captain Mason, the Governor, said, "It is of no use, Holyoake, that you address these applications. I have no power to grant your request—the Mgaistrates will not listen to your memorials, and Sir James Graham will reject that to which they have refused to attend. You have discretion, and you had better not pursue a course which can only annoy those who may otherwise be favourably disposed." My dear Sir, I replied, for I had grown familiar with indignation, "though you should burn every memorial I draw up, before my eyes, the moment it is finished, yet will I continue to do them in the best and most fitting manner, and address one to every official over me. I would tell those stone walls my wants, and shout my requests through those iron bars—for when I leave this place, if leave it I shall, and complain to the public of my treatment here and at your hands, you will be the first person to say, 'Well, why did you not complain?' and the magistrates will re-echo, 'Why did not Holyoake apply to us?' and the public will remark, 'if Holyoake had grievances it is only natural that he should have made them known.' Captain, it is my place to apply—yours to refuse, if you please." Wily devils were those Gaol people! they thought to discourage my complaints that hereafter they might swear there could have been no occasion for them. But I did apply, and I need scarcely add, that my applications were not burnt, and that my condition was soon improved. So if such matters as I have recited are not published now by some one, at the next social Congress the argument will leap to the mouths of men there, "Why were not these evils, if they existed, made known before?" For this reason, without enquiring Mr. Buxton's views, or consulting the taste of persons averse to him, I determined to make known on my own responsibility such facts as to me appeared to bear upon the future existence of our young Community.

The opinion on many points which I have given in these papers on Harmony, differ from those I formerly held. When in the provinces, I had few opportunities of knowing the truth, and being, in common with others, guided chiefly by the *New Moral World*, I was in the simple condition of Burn's ploughman, who could not conceive how a lord could be a fool, or a godly man a knave. Overwhelmed by the cant of prime minds I could not believe in the deficiency of common sense, but piercing the veil of all this orthodoxy and vanity, I confess to having arrived at opinions somewhat different from those expressed in my view of the "Socialist Parliament," in *Movement* 27, in which I characterized its changes as "something that was not expected, and also something that was not desired."

As I turned to gaze on Queenwood for the last time a thousand thoughts thronged for utterance. It seemed as though the spirit of progression, first refulgent in the gardens of Plato, had sent its genial rays down time's broad stream, to nurture a young republic in the nineteenth century. What proud efforts were making within for its success—what hopes without were concentrated there!

Probably no spot on this unconquered land, sacred to antiquity,
poetry, or political struggle, is more full of interest to humanity
than that place on which industry has fixed to work out its eman-
cipation. Even wretchedness smiles as community is named, and
out of the otherwise pathless desert of life a way opens there to
independence. Toil-worn men, at the anvil and the loom, turn to
that place as the happy land where the craven spirit will no
longer submit nor the Jew spirit torture industry for gain, nor
the scoundrel spirit longer laugh at the mortal agony of the poor.
Onwards, Communists! to success or failure, that we may the
sooner know whether the creed of labour is to be peaceful or sanguinary—for the iron maxim of those who rule is, that *no man
suffers while he endures.*

VINDICATORY CHAPTER.

IV.

Look closer to't; you make the evil first;
A base, then pile a heap of censures on it.
'Tis your own sin supplies the scaffolding
And mason work: you skilful, rear the grim
Unsightly fabric, and there point, and say
" How ugly is it." You meanwhile forget
' Tis your own handy work. I could say more ;
But there's a check within : 'tis such an one,
As you I trow, have banished from its birthplace.—*Old Play.*

MANY times have I had to castigate that sickly sentimentalism we call our
charity. I foresaw it would never last—that it was a thing of show rather than
wear. " My heart laments," cried old Artemidorus, " that virtue cannot live
out of the teeth of emulation," and the same may be ejaculated of Socialists'
charity, which lives not out of the teeth of prosperity. Like Christians' charity,
it only lasts while they have all their own way. Recent events have demonstrated the necessity of a healthier virtue, for the letters of the Late Acting
Governor and Mr. Lloyd Jones, in the *Movement,* and the Sunday morning
discussions at Branch A 1, respecting my " Visit to Harmony Hall," justify
the apostrophe—Frailty, thy name is Charity !
  " Look to the motto," Cobbett used to exclaim—look to the motto, reader,
and there you will see depicted the kind of criticism to which my " Visit" has
been subjected, and that, too, in quarters where it was little to be expected, and
by parties in whom such conduct is little creditable. The frank testimony I
bore to the rural beauty of the place, the high sense of independence I commended, the aid I entreated, and the dying interest I endeavoured to resuscitate
are all overlooked, and nothing is seen but prevarication, and nothing discovered but malevolence.
  Of my " Visit" some have said it is political and others that it is personal.
One gentleman declares I want to bring out the old Executive, and another
gives it as his opinion that I intend to draw out the new in the *Movement.* My
description of the nudity of the surrounding country, and the beauty of the
estate are pronounced to be flat contradictions. It is hinted that my sojourn
at Farnboro' was an invention to enliven my papers, and that I was never there
at all—and by others it is suspected that I never went beyond—until I shall
be under the necessity of making my " Visit" over again, or obtaining an affi-

davit sworn by Mr. Buxton, formally setting forth whether I have been to Harmony or not.

Now I undertake, if nothing less will satisfy, to procure a certificate from the Superintendent of the Farnboro' Station, or from the A Division of Scotland Yard, or from the Prince with the saucer optics, or the man with the pear-head, that I really *was* at Farnboro' on October 14, 1844. One fact of that day which I can verify is that the respectability who assembled in the back rooms of the station house to witness the arrival of the royal *cortege*, were so intent on seeing, that they forgot to cheer—not a single sound broke on my dilated tympanum. The mob who stood on the eminence in front of the station, did indeed set up something intended for a shout, but their loyalty seemed to take themselves so much by surprise, that they suddenly broke off like the old lady, who ejaculated, " Lord bless me, I have spoken in church." Their *hu hu rae* died on the hedge in which it was born, and was such a welcome as Smike and his pupils would have given Old Squeers. Louis Philippe must have departed highly elated with his British popularity.

Cynics may say what they will, but I shall not soon forget those lone trees that were shivering on the Hampshire hills. The society for the prevention of cruelty to animals would do well to look after cruelty to trees. Poor things, they were as lean, as ragged and as starved, as workhouse children. Usually the trees of autumn, tho' less gay than those of summer, appear more hardy, but these were delicate, and shivered in the wind like Spitalfield weavers. Had I been staying the night among them, I should have thrown my cloak over their shoulders.

As I have admitted (Chap. I.) though earth and sky seemed in league against fertility and beauty—though such weather prevailed when I left Stockbridge on the morning of the 15th, that even the smoke refused to " turn out," and instead of ascending the chimney, crudled itself up round the fire-place, as the landlady of the Queen's Head is prepard to testify—though the land on the Tytherly estate looked as though it had been the burying place of overseers and country magistrates, from the flinty remains around—yet I admitted that it *does now* fructify, another emblem of that progression destined to be accelerated there, telling us with sweet voice that there is nothing of physical or human nature which art cannot reclaim, or kindness recover.

Call it flat contradiction if you please, but still I adhere to my representation of the estate's glorious variety of hill, forest, brake, and bog. Standing on an eminence, a few days after the rain, I was delighted with the files of bushes, running out in all directions, begemmed with blackberries, bewitching, like so many gypsies' eyes, the rambler from his way—matronly hares skipped over the fields on morning vists to neighbouring burrows—wild birds darted through lofty boughs in very joy because they were wild—young shrubs gratefully tossed their heads to the giant trees, who stretched their huge arms in the gale and sheltered them from the blast—above, the sly sun was glancing through a crevice in the eastern sky, to see if the ground was fit to shine upon, and the clouds, like a cluster of merry coquets, were laughing at his late appearance. Indeed the whole scene resembled that which Ovid painted, when he wrote

> No walls were yet, nor fence, nor mote nor mound,
> Nor drum was heard nor trumpets angry sound,
> Nor swords were forged, but void of care and crime,
> The soft creation slept away their time.

Feeling desirous, as who would not? for the success of that place, was it wonderful that I should write earnestly in deprecation of that policy which was then so blindly cherished, but which, in realising our favourite dreams, had so ill succeeded.

The great services of Mr. Owen, which no one has been more prompt to acknowledge than myself, would have induced me to pass him by had I not known that his influence over his disciples was such as *he*, if a philosopher, must lament. In the very first address of our new Executive, in the *New Moral World* of August 31, 1844, they say, " Our venerable founder has often declared that as a body we do not understand our principles, and that, therefore, our policy is crude and undigested." They do not complain of this treatment at the hands of Mr. Owen, by which he publishes his chief coadjutors and adherents as ninconpoops. And the Central Board take it as a true state ment of their case—but if so, what a farce are their pretensions. What leaders of a bold, popular, and revolutionary party! Brutus! Buonarotti! Babeuf! Darthe! hide your heads! Who will say that that influence ought not to be shaken, which makes our leaders reason like simpletons, and look like children?

The denial of a resurrection to the late Executive (Chap. 2) would not have been repeated had not all report of the meeting at which it was pronounced, been so industriously kept out of the *New Moral World*. It pained, at the time, a very excellent member of that Executive—a gentleman, whose feelings I would on no account wantonly injure. It was he, who, when some of those irregularities, of which I complained, were being enacted at Harmony, thus wrote—" I value not the thousands, I fear I shall never see again, one tithe part in importance to the value of one child in the establishment. With money we may trifle as we please, and start speculation after speculation until we lose all—but for the sake of humanity let us not trifle with the welfare of one human being." Plutarch has not recorded a nobler sentiment than this. Neither patriotism nor philanthropy has any thing more generous on its pages. But because I thus appreciate, must I be blind—because of personal regard, must I connive at erroneous policy? No! *I* also reason for humanity, and though " I would make it kind, yet I must make it true."

The Late Acting Governor I have known since I was a child. That he should have been attacked by a Bishop would alone commend him to my favour. A man who has been respected wherever he has been known, and whom the Corporation of Birmingham specially honoured on his leaving that town, I am not weak enough to think I could injure, had I malevolence enough to attempt it. But though this gentleman may always be estimable, may he not sometimes be mistaken?

Many lusty knocks both Mr. Jones and Mr. Fleming have dealt against the citadel of superstition, and they have rendered some signal services to our common cause—but though I would never forget this, it forms no reason why I should write homilies for criticisms. The many have feelings as well as the few, and we cannot but remember that the order of industry has been consigned to contempt. What sneers at their rashness and inexperience. How ceaselessly has Mr. Owen disparaged them. How systematically have their endeavours been discouraged as vulgar, crude, and illdigested. It is to be expected that moral, as well as physical murder, will sometimes out.

Intellect is always aristocratic. It never descencs to the common level, and never will, it is therefore of no use telling us to be quiet—we must parley, and treat with it, and make the best bargain we can with it. When respectable people meddle with our affairs they do it as a *condescension*, and any questioning of their doings they pronounce downright factious and ungrateful rudeness. It is designated as " the way the working classes always requite those who serve them." Whatever is done for us it is expected we will thankfully receive, however it may be intended, and whatever it may prove. It is not openly avowed, but it is acted on, that we should open our mouths, shut our eyes, and respectfully accept whatever is sent us, Now I want to show the gentlemen who recently conducted our affairs, that we are not insensible to their merits—that we gladly, proudly, promptly acknowledge them—but while we praise we must discriminate—while we welcome their co-operation, we must demur to their dictation—something is due to ourselves as well as to them.

Talk of the Bishop of Exeter being a tactician! When he had an advantage he did not know how to use it. Had he pushed the consternation he created a little farther, Mr. Owen, the Central Board, and the Socialists of London would have marched in a body to St. Paul's to be confirmed. Socialism became a bye-word—synonymous among shrewd men with shuffling expediency. We should be failing in manliness not to provide against another contingency like this. I charge nobody with cowardice. Men have nothing to do with danger but duty, and that duty should be—shall be—better understood than hitherto.

There is the *New Moral World*, the should-be-organ of the Society—in its pages no complaint is noticed, no question answered. The earnest Socialist is treated alike by friend and foe—silent contempt on the one hand, and silent contempt on the other. The conclusion I have come to is that friend Fleming is qualifying for a governorship of the Pentonville prison, he is such a persevering practiser of the *silent system*.

A chief object of my "Visit" was to draw attention to the condition of our new Executive, both within and without, that we might properly understand and vigourously help. I desired to awaken the society from the sleep of paternal despotism, and open the Argus eyes of democracy. Instead of seeing our Branches represented by one man—more inclined, from his position, to tamper than to struggle—instead of our power being tapered down to a presidential point, too fine by far to perforate the hard hide of oppression; I wished that we should war against error and battle for truth, like the giant Briareus with 50 heads and 100 hands.

To tell us that we cannot discuss such topics without distraction*—that we cannot differ without dividing—is to proclaim our principles a dead letter, and our philosophy a lie. Is it come to this that we cannot enquire into our own affairs without falling into the error of those politicians who have ruined their cause by angry imputations and wretched rejoinders? *If* I have been personal, it was because it was a less evil to be personal than mean, for mean and cowardly it is to stigmatize men by innuendoes, and leave them to writhe under implied censures, from which they cannot escape, and to which they cannot reply. It is not my forte to imitate the conduct of those

> "Who show to circling eyes they're too genteel
> To laugh, or smile—to weep, or sigh, or feel :
> Convey in placid tones, their bitterest spite ;
> To prove while stabbing hearts they are polite,
> And coat decocting venom o'er with ice—
> For such is dignity."

It is necessary to notice that Branch A 1 has published a report in the *New Moral World*, expressive of the opinion that my "Visit" is of "*evil* tendency," that it "*maligns* the characters of others," "retails *undigested* statements, not altogether founded on truth," and "is derogatory to the *honesty* of individuals once in power." This wholesale imputation they are pleased to say is "correctly and very mildly expressed"—meaning that they were justified in using harsher terms. Of the "evil tendency," and the "derogation of the honesty" of individuals referred to, the Visit itself, and the remarks already made†, are a sufficient answer. The "maligning and truth of the statements" will be best shown by narrating the attempts made to invalidate them. During four Sundays the Visit was beset at Branch A 1, after the following manner :—

Mr. Lloyd Jones—I deny that the Late Acting Governor had any roads made as stated by Mr. Holyoake in his "Visit." They were all made before the Late Acting Governor took office. So much for what Mr. Holyoake knows of the matter. Where were the roads? He would ask Mr. H. that.

Mr. Holyoke—If Mr. Jones will turn to the last Congress report, page 390, *New Moral World*, he will find that Mr. Buxton asks the Late Acting Governor "if he did not think that the money spent in roads and avenues would have been better expended elsewhere?" If the Late Acting Governor had made no roads, his reply would contain a denial of it, but the answer was a justification of it. "He did not, under all the circumstances, think that it would." With respect to where the roads were, he (Mr. H.) would read from a letter from Mr. Joseph Smith, General Missionary, who had *often* walked over them. "Walks were laid out during the Late Acting Governorship, beginning about 800 yards up the hill leading to Broughton, thence through the wood, behind the Hall, and in other directions, but for such proceedings we should not have been under the necessity of purchasing vegetables from farm labourers in the village, who had only a few yards of ground, while we had 100 acres ourselves. These facts are so plain, that I wonder any one will deny them—we have had them over so often that they are to me truly heart sickening."

Mr. Jones—But Mr. H. has told us that hundreds of pounds were expended on the roads—now the Rose Hill road, the most expensive of all, did not cost but from £90 to £100, he resided there seven months and he saw the Bills.

---

* See Resolution of the Sheffield Branch, *Movement* 53.

† See Reply to the Late Acting Governor, *Movement* 51.

Mr. A. Campbell—It only cost from £70 to £80, I saw the accounts at Congress.

Mr. Jones—They would know in future what credit to attach to Mr. Holyoake's assertions. Mr. H. had made statements which no honest man would make.

Mr. Holyoake read a letter from Mr. Simpson, General Secretary. "I write for the purpose of saying that the *whole* of Mr. Holyoake's statements relating to operations &c. at Harmony, are, I believe, from *actual* knowledge, facts—with the exceptions I stated in a former letter, [that the members' 1s. is allowed by *law*, that they *give* it up—that the walls of the dining room are ribbed *entirely* with mahogany]. You will find from a statement of accounts which I prepared from the books of the society, for the 1843 Congress, that the expences of ' Road making' up to that time was £216, and this be it remarked for the *Rose Hill* road alone. This item is a cash one only—it does not include a single shilling for the value of members' labour, or any thing from our own estate, our own horse labour, or any thing in fact but bona fide outlay of cash for hired labour. The cost of that and other roads that have been made *since*, if *all* were charged, namely, our own horses, fencing, and manual labour, would be *double* or *triple* that amount, because that statement was only up to May, 1843, and roads were extensively gone into last year." Mr. Holyoake then laid on the table the identical statement of accounts referred to by Mr. Simpson, and called on Mr. Jones as an honourable man to retract the reflection he had cast on his (Mr. H's) honesty —it was due to him alike from the courtesies of society and from the facts he had established.

Mr. Jones rose, but instead of doing so, said that the statement Mr. H. had produced had nothing to do with the case—he (Mr. J.) had called on Mr. H. to prove that the rent was accumulating in arrears during the Late Acting Governorship. Let him prove that, and correct his misrepresentation about the Loan.

Mr. Holyoake said that Mr. Jones had put himself out of the pale of courtesy by the gross personality in which he had indulged. By the etiquette of society he (Mr. H.) would be justified in taking no further notice of Mr. Jones—but that discussion should not be stopped by his introduction of personalities. With respect to rent accumulating, etc., he would again refer to what the Late Acting Governor called the "highest authority." He would read the evidence of the General Secretary. "At the Congress of 1843 the rent due to Sir I. L. Goldsmid was £283, and by the Congress of 1844—(the interval being the Late Acting Governor's year of office) it had increased to £534." Since his (Mr. H's) statement concerning the loan of the Late Acting Governor had been called in question also by Mr. Jones, he (Mr. H.) had to say that persons best acquainted with the matter believed that the Late Acting Governor lent his £500 to Mr. Galpin, and when he found it not forthcoming in that quarter he looked to the Home Colonization Society for it, but finding that a shadow he claimed it of them, and his claim was first recognized in a minute of the Central Board. He (Mr. H.) would take that opportunity of saying, that since what he had stated had been so rudely called in question, what he had omitted might be heard in his favour. Upon the past state of the schools much might have been said—but as he had confidence in their future management, he had passed the subject by with a hope where he might have dealt a censure. He had spoken as though it was a doubtful case (Chap. 3) whether the Community fund was not being appropriated to the support of Missionaries; [and Mr. H. was about to say that from the printed documents of the society, published in the *New Moral World*, and sold to any one at 2d. each, it appeared that the Central Board were insolvent, that they did employ the Community fund for the support of Missionaries*, and that (according to law) Mr. Lloyd

---

* For more reasons than my own justification I think these facts ought to be known. Surely, when the Branches are aware of the precise state of their Board they will at once endeavour to place them in an independent position. The Central Board, I know, feel themselves quite justified in their present course, but I think that the Community funds ought to be kept inviolate.

C

Jones himself did not know where his own salary came from]—but before he could do so—

Mr. JONES rose and said that Mr. H. had better proceed with what had been questioned. Mr. H. had stated that Mr. Buxton had paid £800 of "*bad* debts." He called on Mr. H. to prove that.

Mr. HOLYOAKE said he was quite content to proceed with any thing. He called all debts bad debts. But they should hear their General Secretary. "I am of your opinion that all debts are *bad ones*, but if we take the view that tradesmen do, I think our debts cannot be called bad ones, for the tradesmen could sell the property, and we know there is sufficient to pay them." So far, all was in Mr. Jones's favour, but let them listen—the General Secretary continues, "but there is not sufficient to pay the Society and the Loans." Would that satisfy Mr. Jones?

Mr. JONES said that the Secretary ought not to have given Mr. H. any such information. He adduced Mr. H.'s statement that "what the old Executive borrowed they did not know, and what was spent they could not tell." That was entirely false, and he (Mr. J.) would appeal to the Finance Committee to say if the books were not found in perfect order.

Mr. WHITAKER (the Society's auditor) rose and said that the Finance Committee did all they could to make them out, but were obliged to give them up as a bad job. No man in the society but Mr. Simpson could have reduced them to order. He (Mr. W.) would not have undertaken the task for £50.*

Mr. JONES—Mr. Holyoake had only made second-hand statements. He knew nothing at all about what he wrote of. He (Mr. J.) would repeat that Mr. Simpson might tell him this, or that, but it was nothing more than "tittle tattle."

Mr. HOLYOAKE—Second or seventy-hand statements, the question was were they true. Mr. Jones asked for evidence, but how was he to be suited if facts and figures, balance sheets and printed documents, were to be set down as no authorities whatever. What had he (Mr. H.) said of the society that put it in a more contemptible light than Mr. Jones's declaration that their cash books and documents were but mere "tittle tattle." It was saying their ledgers were inventions. Their appeals to the public were indeed founded on *business-like* data.

Reader, it was after these discussions that Branch A 1 published in the *New Moral World* that my "Visit maligned the characters of others and retailed undigested statements, not altogether founded on truth." In what respect they failed can be seen, and how far they were from maligning can be judged. Their latest report says that the remarks I complain of were "intended only as an exposition of the opinions expressed by the various speakers," —then *my* opinions ought to have appeared in the exposition also. But finding these carefully omitted, I called on the Branch to retract their report, or publish the facts on which it was said to be founded. They refused to do either. Men who had confidence in their own verdict would not have acted thus.

It was on this occasion that Mr. Tiffin, a member of the Central Board, said it was easy to see why I had made my statements—it was to sell a "*certain periodical.*" Some men are so sordid as only to be moved by pounds, shillings, and pence considerations, and can never conceive how any one else can be actuated by higher motives. Had the mere sale of the *Movement* been an object—articles would have been selected of a very different character than those that have appeared—we should not have dealt impartial criticisms to friends as well as foes, nor should we ever have noticed Socialism approvingly. Mr. Ironside is one of many who can bear witness how we have refused friends whom we regarded, and whose bounty supported our

---

* This was very generous evidence on the part of this gentleman who had been wounded by the letters. If all the proceedings of the Board were consistent with this example, they would, however their judgments in some cases might be impugned, command respect as men of honourable sentiments.

paper, when our judgments disapproved of their articles. The papers on Harmony did not appear until M. Q. R. (generally adverse to such criticisms, and whose cool and shrewd judgment I always consult) was convinced of their necessity and satisfied of their truth. The *Movement* never published a line for the sake of selling a number. Upon its pages, from first to last, no stain or trick is found. Want has never driven, interest has never swerved, nor danger drawn us from the path of integrity. Nor will ungenerous imputation now induce us to depart from our usual course of honest duty.

One proof that I am not wholly in the wrong is that the Central Board have passed a resolution, enjoining the General Secretary not to furnish me with any more information.* So that when the Late Acting Governor demands of me the "highest authority," and Mr. Jones accuses me of making "dishonest" statements, and I refer in my vindication to the documents in the society's possession, I find the Central Board locking them up. While they find it necessary to pursue this course, it would at least be but decent not to permit their officers to stigmatize me for not producing "authorities" which they are determined I shall never get.†

But despite these difficulties only one allegation, of all those called in question in Branch A 1, has been disproved, the appointment of Mr. Oestriecher by Mr. Owen. One other instance was cited which I have not yet cleared up, owing chiefly to the unsteadiness of the case—that of Mr. Jones "shaking his head," etc. But on this important point, when I have collected and collated evidence, I shall favour the world with a special dissertation.

In conclusion I will again gratuitously repeat my partiality for the Socialists party, my admiration of its philosophy, and friendship for its leaders. I counsel no unkindness. no ingratitude, no intolerance. To infallibility I make no pretensions, and never forget that I *may* be in the wrong. I am not impatient that my views should prevail. I am only anxious that they should be heard —because they appear to me calculated to infuse vigour into our policy and accelerate our progress. Had not the *New Moral World* been closed against all discussion of these vital topics they would never have been mooted in the *Movement*. But I will never be one of those who complain of what they make no effort to amend.

Having in these letters elicited what of warning the past seemed to afford, my future papers in the *Movement* will chiefly teem with advice for the future.

The rudeness with which I have been treated, and the imputations to which I have been subjected have neither taken me by surprise, nor given me uneasiness. Burke long since taught me that, "It is an undertaking of some degree of delicacy to examine into the causes of public disorders. If a man happens not to succeed in such an enquiry, he will be thought weak and visionary; if he touches the true grievance, there is a danger that he will come near to persons of weight and consequence, who will rather be exasperated at the discovery of their errors, than thankful for the occasion of correcting them. If he should be obliged to blame the favourites of the people he will be considered as the tool of power; if he censures those in power, he will be looked on as an instrument of faction. *But in all exertions of duty something is to be hazarded.* When the affairs of a society are distracted private members are justified in stepping a little out of their ordinary sphere. They enjoy a privilege of somewhat more dignity and effect than that of idle lamentation over the calamities of their cause. They may look into them narrowly, they may reason upon them liberally; and if they should be so fortunate as to discover the source of the mischief, and to suggest any probable method of removing it, though they may displease the rulers of the day, they are certainly of service to the cause of truth."

G. J. H.

---

* This was done on December 10.

† I have great pleasure in stating that I have received this evening [Dec. 21] a letter from the Central Board, apprising me that they have come to the resolution of rendering any information in their power, and free access to books in their custody to any member or friend of the society. This is as it should be, and is a gratifying sign that these discussions have not been useless.

J. G. Hornblower, Printer, 4, Wellington Street, Goswell Street.

REPORT

TO A

MEETING OF INTENDING EMIGRANTS,

COMPREHENDING

A PRACTICAL PLAN

FOR

FOUNDING CO-OPERATIVE COLONIES

OF

United Interests,

IN THE

NORTH-WESTERN TERRITORIES

OF THE

UNITED STATES.

BY THOMAS HUNT.

London:

PUBLISHED BY W. OSTELL, 24, HART STREET, BLOOMSBURY;
CLEAVE, SHOE LANE, FLEET STREET; AND VICKERS,
HOLYWELL STREET, STRAND.

1843.

INTRODUCTION.

MUCH surprise will doubtless be felt by those who have witnessed my zeal and anxiety in the cause of Socialism, when they shall hear that I have become an advocate of emigration, and that my conviction now is, that the United States of America is the best field for the future operations of those who are desirous of a speedy realization of the PRACTICE of our system. It will be expected that I should state the reasons which have brought me to this conclusion, and also to explain why I am dissatisfied with the practical proceedings of our society. This it is my intention to do.

After a patient review of the past and present state and future prospects of Harmony, which I felt myself called upon to take in consequence of the evident apathy and want of confidence pervading the working portion of the members of the society, in the promotion of whose objects I feel especially interested, I have been reluctantly brought to the conclusion that that establishment has not answered their expectations, inasmuch as, after an existence of more than three years, and after an expenditure of upwards of £30,000, not more than seventy persons have been enabled to obtain a residence there. It has been contended by many parties that this sum has been judiciously and economically expended. I wish I could see this in the light that others do; and, above all, I wish I could discern in the establishment even the embryo of that wished-for future growth—a community of men and women, usefully employed and wisely directed, and whose every-day existence should give evidence of the fact, that they were approaching nearer and nearer that important and eventful period, viz. the self-supporting stage of their progress, instead of hearing its occupants making an incessant call for external support. This would have been made manifest from the beginning, if the end had been seen, and the means properly proportioned to it. As the means were limited, the object should have been proportionately small. The error of aiming at too much has been fallen into, and, in consequence, it may fairly be anticipated that little or nothing, in an industrial point of view, will be effected.

Impressed with this conviction, and having a strong desire to see a successful experiment upon the land, in order that the path to permanent relief may be opened to the members of our society, it cannot be surprising that a question like the following should have presented itself to my mind for solution :—" How is it, that after such an expenditure of time and money, our society has not succeeded in making 100 persons independent of external aid ; while the Rappites, in America, with little more than £3,000 to begin with, made themselves independent of the outward world after the first harvest, and at the end of eight years they numbered 800 persons, whose property was estimated at upwards of £45,000 ?" I could hardly conceive that it would be contended that these persons were either more skilful, more industrious, or more economical than an equal number of persons professing the Social principles, and was consequently led to inquire whether this discrepancy might not arise from national causes, and whether America was more favourably circumstanced than this country for such an undertaking. I therefore resolved to inquire into the nature of these circumstances, and to ascertain their probable effects upon a colony of 100 persons established in that country, with a view to contrast its results with what has been effected by us in this country, taking for granted that what has been done is the best that could have been done under all the circumstances. This limited number I knew to be unfavourable to the American side of the argument, the cost of maintenance being so exceedingly low, when compared with the value of labour; but I nevertheless adopted it as the most desirable, because the most controlable number ; and, further, because it corresponded more closely with the greatest number of residents at any period admitted into the Harmony establishment. I was aware, too, that one year would not give a satisfactory solution of the question, and I therefore made a series of estimates of production and consumption upon a farm of 200 acres, extending through a period of three successive years, in order to ascertain, first, the sufficiency of the original outlay ; secondly, the amount of production and consumption in each year ; and, thirdly, whether any and what amount of surplus remained.

It will be seen by the detailed statements to be hereafter given, that at the end of three years the whole of the original outlay will be returned, after supporting the residents, improving the land, erecting a number of buildings, and greatly increasing the implements and stock of the farm. Thus, in three years, would 100 persons become possessed of a highly-improved freehold property, capable of supporting double or treble their number.

I was surprised and delighted at this result—not because it was favourable to America as a field for working out the co-operative principle, and therefore greatly to the disadvantage of our own country in this particular, but because I felt it to be a happy circumstance that any country, and more especially one possessing liberal institutions, should present to the industrious man of small capital the means of securing a permanent existence immediately, and the certainty of being enabled ultimately to surround himself with everything essential to complete his happiness, requiring only the exercise of his skill and labour upon the raw material which exists there in great abundance, which he will find himself at full liberty to use to the extent of his power; for there nearly the entire value of a commodity is labour.

Satisfied as to the accuracy of the estimates from which the result I speak of was obtained, I at once resolved upon making them the basis of a plan for an experiment on our principles in America. A rough draught of the plan having been prepared, it was quietly submitted successively to various individuals of congenial minds, and their co-operation in carrying it into practice invited and secured.

The expense of locating a single family of five persons in the north-western part of America I calculated to be about £72, including travelling, share of purchase-money of estate, &c. The cost of locating twenty families, comprising 100 persons, would therefore be £1,440. The sum expended upon the estate in Hampshire is £30,000, by means of which, in three years, about seventy persons have been admitted. This £30,000, expended in America instead of England, would have established twenty-one sections of a community similar to the one I propose, these sections comprising in all 2,100 persons, possessing freehold land to the extent of 4,200 acres.

It may be in the recollection of the members of the society, that at the Congress held in Manchester, in 1841, a series of propositions were brought forward and passed, having for their object the facilitating the introduction of members into community, but which, for certain reasons, were not carried into effect. The terms of admission there laid down were as follow:—For a man £50, his wife £30, and each child £20. Having seen the data upon which these terms were made, I feel satisfied that they could not have been lower; and perhaps the respective merits of home and foreign colonization cannot be better determined than by the following contrast:—

	ENGLAND.	UNITED STATES.
A man and his wife......	£80 0 0	£54 0 0
Three children..........	60 0 0	18 0 0
	£140 0 0	£72 0 0

But the contrast in the condition and prospects of these parties would be still more striking than the original cost of their location, inasmuch as the English colonist would be crippled by a perpetual rent and an enormous taxation; while the American colonist, upon an unincumbered and far more fertile soil, and retaining for his own use all its productions, would find the labour of three days more productive to himself than would his English competitor the labour of six.

These facts will be sufficient to account for the alteration which has taken place in the mind of one who has always attached so much importance to a practical experiment, being convinced that our principles can produce but little practical effect upon minds ill at ease in all that relates to their present and prospective physical condition.

As many objections to emigration are afloat in the public mind at the present moment, I propose, in this place, to answer some of them, and shall then bring under your notice the details of the plan you have met to consider.

Some of these objectors have their own peculiar remedies for existing evils. The remedy of one class is the employment of the surplus population at home on the waste and other lands; but I am not aware that any parties (except those entertaining our principles) propose to adopt the only true mode of making man permanently secure and truly happy—that is, by establishing SELF-SUPPORTING COLONIES OF UNITED INTERESTS; while the remedy of other parties rests upon an increased demand for the manufactures of the country, to be brought about, amongst other means, by a repeal of the corn-laws. Among these parties, we find the objections of a number of individuals formerly friendly to the principle of emigration; who, having tested the value of emigration by actual experience, and finding the competitive system as prolific of evil at New York and its vicinity, as well as at all the frontier cities and towns in the United States, as they had experienced it in England, have returned to their own country, spirit-broken and bereft of hope, exclaiming bitterly against the "promised land."

On the objections urged by these parties I propose to make a few remarks, in order to establish the fact, that the evils which the objectors apprehend, and, in some instances, have experienced, are the offspring of an unnatural state of society, which has produced, is producing, and must, in its present form, continue to produce, the same bitter fruits everywhere.

It will be seen, upon examination of the grounds of their various objections, how completely they prove the erroneousness of their own course of proceeding, and the necessity that exists for a change from the competitive to the co-operative principle.

Let us first apply ourselves to the waste-land objectors, and we will take Mr. Burn, the author of "Familiar Letters on Population, Emigration, &c.," as the representative of his party. This writer assumes that a redundant population is the only excusable ground for emigration, and satisfactorily establishes the fact, that the population is not redundant, by referring to the millions of acres of waste land in this country, inviting the labour of man—a fact which has been proved by many writers before his time. I admit, then, that with respect to England a redundancy of population, which implies a *want of means* to employ and support it, cannot be used as an argument in favour of emigration, and most assuredly is not my argument, as I believe there is no lack of means to provide for a much greater population than ours at home.

But, though this fact be admitted, the whole argument against emigration is not thereby conceded, since the *power to command the use* of these millions of acres is not in the people, but in the government, which, in its turn, is subject to the influence of those who believe that their interests would be affected materially by the produce obtained from an extensive cultivation of these lands in the way proposed. Besides, the conviction sought to be produced in the minds of the parties interested, that a concession of this nature is indispensable to the tranquillity of the country, will consume a lengthened period of time employed in discussion; and let it be borne in mind, that while the different interests are engaged in disputation, the people are either starving, or, in order to avoid it, are driven to emigration as a means of bettering their condition—absolutely thrust out of the country, as it were, into a state of more complete isolation and self-dependence than before, in ignorance of the nature of the country to which they are driven, and, in most instances, destitute of means to enable them to encounter the difficulties with which they find themselves beset. Hence the altered tone of some of these parties, on their return from a country which had so worked upon their imaginations as to lead them to expect that a home was in readiness to receive them, and that they might pursue their accustomed manufacturing avocations, and find a ready market for their various productions.

I know that, in a national point of view, emigration is an evil—not to those who emigrate systematically and unitedly, (and none ought to emigrate in any other way, if they can avoid it,) but to the nation they leave, that nation having resources within itself to maintain them; because, in the first place, the nation is deprived of so much of its natural strength; and, secondly, that strength is turned against it, whether the emigrant go to a colony or to an independent state; and this is a part of the argument upon which Mr. Burn lays the greatest stress. Whatever effect that argument may have upon the minds of the powers that be, it is undeserving the attention of those who are evidently *not cared for by the nation.*

The government which resorts to and encourages emigration, as the government of this country has done and is now doing, must bear the imputation of being either grossly ignorant of the resources of the country whose interests it has undertaken to promote, or, if fully sensible of them, unpardonably cruel and wicked in allowing the interests of a section of the people to stand in the way of the adoption of a broad measure of justice, by which the vast resources of this country would be opened up, and all the wants of the people fully satisfied. But the government will not concede, and the nation is not sufficiently alive to its true interests to demand, the adoption of the only measure calculated to relieve the country, and render emigration unnecessary for many years to come, viz., the establishment of INDEPENDENT, SELF-SUPPORTING, and SELF-GOVERNING HOME COLONIES; and those who oppose emigration do not appear to entertain the remotest idea of claiming for the people this GREAT AND MIGHTY GOOD.

The "National Employment and Education Society," whose circular has been some time before the public, aim at relieving the country by means of "*home colonization*," as they call it, but which, upon examination, dwindles into a species of the *allotment system*, or, as the circular afterwards expresses it, "*little spheres of manageable cultivation.*" The author of the circular, with the view, I suppose, of giving strength to his argument, endeavours to excite the prejudices of the people against emigration, as will be seen by the following extracts from it:—

"Let it be fully borne in mind that home colonization presents immediate advantages which cannot be expected to co-exist with the clearing of lands in the backwoods of America, or in the boundless plains of New Zealand. In England we have markets at hand for the primary produce of every acre of reclaimed soil, which the most fortunately located emigrants cannot hope to have for long years to come. Nor should the expense of emigration be omitted when we are called upon to contrast that mode of relieving our population with a judicious system of home employment. The funds required to transport emigrants to the shores of our Australian possessions would suffice to put in motion a quantity of agricultural labour in any given spot of sterility in Great Britain or Ireland." * * * * "Colour and qualify emigration as we may, it is a harsh inversion of the social system—it is, in fact, consigning the children of civilization to the remotest recesses of barbarism. They have to recommence life by recurring to the naked hardships of a savage state in their first years of discomfort and dreariness." * * * "Instead of expatriating our unfortunate fellow-countrymen to some savage region of the southern Pole, the society would invite them to a favourable location in their native land, where the reclamation of waste soils should proceed with all practical vigour and celerity—where allotments would be made so as to suit the habits of individuals and the size of families—and where spade husbandry, that precious protection from pauperism, would diffuse fertility through little spheres of manageable cultivation."

Now, emigration and the "clearing of lands in the backwoods" are not necessarily connected, nor is it necessary to incur the expense of a voyage to the "boundless plains of New Zealand," nor to be "transported to the shores of our Australian possessions." There happen to exist in the free republic of the United States "boundless plains" of prairie or meadow land, of inexhaustible fertility, of easy culture, and at a low price, which, in my estimation, possesses greater attractions than "any given spot of *sterility* in Great Britain," or any of its land-jobbing, speculating, or tax-consuming colonies. In the United States a man feels that he has "elbow-room," as Mr. Charles Lane expresses it; and any attempt to excite prejudice against emigration by dragging into the question a catalogue of evils which, under judicious arrangements, are more easily removable in a "boundless plain" than in a thickly-settled country, evinces in those who resort to it such deplorable ignorance of the real nature of the evils they seek to remedy, as to disqualify them for the task they have undertaken. Mr. Burn, the author before referred to, truly says, that "Produce depends not on few, but large numbers, applied to agriculture; and the risks of destitution, like the risks of insurance, are actually diminished by increase of numbers." Apply this truth to the entire business of life, instead of confining it to the cultivation of the soil—let it be seen in congregated numbers mutually supporting and protecting each other against the evils inseparable from a state of isolation—apply it honestly in every department, and, above all, let it be seen in an *equal distribution* of the produce obtained, and abundance will be seen everywhere—destitution nowhere. Apply large numbers to agriculture, by all means—bring into cultivation every acre of the soil of Britain, but let those who cultivate it see the certain prospect before them of becoming independent of those who may furnish the means of enabling them to do so; for without the fulfilment of this condition, no permanent good can be effected for the people.

It would be well for those who advocate the cultivation of our own soil not to attempt to depreciate the facilities afforded for the cultivation of that of other countries, and thus provoke comparisons by no means favourable to our own. A gratuitous and most outrageous specimen of this description is given in a letter by "One who has Whistled at the Plough," in the *Morning Chronicle* of the 29th December last. The writer says, "When we see before us the fact that £100 capital applied to ten acres of almost any of the arable soils of England would bring in return *twenty times greater* than on ten acres of the back settlements of the colonies, for a period at least equal to one generation, we may well throw aside emigration as a secondary consideration." I ask this writer, is the cost of the land in America twenty times greater? Does the taxation amount to twenty times more? Does the land produce twenty times less? or do those employed upon it require to consume twenty times more? If these questions cannot be answered in the affirmative, how is the assertion substantiated? Admitting that the produce is more valuable in England than in America, as fetching a higher price in the market, we must also consider that those who raise it must or ought to consume a large portion of it, and that the rest will go to pay a heavy rent and heavy taxes—a perpetual drain upon the industry of the producers; while the surplus of the American producers, having no rent and few taxes to pay, would be so much saved; and if the surplus would fetch but little money in the market, it would bring its value in exchange for articles of utility not produced on the farm.

I confess, however, that so far from being anxious that the government of this country (which is but the breath of the landed interest) should undertake to relieve the distress of the people by establishing home colonies, instead of the " little manageable spheres" before spoken of, I would much rather see the landed interest utterly swamped by a free importation of foreign commodities, that the people, by this means, finding the land cheaper, might have it in their power to found colonies for and by themselves, upon the principles of liberty and equality; for it is quite certain that those who never labour at all, but live upon the industry of those who do, can never desire, but, on the contrary, would, to the latest moment, strenuously oppose any change having a *tendency* to reduce them to the necessity of labouring for their own subsistence.

These parties, possessing as they do all the substantial wealth of the country, and with it the tremendous influence which that wealth gives them, may be said to have the power in their own hands of deciding, if not whether a change of system shall or shall not take place, at least of *determining the nature of the change*, since some change is clearly inevitable.

It is thought by many persons attached to our system, that as there are but two principles upon which society can be founded—the competitive and the co-operative —and that as the abandonment of the former would necessitate the adoption of the latter, so would it also, in their estimation, imply the adoption of the fundamental principles of the Rational System of Society. This is a complete delusion; for, should a change from the competitive to the co-operative principle take place—should the landed interest, who have hitherto resisted all permanent improvement, give a preference to home colonies, as a means of giving employment to the surplus labour thrown off from our now paralized manufacturing system, by which an abundance of agricultural produce would be raised in this country, rather than be forced into a repeal of the corn-laws, and with it an extensive depreciation in the value of their land and its productions—should a change of this description be preferred by them (and they would prove themselves worse tactitions than they have hitherto had the credit of being, should they throw away the opportunity offered them), they would have the power, in organizing this new system, of stamping upon it whatever character they might desire to give it.

The physical condition of the people might in some degree be improved by the change; but as this change would not have been produced by the people themselves, but by the tyrants in heart and the depraved in morals—as it would have been imposed upon these tyrants by an uncontrolable necessity, and adopted, like every other measure, as a choice of evils, rather than from principle—as the thirst for individual gain would not have been extinguished, nor the love of dominion eradicated from the minds of these old tyrants of the world, there is not a glimmer of hope that an enlightened and humanizing philosophy would shed its equal and genial rays over colonies of their formation, or that any but a stultifying education would be given to the people. On the contrary, a despotism more complete—a tyranny more enduring than any hitherto existing in the world would be established in these colonies, because the power of resistance on the part of their inmates would be utterly destroyed by the fact of their being wholly dependent upon the landed aristocracy, and subjected to the every-day influences of a clerical domination.

The clerical plan of Mr. Morgan is exactly to the taste of these parties, as evidenced by the high enconiums recently passed upon it by some of the Tory journals. The fact of its being palatable in this quarter is enough to create suspicion that the plan is any thing but favourable to liberty and equality. Nay, an examination of it will satisfy any one that it is designed to perpetuate slavery, inequality, and superstition; and those who come within its sphere will find, (what M. Rousseau, in his "Crusade in the Nineteenth Century," insists upon,) that the "blessing of liberty can only be conferred on those who have passed under the *yoke of authority*." What time it will require, by this process, to qualify a man for the enjoyment of liberty, is a question to be mooted some centuries hence, should the human race, in the interim, get into these clerical folds.

Could any man embued with the Social principles endure a colony of this description? I am confident he could not. Then, of what value is the founding of these colonies to the advocates of liberty and equality? We have still the task to perform of setting an example of a superior system, founded upon our own principles; and the colonies of the clergy, by stultifying the minds of the people, would retard, rather than assist us. Nay, an extensive adoption of the plan of clerical colonies by the aristocracy, with the powerful means they possess, would enhance the value of land in this country, and thus throw a still more serious obstacle in the way of founding colonies upon liberal principles.

As to the repeal of the corn-laws, and the expected revival of trade through that means, what will it amount to as a means of improving the condition of the people? Why, precisely to this: the manufacturer will again put forth his energies—pursue his reckless, his unnatural, his self-destroying course—again glut the few markets that may be opened to him by a repeal of these laws, and finally complete the destruction of the millions who have been made to believe that a system exclusively manufacturing would last for ever. Great misgivings are, however, discernable among them; but they still believe themselves to have been made for the system, and that its destruction would be their destruction, as they cannot conceive themselves to be convertible into any other uses than that which the system has made of them.

Not expecting from the blind policy of the rulers of this nation's destinies any prudent, liberal, and organic changes, by which the awful calamity referred to might be averted, and believing that the mass of the people are so completely under the hoof of despotism as to be unable to demand and enforce their own deliverance from bondage—believing that the few who are liberally inclined are wasting their energies in an ineffectual struggle against the incurable institutions of this country, and knowing the only secure refuge to be THE LAND, I feel it my duty to recommend emigration to that section of the globe which offers it upon the easiest terms; and this I do, notwithstanding the great complaints that have reached us through the public press, from returned emigrants, as well as through other channels, against the United States, alledging that there exists as much distress in that country as in this. Upon examination, we find that nearly all the distress is confined to the trading and manufacturing interests.

In a letter from New York, dated August 4, 1842, which appeared in the *Morning Chronicle* a few weeks afterwards, it is, however, stated that the FARMERS in the western states are greatly embarrassed; and the principal cause of their embarrassment appears to be the want of markets for their produce, or, in other words, they are unable to obtain *money* for it. The following extract from that letter exhibits the folly of the individual system in a remarkably striking point of view, and furnishes a powerful argument in favour of the views of united production and consumption. The writer says :—

"Domestic trade in the interior of the country is reduced, from the want of a circulating medium, to barter; a farmer gives two pounds of wool to a weaver for one pound of the same wool made into homespun, and sends four bushels of wheat to the miller in exchange for the flour of three bushels.

"There is everywhere a superabundance of natural productions—wheat, Indian corn, pork, beef, and lumber; and yet the people in the agricultural districts are everywhere wretchedly poor, as respects the power either of paying old debts or purchasing new commodities. ——, who has just returned from his tour to Niagara, &c., says that the forced stoppage of consumption of all imported or city manufactures, is going on to an extent which it is difficult for an Englishman, unacquainted with the singular changes which occur here, to realize to himself. The farmers tell him they do not use tea or coffee above once a week—they make maple sugar in great quantities to avoid the necessity of purchasing sugar—and they wear nothing but homespun, made from their own wool, and spun by their wives and daughters. The abundance of provisions of all kinds was great before this harvest; and this harvest is said to be greater than any that has preceded it, the injury done to the wheat by rust and floods having been entirely confined to some districts in Virginia, Indiana,

Pennsylvania, and New York, the season elsewhere having been very favourable, and the breadth of land sown greater than was ever known, owing to new labour and capital having been turned to agriculture, from which they had been diverted by the speculations, and public works, and planting mania of former years. You may suppose, therefore, that there is a positive glut of provisions of all kinds—the farmers find their stores and the wharfs of the inland ports loaded with their produce, for which in the interior they can absolutely obtain nothing in money. The reason of this is, that having already over-supplied the New Orleans and New York home demand, they have reduced the price so low, that the expense of transport for so many hundred miles—an expense which remains nearly fixed—swallows up the whole of the price. In this state of things, having glutted the home market, and finding it very difficult to force an increased export trade to take off the surplus, the western farmers have brought home directly to them the truth, that their power either of paying old debts, or obtaining new supplies, their wealth, in fact, is exactly in proportion to the extent to which they can secure purchasers for their produce.

"Facts like these will explain to you how the western states, the most thriving in all natural resources, are for the present utterly unable to pay the interest on their debts."

Now, what is the amount of all this suffering? We gather from this quotation these facts:—That domestic trade is reduced to *barter*—that there is everywhere a *superabundance* of *natural productions*—that, nevertheless, the farmers are *wretchedly poor*—that they do not use tea or coffee above once a week—that they *make maple sugar in great quantities*, to avoid the necessity of purchasing sugar—that they wear nothing but home-spun, *made from their own wool, and spun by their wives and daughters*—and that the farmers find their *stores* and the *wharfs* of the inland ports *loaded with their produce*, for which, in the interior, they can absolutely obtain nothing in the shape of *money*.

After attentively considering this catalogue of grievances, the only remedy I can suggest for this *afflicting* condition of the farmers of the west is, that as the produce cannot find the mouths, they should give the mouths an opportunity of finding the produce. It is by no means surprising that we should have anticipated, in our arrangements, a state of things similar to that described by the author of the letter in question, as we knew it to be the necessary result of an unnatural and vicious state of society, which, as far as regards ourselves, we have undertaken to correct; for upon 200 acres of land we propose to locate about 100 persons, whereas the American farmer contents himself with about half a dozen persons, and hence his cry for markets. So that we shall make sure of a market, to a very considerable extent, by taking it with us, and shall therefore only experience the much-dreaded evils of barter in a very limited degree. We expect, in a short time, to be enabled to grind our own corn; but, in the interim, we shall not consider it a very great hardship to give "four bushels of wheat to the miller in exchange for the flour of three bushels;" because, if a bushel of wheat be worth 3s. in the market, either ourselves or the miller can obtain that price for it, and it will signify but little to us whether we give a fourth part of our produce in money or in money's worth, since that amount, in some shape, the miller must have. As to the tea and coffee, if we cannot obtain them in exchange for our produce, we must endeavour to find out a substitute for them. Then there's the sugar—the cruel alternative of either doing without it, or "*making maple sugar in great quantities.*" It is also exceedingly inconvenient that the wife and daughters of an isolated farmer, short-handed as he is, should be employed in converting their own wool into home-spun for the use of the family, when their services are so much required to assist in the production of commodities *to be sent away from the farm for the consumption of others.* This difficulty we shall easily get over, by reason of our greater numerical strength. But the produce, it appears, will absolutely fetch nothing in the interior in the shape of *money*, or, in other words, the representative of wealth. So that we shall have to content ourselves with the *substance*, and leave the pursuit of the *shadow* to those who sicken, and pine, and die in quest of it.

The state of isolation in which the American farmers exist is the great producing cause of all the evil of which they complain; for, however absurd it may appear that men in the midst of abundance should talk of distress, bankruptcy, and ruin, their distress is by no means imaginary. But their disease is not so inveterate as that of the manufacturers, as the farmers have the remedy in their own hands, and may instantly relieve themselves by increasing their numbers in the agricultural department, and by adding to their farming arrangements a number of useful handicrafts, all working into each other's hands—producing and consuming in common.

In "Chambers's Information for the People," the following advice is given to emigrants:—

"As a further advice to settlers entering into the woods or new lands, we would say, that if two or three can go together, it assists them materially: a family with several stout sons has a very great advantage in this respect. A few acquaintances joining together, and taking a piece of land to divide among them, can assist one another in clearing it, or in getting in their harvest; and if any accident happens in one of their families, the good offices of the rest serves greatly to relieve its inconveniences. It may happen, for instance, that some of them gets a hurt, or is laid by for a week with sickness; and if this were to occur during harvest, or in seed time, every thing would be lost, without the assistance of the rest of the company. If such partnerships cannot be formed before leaving home (which, when the emigrants are not from the same neighbourhood, cannot be expected), they may be, and often are, arranged to much advantage during the passage; and intending settlers will often find it advisable to sacrifice some of their own views as to the district in which they mean to settle, in order to have the assistance of steady companions elsewhere."

Observe the shifts resorted to here, in order to obtain by stealth some of the advantages of co-operation, rather than recommend the adoption of the broad principle; but at the same time admitting, in so many words, that the individual system is utterly helpless. The Germans, Dutch, and Swiss, however, were not satisfied with this sneaking recognition of the co-operative principle, but adopted it to the extent of a complete union of interests; and Mr. Bradbury, who has travelled in the United States, bears the following testimony to the success of their enterprising spirit:—

"Emigrants to this country are almost of every nation in Europe; but it is a remarkable fact, that the Germans, Dutch, and Swiss succeed much better than those from other countries. This is not so much owing to their greater industry or economy, as to the more judicious mode they adopt in settling. These people EMIGRATE IN COMPANIES, LAY DOWN PLANS, AND SEND AGENTS OVER IN WHOM THEY CAN CONFIDE. They purchase a suitable quantity of land, and prepare the way. When their arrangements are made, they go over in a body. This mode has many and great advantages, and its beneficial effects are conspicuous in almost every part of the United States, particularly in the states of New York, New Jersey, and Pennsylvania, in all of which states they are in possession of the best lands."

This, then, in a few words, is the great secret of their success, and the mode they have chosen ought to recommend itself to all those who seek the attainment of similar advantages. But why did these people leave their native country? Why not establish themselves in colonies at home? It is said that some of them were persecuted, and therefore they left their homes. But if they had not been persecuted for their opinions, and had remained at home, would they have risen from the degraded condition in which they were? With the slender means at their command, would they so speedily and successfully have made head against the landed monopolists of their own country, and have established themselves in the state of independence and real security in which they now find themselves in the country of their adoption? And this question may be asked of all the old-established countries in Europe, and more especially of England, where arbitrary power, as respects the tenure of land, is more offensive, burdensome, and insecure than in almost any other country. A correspondent of the *Morning Chronicle*, "One who has Whistled at the Plough," speaking of English tenures, with great truth says—"Bring from Scotland the best farmers with the best implements of husbandry, and set them down with their hinds upon any farm in England they might choose. But let all the complication of English tenures exist; all those quirks and cranks of the law, which render it more necessary for an English farmer to be a skilful lawyer than a skilful cultivator; let the lease or the annual agreement be that which an English lawyer draws out, and an English nobleman exacts adherence to from his tenant; let all these be the conditions for the Scotch farmer, and he would find himself reduced to the limited operations of his English neighbour."

Contrast the complication, insecurity, and expense of English tenures with the simplicity, security, and, if it be preferred, total absence of cost in the mode of conveying land in the United States, as I find it stated in a letter by "An American Citizen," inserted in the *Preston Chronicle*:—"In the purchasing of land, the deed that transfers the right of property from the general government to the individual purchasing is very simple: it is contained on a piece of parchment less than half a sheet of letter-paper, with the date, the locality of the land, the purchaser's name, and then subscribed by the President of the United States, and the agent of the general land-office. This is given free of all expense, and may be transferred by the purchaser to any other person, without the aid of a lawyer, or that of stamped paper."

It has long been a practice in the United States for those who were too poor to purchase, to take possession of unsurveyed land, and consequently all the labour they might have given to it was entirely at the mercy of the government. But a law was enacted to protect these little properties, by giving their occupiers a priority of right to purchase, at the Congress price of a dollar and a quarter per acre, whenever the land they occupied should come into the market, and whatever might have been the extent of their improvements, provided these improvements included the erection of a dwelling-house of certain small dimensions.

In short the obstacles in the way of obtaining land in this country, by small capitalists, are so great as almost to amount to an absolute prohibition of its use; and even if attainable, it is so beset with legal entanglements, burdened with such a high rental, and taxed in so many different forms, as to make any experiment on the land, however well supported, lingering in its progress, doubtful as a measure of relief to those who may support it, and uncertain as to its protracted results.

To meet the never-ending exactions to which land in this country is subjected, two-thirds of the produce of the labourer's toil is drawn from him. If he take a farm at a rental, he and his fellow-slaves can only call the produce of every third acre their own, although none of these acres possessed any value without their labour. They alone have given value to them, and they alone ought to reap the fruit. This they can never do under the system which has produced the injustice. They are, and ever must be, the bond slaves, socially and politically, of the monied interest, so long as they continue under its influence. Of what value to the working man is the knowledge of a happier state of human existence, when he is met by insurmountable obstacles at every turn in his endeavours to improve his condition by the application of superior principles to practice?

It is intended to be shown that the proposed plan is not only exempt from all the objections I have stated, but that in two years from the commencement of operations, at a comparatively trifling outlay, every individual interested in the undertaking, by a safe and simple process, may be so placed as to commence a career of uninterrupted prosperity and real independence. And when it is considered that in addition to this comfort and independence the individuals thus located upon American soil will have the means in their own society for educating their children in knowledge and virtue, no further persuasion will be necessary to convince the thinking portion of the public of the utility of the Plan detailed in the following Report.

THOMAS HUNT.

London, January 1, 1843.

*** I cannot allow this Report to pass through the press without observing, that the mere announcement of its publication has excited feelings and prejudices which were never intended to have been awakened, and which have been manifested in words and actions inconsistent with the spirit of free inquiry, inimical to the free discussion of the best mode of promoting human happiness, and contrary to the motto—"Truth without mystery, mixture of error, or fear of man." I pity the weakness of the parties alluded to, and shall only say—Let them be forgiven, for they know not what they do.

THE PLAN OF PROCEEDINGS,

AND

ITS RESULTS IN PRACTICE.

HAVING, in the foregoing remarks, given what I conceive to be sufficient reasons in favour of emigration to the United States, and having given in an appendix to this report much information respecting that part of the country known as the north-western territory, bordering on lake Michigan, I shall at once proceed to state, as briefly as possible, the nature of the plan recommended, and shall afterwards give a detailed statement of its results in practice.

It is proposed, in the first place, that the society shall consist of twenty families, which number may be increased to twenty-five, should circumstances render it desirable; but the calculations are all made relative to the former number. Secondly, that an improved farm, consisting of about 200 acres, shall be purchased in the United States of North America. Thirdly, that from 15 to 20 persons shall proceed to the territory of Wisconsin, near lake Michigan, in the month of June next, or as soon after as possible, with full power to make such purchase there, or in some more eligible situation, should it present itself. And, fourthly, that these twenty persons, composed, as they necessarily must be, of men, women, and children, should contain among them persons capable of acting in the following capacities:—

1. A person capable of acting as general superintendant of the affairs of the society, who may have the full confidence of all the other proprietors.
2. A person qualified for the duties of farm-director.
3. A person capable of directing the building department.
4. As many others as can be found in the number selected capable of working in the agricultural, building, and other departments.

The purchase of land having been made, some of the party will proceed to erect such temporary accommodation as may be necessary for themselves, as well as for the stock they may purchase, should they not find sufficient accommodation already existing; while the others will turn their immediate attention to the land brought into cultivation by the previous proprietor; and the next object will be the breaking up of a portion of the new land.

The principal object of the society will doubtless be the location of as many of its members as practicable at the earliest possible period; but before this object can be safely effected, there must be a sufficient supply of food for twelve months, and lodging accommodation for every individual prior to his location. It appears by the evidence of many settlers in America, that the first crop upon land newly broken up seldom produces more than half a crop, but that the subsequent crops are most abundant. It is therefore of great importance, at the commencement of operations, that a portion of the land should have been cultivated before it comes into our possession, in order to secure a good average crop at the end of the first year, for the consumption of those who may arrive at that time.

For this reason, the purchase of what is called an "improved farm" is recommended, consisting of about 200 acres, being partly fenced in, and having some domestic and farm buildings upon it. Such a farm, while it would give immediate domestic accommodation to some, if not all, the pioneers of the party, would, at the end of the year, afford an abundant supply of provisions for the support of the second draught of members.

If we calculate the cost of an improved farm of 200 acres at five dollars per acre, we ought to expect to find some real " improvements," since this is an advance of 3¾ dollars upon the original cost of the land; and it should be recollected, that being prairie land, the labour of cutting down timber will form no part of this increased value. We shall therefore, in all probability, find that half the land has previously produced crops; but, to be safe, we will say seventy-five acres have been brought into cultivation, and upon that assumption we will make our estimates of production. The cost of the farm will be 1,000 dollars, or £208. 6s. 8d.

We will suppose our first winter to be approaching; that during the autumn every attention has been paid to the land, in order to secure good crops next year ; and that all parties are as comfortably sheltered from the weather as circumstances will admit, and as they can reasonably expect. In the course of the winter, the labour of the field being in a great measure suspended, a favourable opportunity will be presented for carrying on the building operations, preparatory to the introduction of more members.

The first consideration of the party will be to erect a building measuring sixty by twenty-four feet, which will be sufficiently large to afford comfortable accommodation for at least 100 persons, to be used as a dining room, an assembly-room, a school-room, and, in fact, for all public purposes. As the first and second draught of members will not exceed half the total number, and as the building will be equal to the accommodation of the whole, at least one-half the building may be converted into sleeping-rooms for those who may be introduced at the end of the first year, and we will suppose that number to be twenty-five. Taking thirty feet from the large room, we shall get six double-bedded rooms, ten feet square, leaving a passage of four feet between the two sets of rooms. This space of thirty by twenty-four feet may either be divided into rooms by slight temporary partitions, or remain as one large room. In either case, lodging accommodation for twelve single male or female members will be obtained. To provide accommodation for the remaining thirteen, it will be necessary to erect two cottages of four rooms each, forming part of the permanent plan intended to be adopted. The cottages will be detached, as the best protection we can have against an extensive destruction of our dwellings by fire. It is intended to allow one room to each single person who shall have attained his or her twenty-first year, and two rooms to a married couple, in addition to the use of the large room. Each of these detached cottages will consist of two rooms on the ground floor and two above, with a recess behind each room capable of holding a bed, and a smaller one for a washstand and other conveniencies. A sufficient number of these cottages will be built to aaccommodate all the residents, who will leave their old abodes as soon as the others can be got in readiness.

These cottages it is proposed to arrange in the form of a crescent, so that the required number may be added at convenient intervals, without destroying the original form. In the centre of the crescent a large public building of two stories will be built as early as possible, to supersede the public building first erected, which may then be converted into workshops, &c.

In front of the cottages, there will be a lawn and flower garden, and beyond these the orchard and kitchen garden. Behind the cottages, and at a convenient distance therefrom, the farm-yard and buildings will be placed, and close by a series of sheds, &c., for workshops. The domestic and business arrangements will be separated by small fields or paddocks in the rear of the former.

Before I could satisfactorily ascertain the average amount of produce per acre obtained from land in the Wisconsin territory, as well as the market value of the same, I consulted many authorities ; and, after all, it occurred to me that the best authority in this matter is the experience of those who, residing in the district, instead of hastily travelling through it, are practically engaged in the business respecting which information is desired. For this reason, I gave a preference to the unvarnished statements of some of the humbler settlers in that and similar districts of country, as contained in letters to their friends, they having no interest to serve, and consequently no motive to deceive.

In adopting the following as the basis of my calculations, I have kept considerably within the average of the different authorities I have consulted, as all those who have a practical knowledge of the subject will readily perceive, when they consider that it is admitted on all hands that the soil referred to is the richest in the world, and when they also consider that the statement is founded upon what *is*, not what *may be*, the produce of that soil ; and its estimated price is given with the same desire to avoid exaggeration :—

Commodities.	Bushels per Acre.	Price per Bushel.
		s. d.
Wheat	25	3 0
Barley	30	2 0
Oats	40	1 3
Indian Corn	30	1 9
Potatoes	360	1 0

In the following elaborate, and, I am fearful, tedious detail, I shall rely upon the accuracy of the above statement.

Unlike anything mechanical, agricultural results are slow to manifest themselves, and more especially so upon an impoverished soil, which, fortunately for us, we shall have no need to be troubled with; but, even on the richest soil, the first or second year, in an undertaking like ours, can scarcely be taken as a criterion by which a correct opinion can be formed of its real progress. I have therefore made three sets of calculations, one for each of the three first years of the society's operations, in order the more clearly to exhibit the progressive development of the powers of the establishment, and the independent position which every individual composing it will feel himself placed in at each successive stage.

THE FIRST YEAR.

If we suppose seventy-five acres of the land to have been brought into cultivation by the owner of the farm we may purchase, and if we appropriate forty acres of it to wheat, ten to barley, ten to oats, and fifteen to potatoes, and break up twenty-five acres of new land in the course of this year, and plant it with Indian corn, making 100 acres in the whole, the produce and its value will be as follows:—

	£	s.	d.
1,000 bushels of wheat, at 3s. per bushel	150	0	0
300 ditto barley, at 2s. ditto	30	0	0
400 ditto oats, at 1s. 3d. ditto	25	0	0
375 ditto Indian corn (half a crop), at 1s. 9d. per bushel	32	16	3
5,400 ditto potatoes, at 1s. per bushel	270	0	0
5 hogs, producing in the course of the year, 640 stone of pork, at 1s. 4d. per stone	42	13	4
250lbs. of wool, at 9d. per lb.	9	7	6
Total value	£559	17	1

The produce of the first year will not be ready for consumption during that year, except the meat, estimated at 640 stone, from which I have taken 345 stone for the family consumption, leaving 295 stone to dispose of.

The establishment will have to dispose of, or retain for next year's consumption—

	£	s.	d.
1,000 bushels of wheat, at 3s. per bushel	150	0	0
300 ditto barley, at 2s. ditto	30	0	0
400 ditto oats, at 1s. 3d. ditto	25	0	0
375 ditto Indian corn, at 1s. 9d. ditto.. ..	32	16	3
5,500 ditto potatoes, at 1s. ditto	270	0	0
295 stone of pork, at 1s. 4d. per stone	19	13	4
250lbs. of wool, at 9d. per lb.	9	7	6
Total value of surplus..	£536	17	1

The expenditure during the year will be—

	£	s.	d.
200 acres of land, with improvements, at 5 dollers per acre	208	6	8
Seed for 100 acres	55	0	0
Maintenance during the year, say 15 persons, at 2s. 6d. per week..	97	10	0
Materials for the erection of buildings during the year	50	0	0
1 horse £12, and 3 pair of working oxen, at £8 ..	36	0	0
3 cows, £2 10s. each	7	10	0
50 sheep, 8s. 4d. each	20	16	8
5 pigs, 12s. 6d. each..	3	2	6
Carried forward	£478	5	10

Brought forward	£478	5	10
2 carts	18	0	0
3 ploughs	6	0	0
Harness	8	0	0
3 pair of harrows	3	0	0
A number of minor implements, &c.	25	0	0
A quantity of iron	10	0	0
Oats, potatoes, Indian corn, and hay, for stock	31	16	3
Medical attendance and medicine for 15 persons ..	5	0	0
Expenditure during the year..	£585	2	1

I have supposed that 200 acres of land might be purchased; but there is every reason to believe that 160 acres would be the most likely quantity; so that a saving in the expenditure of £41 13s. 4d. would be effected on this item, making the total demand upon the funds £524 8s. 9d. This would make £75 11s. 3d. available for items not specified in the foregoing estimate of expenses; to which £60 may be added, being 10 per cent. exchangeable value upon an outlay of £600. Without this reduction, however, the account will stand thus:—

Produce	£536	17	1
Expenditure	585	2	1
Deficiency	£48	5	0

It will thus be seen that the value of the first year's produce is only £48 5s. below the expenditure of the most expensive and least productive year.

THE SECOND YEAR.

In the course of this year, all the labour that can be spared from the agricultural department must be employed in the erection of buildings for the accommodation of the remainder of the members; and when we consider the amount of useful labour, agricultural and mechanical, to be found amongst forty-five persons, judiciously selected, the improved state of the land broken up the first year, the quantity of new land to be taken into cultivation this year, and the great increase of the stock upon the farm, it cannot be doubted that the estate will be in a condition to receive, in the course of the year, all the parties interested in the experiment.

We now propose to bring into cultivation fifty additional acres of land, making 150, and we shall suppose them to be cropped as follows:—The forty acres of wheat of last year (after a crop of tares and rye in the spring, for the cattle,) will be succeeded by twenty-five acres of turnips and fifteen of barley; the ten of barley by ten of oats; the ten of oats by ten of Indian corn; the fifteen of potatoes and twenty-five of Indian corn by forty of wheat; and the fifty acres of new land to be broken up will be appropriated to twenty-five acres of Indian corn and twenty-five of potatoes. The produce and its value will be as follows:—

	£	s.	d.
1,000 bushels of wheat, at 3s. per bushel	150	0	0
450 ditto barley, at 2s. ditto..	45	0	0
400 ditto oats, at 1s. 3d.	25	0	0
675 ditto Indian corn (estimating the 25 acres of new land to produce only half a crop), at 1s. 9d. per bushel	59	1	3
5,000 ditto potatoes (estimated at little more than half a crop, being on new land), at 1s. per bushel	250	0	0
20 hogs, producing in the course of the year, 2,560 stone of pork, at 1s. 4d. per stone	170	13	4
500lbs. of wool, at 9d. per lb. (from 100 sheep and lambs)	18	15	0
Total value	£718	9	7

The production and consumption will be as follows:—

	Wheat.	Barley.	Oats.	Indian Corn.	Potatoes.	Meat.
	Bushels.	Bushels.	Bushels.	Bushels.	Bushels.	Stone of 8 lbs.
Produce.......	1,000	450	400	675	5,000	2,560
Consumption ..	400	150	160	75	2,000	926
Surplus........	600	300	240	600	3,000	1,634

The establishment will have to dispose of—

	£	s.	d.
600 bushels of wheat, at 3s. per bushel	90	0	0
300 ditto barley, at 2s. ditto	30	0	0
240 ditto oats, at 1s. 3d. ditto..	15	0	0
600 ditto Indian corn, at 1s. 9d. ditto	52	10	0
3,000 ditto potatoes, at 1s. ditto..	150	0	0
1,634 stone of pork, at 1s. 4d. per stone	108	18	8
500lbs of wool, at 9d. per lb.	18	15	0

Total value of surplus £465 3 8

The expenditure for the second year will be—

	£	s.	d.
Field and garden seeds..	£135	6	3
2 horses, £12 each	24	0	0
3 cows, £2 10s. each	7	10	0
Addition to implements	30	0	0
Flour mill, capable of grinding and dressing a bushel and a half per hour	30	0	0
Iron-work for a patent mangle	4	10	0
Ironmongery..	20	0	0
A quantity of iron	15	0	0
Articles for family consumption not produced on the farm, such as tea, coffee, sugar, &c.	50	0	0
Medical attendance and medicines for forty-two persons	10	0	0

Expenditure during the year.. .. £326 6 3

The account will stand thus:—

	£	s.	d.
Produce	£465	3	8
Year's expenditure	326	6	3

Profit on the year £138 17 5

THE THIRD YEAR.

We have now completed our second year, brought 150 acres of land into cultivation, and we will suppose all the members attached to the undertaking to have been located on the farm.

We now propose, in commencing the third year, to bring the remaining fifty acres under the plough, completing the 200 acres, by which we shall be enabled to ascertain, in some degree, the tenature of our resources in land and labour, by exhibiting, in the first place, the produce of the farm when wholly cultivated; secondly, the number of persons required to raise such amount of produce; thirdly, the surplus labour available for domestic, manufacturing and other purposes; fourthly, the money value of the whole of the agricultural produce raised during the year; fifthly, the quantity of produce required for the maintenance of the 100 persons forming the establishment, as well as to feed the stock upon the farm; sixthly, the disposable surplus; and, lastly, the profit of the third year.

The establishment, as has been already stated, is estimated to amount to 100 persons, men, women, and children, and the result of their industry is calculated as follows :—

No. of Acres.	Crops, &c.	LABOUR.			PRODUCE.			
		Days per Acre.	Total Days.	No. of Labourers.	Bushels per Acre.	Total Bushels	Meal per Bshl.	Total Meal.
50	Wheat	32	1,600	8	25	1,250	46	57,500
20	Barley	30	600	2	30	600		
10	Oats............	30	300	2	40	400		
20	Indian Corn......	50	1,000	3	30	600		
20	Potatoes	70	1,400	5	360	7,200		
20	Clover and Grass..	5	100	1				
10	Vetches	30	300	1				
24	Turnips..........	40	960	4				
20	Meadow or Pasture	6	120	1				
4	Garden and Orchard	80	480	2				
	To feed Pigs, &c..			1				
2	Buildings, &c....							
200	Acres cultivated in		6,860	by 30 labourers, in 224 days each year.				

By the above table it will be seen that thirty persons will be required to work 224 days each year, in the production of the various commodities therein enumerated, being eighty-nine days less than the year, after deducting fifty-two Sundays; but we will suppose these thirty persons to be wholly occupied in these labours throughout the year ; and out of the entire family of 100 persons, we will further suppose the children incapable of labour to amount to thirty-three, and the sick to average two persons annually, which, with the thirty employed in agriculture, will dispose of sixty-five persons, and leave us the labour of thirty-five men, women and children, for domestic, scholastic, manufacturing, and other purposes. Supposing eight to be required for domestic purposes, such as cooking, washing, cleaning, &c., two for the school department, book-keeping, &c., and two for the dairy, we shall have twenty-three persons remaining for manufactures of various kinds, whose labour, in proportion to their number, we may estimate as being equal in value to that of the thirty individuals employed in agriculture, and we shall therefore carry forward the amount to a subsequent estimate, as so much value given to the farm; for whether these persons are employed in fencing in the estate, or in erecting buildings, manufacturing articles for the use of the family, or for sale in the public market, they are equally contributing to the wealth of the establishment.

I now proceed to give the estimated amount of produce, with its value, which is as follows :—

	£	s.	d.
1,250 bushels wheat, at 3s. per bushel	187	10	0
600 ditto barley, at 2s. ditto	60	0	0
400 ditto oats, at 1s. 3d. ditto	25	0	0
600 ditto Indian corn, 1s. 9d ditto	52	10	0
7,200 ditto potatoes, at 1s. ditto	360	0	0
200 sheep, producing 2,000 stone (8lbs.) of mutton, at 1s. 8d. per stone	166	13	4
10 bullocks slaughtered, producing 1,000 stone of beef, at 1s. 4d. per stone	66	13	4
50 hogs, 30 stone each, producing 1,500 stone of pork, at 1s. 4d. per stone	100	0	0
10 cows, producing 8,126 gallons of milk (partly made into butter and cheese), at ¼d. per quart	67	14	2
1,000lbs. wool, at 9d. per lb.	37	10	0
Poultry, eggs, &c.	20	0	0

Total value £1,143 10 10

Allowing each individual of the men, women, and children to consume daily a pound of flour, two pounds of potatoes, half a pound of meat (with fish and poultry), a quart of ale or cider, a pint and a half of milk (or what it will produce in butter or cheese), eggs, and a sufficient quantity of fruit and vegetables from the garden, the produce and consumption will stand as under:—

	Wheat.	Barley.	Oats.	Indian Corn.	Pota- toes.	Meat.	Milk.
	Bshls.	Bshls.	Bshls.	Bshls.	Bshls.	Stones of 8lbs.	Gallns.
Produce	1,250	600	400	600	7,200	4,500	8,126
Consumption	793½	365	312	100	3,200	2,281	6,844
Surplus.....	456½	235	88	500	4,000	2,219	1,282

This surplus is obtained, after deducting from the wheat, barley, potatoes, meat, and milk, what 100 persons will require to consume, according to the scale of allowance given; and also after deducting from the oats 312 bushels for the six horses, giving to each horse one bushel weekly; from the Indian corn 100 bushels, and from the potatoes 825 bushels for the pigs, &c.

It may be necessary to observe, that in defining the quantity of provisions to be given to each member of the establishment, it is not intended in practice to establish any scale of allowance, the sole object being to arrive at a probable estimate of the consumption of the family. In the midst of such abundance, the bare idea of a limitation of food, would be an absurdity. But supposing the estimated consumption here given to be sufficient to satisfy the wants of the members, it may not be out of place to s ate, that the money value of the daily allowance of food for each individual will not exceed sixpence; and supposing the clothing, &c., to bear a proportion of one-third of the value of the food, the total cost of maintaining each person per day would be 8d., or 4s. 8d. per week.

The establishment will have to dispose of—

			s.	d.			£	s.	d.
456½	bushels of wheat,	at	3	0	per bushel .. .		68	9	6
88	do.	oats, at	1	3	do.	..	5	10	0
235	do.	barley at	2	0	do.	.. ..	23	10	0
500	do.	Indian corn,	1	9	do.	..	43	15	0
4000	do.	potatoes, at	1	0	do.	.. ..	200	0	0

2219 stone of meat of different kinds, averaging
1s. 4d. per stone.. .. .. — 147 18 8
1282 gallons of milk, producing, at the rate of three
gallons to the pound, 427¾ lbs. of butter, at 8d. per lb. — 14 4 10
1400 lbs. of wool, at 9d. per lb. .. .. — 52 10 0
Poultry, eggs, &c. .. .. — 10 0 0

Value of surplus produced by the labour of 30 persons employed in agriculture, after feeding, educating, &c., 100 persons 565 18 0
32 hands employed in improving the estate, and in manufacturing such articles as may be considered useful to the establishment and saleable in the market, and whose labour, in proportion to their number, we estimate at the same value as that of the 30 individuals employed in agriculture; but say that, in addition to their labour *for,* they bring *to* the establishment two-thirds of the value of the agricultural surplus as above 377 5 4

Total value of surplus £943 3 4

The hides and skins from the bullocks and sheep slaughtered would nearly purchase leather for shoes for 100 persons, had it been necessary to provide that article in this year's estimate; the fat and tallow from the same, and from the pigs slaughtered, will supply candles and soap; and some parts of what is called offal from the slaughtered animals would furnish an addition to the allowance of meat.

c

The outlay for the third year's operations, considering their increased extent, will be comparatively light, since the principal part of the stock will be derived from that of the two preceding years. It will be as follows:—

	£	s.	d.
Field and garden seeds..	128	10	0
3 horses, £12 each	36	0	0
Addition to implements	50	0	0
Articles not produced on the farm, such as tea, coffee, sugar, &c...	100	0	0
Medical attendance and medicines for 100 persons ..	20	0	0
Expenditure during the year	£334	10	0

The account will stand thus :—

	£	s.	d.
Produce to dispose of, value of earnings, &c., after feeding and educating 100 persons	943	3	4
Deduct year's expenditure	334	10	0
Profit on the year	£608	13	4

The profit on the three years will therefore be—

	£	s.	d.
First year	0	0	0
Second year	138	7	5
Third year	608	13	4
	£747	0	9

	£	s.	d.		£	s.	d.
Deduct first year's deficiency	48	5	0				
Do. three years' interest..	90	0	0				
					138	5	0

	£	s.	d.
Total profit on three years	£608	15	9

It will be seen that I have made no allowance for wearing apparel, household linen, &c., as the parties have agreed to provide these things up to this period. The following year this expenditure must be met; and the best way to provide for one important item in the account will be to devote a few acres of land to the growth of flax, the Wisconsin territory being peculiarly favourable to its cultivation. Five acres will produce as much flax as may be manufactured into 2,826 yards of linen of different sorts. This must claim our early attention, as a means of employing some of our surplus labour.

It will also be perceived, on the other hand, that I have made no estimate of the value of the agricultural improvements effected in the course of the three years, because my principal object was to show a sufficiency of the means of enjoying life. This I have not only succeeded in doing, but I have shown a very considerable surplus beyond it ; and, in order to obtain this surplus, I have resorted to no over-estimate in the production, nor under-estimate in the consumption, but the reverse, I hope it will be found, in both cases.

I might have dwelt upon the increased value given to the land by cultivation, and particularly to the 125 acres brought in from a state of nature. The difference in value between cultivated land and land in a state of nature is the difference between 5s. 2½d. and £1 0s. 10d. per acre, the latter being the price at which I have estimated the cost of the farm. Deducting the value of the mechanical improvements in buildings, fencing, &c., which we may fairly estimate at one-half this difference of 15s. 7½d., each of the 125 acres will have been increased 7s. 9¾d. in value, being a total increased value of £48 16s. 6¾d.

In the expenditure of the second year, I have included the purchase of a mill for grinding and dressing flour, which, besides its uses for the establishment, may be rendered a scource of profit in grinding flour for the surrounding neighbourhood. With this and other machines, and the command of surplus labour, which the co-operative principle will secure to us at all times, we may, if we desire it, profit considerably by the necessities of those who live under the isolated, helpless, and "fragmental" system of the outer world. But profit is not our object. We aim at the practice of the great co-operative principle. If profit, obtained by machinery, or by any other honest means, can be rendered subservient to the end we have in view, we shall resort to it for a time, without making it the unceasing business of our lives.

ARTICLES OF AGREEMENT.

The following are the terms of agreement amongst the proprietors of this undertaking:—

1. That the village intended to be established by this society shall be called " ;" and that no persons shall be allowed a permanent residence therein who cannot adopt the principle, ' that the character of man is formed *for* him—not *by* him," and who are not prepared to conform to the practical arrangements of the establishment indicated by that principle.

2. That this society shall consist of twenty, but not exceeding twenty-five, proprietors and their families.

3. That no person shall be admitted a member of this society against whom any individual member may have a decided objection.

4. That each of the proprietors, or heads of families, shall pay £30 into the hands of the treasurer before the departure of the individuals to be appointed to secure an estate.

5. That each proprietor shall have an individual freehold right to an equal proportion of the land purchased.

6. That as soon as all the proprietors shall have arrived on the estate, and the best mode of awarding the different sections of land shall have been agreed upon, the legal titles shall be procured for each of them.

7. That prior to any division of the estate being made, a sufficiency of land for the erection of the farm and domestic buildings and workshops, for the orchard and gardens, and for any other purpose, shall be staked off and set aside as the common property of the proprietors.

8. That the interest of the proprietors in all the property upon the estate shall be common.

9. That any proprietor feeling a desire to retire from the society, may either take to the occupancy of his own section, sell it to some one willing to become a member (if approved by the society), or the society shall have a prior right to purchase the same upon equitable terms, if convenient; but no alienation of any section can take place until the whole of the land shall have been brought into cultivation.

10. That interest, at the rate of five per cent. per annum, shall be paid on the moneys advanced by the proprietors; but that no payment of interest will be expected until the end of the third year, when the interest upon the three years will be paid.

11. That the principal money shall be returned as soon as the profits of the establishment can be made to yield a surplus that can be conveniently applied to that object.

12. That any proprietor, not becoming a resident member, shall claim priority in the repayment of money invested by him.

13. That should the society experience difficulty in obtaining money in exchange for its commodities, they may pay to the resident proprietors, or to any proprietor seceding from the establishment, either the interest or principal, or both, in the produce of the farm, estimating its value at the market price prevailing in the neighbourhood at the time of payment; but that non-resident proprietors shall receive both interest and principal in money.

14. That the business of the establishment shall be conducted by a board of directors, composed of all the proprietors on the estate.

15. That the transactions of the society may be carried on either through the medium of money, or by an exchange of labour, or the products of labour; and that the society shall, as far as possible, avoid contracting debts.

16. That no order for goods, for the employment of labour, or any other act involving an expenditure of the funds, property, or labour of the establishment, shall be considered valid, unless signed by the general superintendent and two of the directors.

17. That individuals and families shall, in every instance, defray their own travelling expenses from England to the place of location in America.

18. That the parties may take with them as many useful tools and articles for domestic use as they may have and can procure; and that the value of such articles as may be thought fit to be taken into use by the establishment shall be ascertained at the time they are so taken, when the party will be credited with the amount, and paid for the same as soon as convenient.

19. That each individual shall take with him or her sufficient clothing and bed-linen for at least two years.

20. That the location of the members shall be in something like the following order:—

	No.
The first draught, say	20
At the end of the first year	25
In the course of the second year, the remainder, in two or three divisions, at intervals of four or six months, say	55
Total	100

Or more speedily, if circumstances will admit.

21. That all disputes between one member and another, as well as those between individual members and the society collectively, shall be settled by arbitration, and that the arbitrators shall in all cases be selected from the members of the establishment, each party in the dispute choosing three arbitrators, who shall be empowered to call in a seventh, to act as chairman, having a casting vote, and their decision shall be final.

Route and Expense of Travelling from London to Milwaukee, Wisconsin Territory, United States, for one adult Person.

The statements I have met with respecting the expense of travelling between New York and Milwaukee, on Lake Michigan, are almost as various as the tastes of the travellers themselves. I offer the following as by no means an under-estimate of the expense:—

	No. of Miles.	£.	s.	d.
From London to New York		5	0	0
Provisions		2	0	0
New York to Buffalo, by the Erie Canal, 2½ cents per mile, with board	523	2	14	11½
Buffalo to Detroit, by steamer, on Lake Erie, in 48 hours	360	0	12	6
Provisions for two days, at 4s. per day ..		0	8	0
Detroit to Milwaukee, or Racine, on Lake Michigan, at 1¼ dollar per 100 miles, in five days..	814	2	2	3
Provisions for five days, at 4s.		1	0	0
Total	1,697	£13	17	8½

In a recent number of the *New York Herald*, it is said, "The price of passage from this city (New York) to Detroit, in the cheap lines, is only two dollars and a half, and about as much more for food." By this statement the cost would be £1. 1s., provisions included. Detroit being more than half the distance between New York and Milwaukee, the addition of 19s. will make the cost of inland travelling £2, which, added to £7 for crossing the Atlantic, will make the total cost £9.

An estimate between these two statements might be relied upon with confidence ; and, in the absence of the exact information I have been expecting from New York, I should be inclined to think that £12 would cover the expense to an adult, and one-half that sum would suffice for children under twelve years of age.

Taking the travelling expense at this rate, the total expenditure for a family of five persons would be as follows:—

	£	s.	d.
Man and wife	£24	0	0
Three children, £6 each	18	0	0
Subscription for land, &c..	30	0	0
	£72	0	0

So that the total expenditure of 20 families, five in a family, would amount to £1,440.

A GLIMPSE OF THE FUTURE GROWTH OF THIS SMALL BEGINNING.

To those who look for the establishment of communities by magic, or through the assistance of those over whom their appeals exert as little influence as they would over the wand of the magician—to those who are indisposed to the labour of making, before they enjoy, a paradise—to those who, while they profess to be followers of nature, disregard the universal mode by which her works gather strength and attain to maturity—to such persons the plan I have just submitted will appear sufficiently mean and contemptible.

To such parties I have not addressed myself. I would much rather repel them by an over-estimate of hardships to be encountered, and privations to be endured, than, by throwing over these hardships and privations the air of a romance, beguile them into realities inconsistent with the pictures painted upon their imaginations.

But, permit me to say that the imagination never conceived—the poet never yet described—nay, that noble of nature, the benevolent OWEN himself, whose entire heart is one intense feeling of desire for the happiness of his species, never yet presented to the world a picture of human felicity more congenial with human nature than is this modest, unpretending, noiseless effort capable of attaining to, when, through the successive stages of its growth, it shall have acquired that strength and solidity—that exactness of proportions, which shall make it harmonize with parts possessing the same properties and proportions.

Being, as it were, the segment of a circle, it will be true in form to the extent of its arch. If we subdivide this segment into a hundred parts, each part will maintain its relative proportion to the whole. But—how fearful our task!—our segment must be described by a hundred sentient beings, beautifully formed, as all are when they first enter the sphere of existence, but, ignorantly and viciously circumstanced, they will have necessarily become more or less unfavourably developed and matured.

If we suppose this segment of a hundred subdivisions, each subdivision represented by a human being, to be the tenth part of an entire circle, nine other similar segments united with it would complete the circle, or bring together one thousand individuals, who, as far as numbers are concerned, would form a community sufficiently varied for all practical purposes. But would this union of form—this mechanical mode of uniting beings so differently organized—bring with it union of feeling, of sympathy, and of sentiment? Would this wholesale method of attempting to unite human beings, *without let or hindrance on their part,* promote or retard that object? Is it the TRUE principle, even supposing these different sections to have had all the advantages of proximity of situation, with opportunities afforded them of frequently meeting together? No, not even then; for, although there might have been nothing decidedly repulsive in the elements thus brought together, the *manner* of bringing them together, and the constraint thereby implied, would be sufficient to create feelings unfavourable to a healthy and harmonious action of the various parts of the machine.

This, then, is not the true principle of congregation, nor can any be considered as such which in any way violates even the prejudices of those whom it is desired to unite.

Well, where shall we find the true principle? If we go back to the formation of the first section (the details of which are given in the foregoing plan, and are equally applicable to any subsequent section,) we shall there find the true principle. It is there resolved, *that no person shall become a member of the family against whom any member may have a decided objection.* If perfect harmony cannot be brought about by this means, the cause will not be traceable to the *mode of bringing the members together ;* for here we meet hostility on the threshold, and oppose its entrance.

Taking universal consent to be the best possible principle of admission, I proceed briefly to sketch out a plan of future and more extended operations than the one already given, which is applicable to the formation of sections, and to an incipient or training stage of their existence ; and in order to show the working of the proposed plan, we will suppose several of these sections to have been brought into operation, and to be placed within a moderate distance of each other.

The differently-constituted minds composing these different sections will naturally lead to different kinds of thought and action, and, as a consequence, different degrees of improvement in the arts of life will be attained.

In order that all the sections may immediately profit by the improvements effected in any particular section, it will be necessary that a system should be established by which this and other advantages may be secured to all, and this object may be effected in the following manner:—

Let an individual be selected in each section, having the largest share of public confidence, but removable at pleasure, and another appointed.

Let the individuals thus chosen meet together at stated periods—not in the character of legislators, but as mutual friends, meeting each other for the purpose of giving and receiving advice upon all matters affecting the well-being of those who sent them, and more particularly as to the best means of drawing closer the bonds of union subsisting between them, as the most attractive and secure mode of interesting the outward world in their proceedings.

By the natural increase of their numbers—by the desire prompted by the improvements already effected, and the rapidly-accumulating means at their command, the necessity for an enlarged sphere of action will be forced upon the various sections. Then will come under the consideration of these representatives of the different sections questions of the deepest interest and importance, and the task of bringing about an agreement between the members of the respective sections it will be their duty to prosecute.

They will have to consider the extent of land to be purchased, its locality, the plan to be adopted, the number of residents to be drafted on it, and the time and manner of their location.

All these matters having been arranged, and the trades required for the first draught determined upon, each section will select an individual or family to form part of that draught, and each person so selected must give his or her consent to reside with all the others, before the nucleus can be said to be formed. This effected, and the nucleus once formed, the approval of every individual member must be had to all subsequent additions to the establishment.

As soon as their numbers shall have been completed, by a strict observance of the same principle of selection throughout, all ties to the respective sections from which the members of this new establishment emanated shall be loosened, and this new machine at once launched into an independent existence, where there will be no external control, and no clashing of external with internal interests.

The void occasioned in the sections, by the withdrawal of members from them, will of course be filled up, where necessary, by new members, who will come into a well-organized school of training, not to be deranged by their inexperience.

This brief outline is sufficient to show the expansive nature of our plan, and that our views are not limited to the insignificant number of persons contained in a single section; but, though insignificant, it is nevertheless in perfect accordance with the natural growth of all existences.

We look forward to higher objects, and shall prosecute our intentions as soon as the materials, animate and inanimate, can be prepared in the sectional training schools; and when we consider the facilities afforded by the great productiveness of the American soil, and the absence of all the oppressive imposts which bear down the energies of the people of this country, we feel ourselves justified in anticipating a rapid increase of our numbers. Nay, we confidently expect, that in a very short time after we shall have gained a secure footing, arrangements may be made by which parties may be introduced into these training schools at a cost of little more than their travelling expenses.

APPENDIX,

COMPRISING EXTRACTS FROM VARIOUS AUTHORITIES IN FAVOUR OF THE NORTH-WESTERN TERRITORIES OF THE UNITED STATES.

It will at once be admitted that the four most important objects the emigrant ought to endeavour to secure are—First, a healthy situation; secondly, a soil not only of good quality, but requiring the least possible expenditure of labour and capital to produce an immediate return; thirdly, an abundant supply of pure water; and, fourthly, (although an object of comparative indifference on the co-operative principle,) easy access to the best markets. It will be seen by the following extracts that all these objects are to be obtained with greater certainty in the territories in question than in any other part of the United States:—

[From the Far West.]

WISCONSIN TERRITORY.—This territory was erected into a separate government in 1836, and for two years afterwards included Iowa within its limits. It stretches from the Mississippi river on the west to lake Michigan on the east, and from the northern boundary of the Union to the states of Missouri and Illinois on the south; being in length nearly 600 miles, and in breadth between 100 and 200 miles. The population is about 25,000. A large portion of this territory is imperfectly known, and is for the most part still in the occupancy of the Indian tribes—the Chippeways, Menomonies, and the Stockbridge Indians.

It is settled by a white population only along a part of its southern and eastern border. Its great mineral resources, fertile soil, and fine climate are, however, attracting such numerous emigrants, that it is probable a few years only will elapse before those portions of the territory most suitable for settlement will number many towns and villages, and be covered with a comparatively dense population.

In some parts of the territory the soil is very fertile, and produces large crops of the various grains common to this section of the Union; but the great riches of Wisconsin are its minerals: lead is found in great abundance, and also copper and iron. Lead mining is carried on extensively, and that of copper is about to be commenced.

Fort Winnebago, a military post of the United States' government, stands at the portage between the Wisconsin and Fox rivers, which, when united by a canal in progress of construction, will form a communication between the Mississippi and the lakes.

[From Chambers's Information for the People.]

The reader will observe on the map a tongue of land, situated between the two lakes, Huron and Michigan; this tract, with another which lies on the west, between Lake Michigan and the Mississippi, has been lately begun to be settled by emigrants from the old states of America. The two together possess great recommendations to agricultural emigrants. The capital is Detroit, a town situated on the river which connects Lake Huron with Lake Erie, and containing 2,500 inhabitants. These lakes, with their rivers and canals, give the district access to the markets of New York, New Orleans, and Montreal.

The climate is temperate and healthy; winter sets in generally about the middle of November, and continues till about the middle of March. At Detroit, in 1818, the mean heat of January was 24 deg.; and in 1820, the mean heat of July was 69 deg., of December 27 deg. The country is situated upon limestone rock, rather hilly, and possesses what the Americans call good water privileges—that is, numerous falls of water for mills, &c. It is better watered than any other in the United States, being finely diversified with lakes and brooks, rising in most parts from copious springs.

The soil is in general a good fertile loam, upon limestone: in some places a calcareous earth is turned up, mixed with the common soil; in others, the loam is mixed with a little sand; both are extremely productive. The country is, in some districts, under heavy timber, and in others an open prairie, where the settler has nothing to do but start his plough. The produce of the land runs from 25 to 50 bushels of wheat, after one bushel of seed. The cotton plant, the grape vine, the sweet potatoe of Carolina, the tomato, and egg plant, have all been successfully cultivated. Rye, barley, oats, peas, beans, and potatoes, as well as all kinds of vegetables usually cultivated in the same latitude, produce here in great abundance. Peaches and pears have been tried, and both produce delicious fruit : near towns, pears sell at from 2s. to 4s. per bushel ; apples vary from 6d. to 2s. per bushel ; currants, blackberries, raspberries, and strawberries thrive exceedingly. Indian corn is less luxuriant than in the valley of the Ohio, the climate being somewhat colder. This country, on the whole, seems more congenial to European constitutions and habits than the other western settlements.

The richest and perhaps most beautiful part of the territory, is generally thought to be that adjacent to the St. Joseph's River, on which twelve new counties are formed. The soil is excellent, and there are numerous falls of water for mills, &c.

Fox River, on the west side of Lake Michigan, is specially noticed as highly desirable for settlers, in regard to quality of soil, beauty, and local advantages : a canal is projected to connect this river and the lake with the Mississippi.

Detroit, the capital of Michigan, is the embryo Constantinople of the inland seas of North America. It is situated in a narrow channel, which connects the two lower lakes, Ontario and Erie, with the three upper, Huron, Michigan, and Superior. Having access in every direction to countries of more fertile soil than those of Greece or Asia, and possessed of an equally favourable climate, it begins its career with political institutions far more propituous to human welfare than were possessed by the celebrated city we have mentioned; and it promises one day to be the abode of a more numerous as well as happier population.

[*From Remarks on the Western States of America.*]

The writer of the accompanying remarks having been repeatedly consulted respecting the comparative advantages of different parts of the United States of North America, and more especially that region now familiarly known as the western country, either as a field for emigration or investment, offers the following sketch to the consideration of all who may feel an interest in the subject, as embracing a few leading and authentic facts relating to the statistics of the Valley of the Mississippi. These he wishes to be understood as more particularly applicable to the northern part of that country, commonly designated the Upper Valley of the Mississippi, for it is only that part which he can unreservedly recommend to the serious attention of a native of England or Scotland.

It would occupy too much space to give a full and detailed account of the works of internal improvement, either finished or partly completed, in the western country. The reader may form some idea of them from the remarks that follow, given on the spot, as evincing the tone of public sentiment on these matters in the states of Michigan and Illinois.

The following extract from the late annual message of the governor of Michigan (which state, it will, perhaps, be recollected by some of our readers, was only admitted into the Union some two or three years since) addressed to the legislature of the state, which assembled the 7th of January, 1839, is taken from the *Times* newspaper, and forcibly shows the enterprise of that infant state. It states "that the railroads and canals commenced within the limits of Michigan embrace a distance of 1,109 miles, that the estimated cost of these great works is nearly eight millions of dollars : that the expenditure up to the 1st January, 1839, amounted to 888,300 dol. (£178,000); that twenty-eight miles of the central rail-road from Detroit to Ypsilanti, the only work as yet finished so as to produce a revenue, have yielded to the state, in about ten months, 81,604 dol. (£17,000); that 28,751 passengers and 9,792,415 pounds of merchandize, in addition to 15,050 barrels of flour, have been transported on the road within that short time. That the same road, and all the other roads and canals, nearly all of which extend from Lake Erie to Lake Michigan, are in progress towards completion. • * • * • *

We have entered above into a more minute detail [of the internal improvements] than may seem necessary, because repeated inquiries have been made of usrespecting the State of Illinois, particularly its north-western part, its facilities for trade, internal communication,&c. by Englishmen and Scotchmen, both agriculturists and miners, some of whom had been across the Atlantic, and had returned to take over their families, and all of whom seem disposed to prefer the northern part of Illinois and the southern part of the Wisconsin territory to any portion of the United States which they had visited. Few will dispute the soundness of their judgment, for, taken *en masse*, Illinois is allowed to be the finest land in the Union: and it is believed that no practical men, whether labourers or capitalists, (and to such only these remarks are addressed) who may contemplate emigration or investment in that part of the western country, will complain of undue prolixity in the details just given.

In some countries stock-farming has taken place of all other business. The Scioto Valley and other districts in Ohio are famous for fine well-fed beef. Thousands of young cattle are purchased by the Ohio graziers, at the close of winter, of the farmers of Illinois, Missouri and Wisconsin. The Miami and White-Water sections of Ohio and Indiana abound with swine. Cincinnati has been the great pork mart of the western country: 150,000 head of hogs have been frequently slaughtered there in a season.

In ascending to the upper Valley of the Mississippi, the traveller comes to the fine states of Missouri, Illinois, and the territory of Wisconsin; and to the native of Britain probably no part of the western world can present such attractions as does this favoured region. The northern part of Illinois, and the southern and south-western parts of the territory of Wisconsin, more especially, are unsurpassed in beauty, enjoy a fine, salubrious, and elastic climate, have a most prolific soil, abundance of clear and never-failing streams, affording excellent mill seats, and several navigable rivers. Some of these rivers, such as the Pekatonica, the Grant River and the Lefevre seem intended by Providence as natural channels for the conveyance of the valuable minerals found in this neighbourhood to the great Mississippi, on which river they may be freighted down the western valley, or else go from Galena, or some point on the Galena and Chicago Union rail-road, to Lake Michigan, on their way to an eastern market. Here is situated the tract of country generally known as the Lead Mine District, lying north of the town of Galena in the state of Illinois and Dubuque in the Wisconsin territory, and extending, it is supposed, some fifty miles. This district of country is unrivalled in the whole of the United States for the abundance and variety of its mineral products.

The land in this district of country is what is known as the rolling or undulating prairie of the western country. From May to October these undulating or dry prairies are covered with tall grass and flowers. In June and July they seem an ocean of flowers of various hues waving to the breeze. The prevalent tint of these flowers in the early spring is the color of the peach blossom, the next a deeper red, then succeeds the yellow, and to the latest period of autumn they assume a brilliant golden hue. These tall flowers and shrubs, growing luxuriantly on the surface, present a striking and delightful appearance. The undulations are so slight, that to the eye the surface has the appearance of an uninterrupted level, though the ravines formed by the rivulets indicate a considerable degree of inclination. These prairies are from one to six miles in width. They are intersected in every direction by strips of forest land advancing into and receding from the prairies towards the water courses, whose banks are always lined with timber, generally of luxuriant growth. Between these streams, in many instances, are copses or groves of timber, containing from 100 to 2,000 acres in the midst of the prairies, like islands in the ocean.

The lead mine region in Illinois and Wisconsin abounds with these groves. The first improvements are usually made on that part of the prairie or meadow which adjoins the timber, and thus we frequently see at the commencement a range of farms circumscribing the prairie as with a belt. The writer before quoted says, " In breaking up prairie land, &c., for cultivation, we usually plough with three or four yoke of oxen. The shear plough turning up about eighteen to twenty-four inches of turf at a furrow in breadth, and from three to four inches deep: the sod turning entirely over so as to lay the grass down, and it fits smoothly enough, furrow to furrow, to harrow and sow wheat. It is usual to sow and break it up in May, and to drop corn (Indian) along the edge of every fourth row. This is called sod corn. No working or ploughing is necessary the first season. The sod is left lying for the grass to decay, and after the next winter's frost it becomes light and friable. The sod corn does not make more than half a crop, and is cut up, stalk and all together, and stacked up for fodder for stock. The next year, the stock of Indian corn is most abundant, averaging fifty bushels per acre; wheat twenty-five to thirty bushels; rye twenty-five to thirty-five, and oats from forty to sixty bushels per acre. Potatoes, hay (timothy), and all the different garden vegetables, yield most abundantly. A man can tend double the quantity of corn that he can in newly-settled timber countries, there being no stumps to obstruct the plough or hoe. The cost of breaking up an acre of prairie is from one dollar fifty cents to two dollars ; fencing, say forty acres, eight rails stake and rider, 6000 rails and stakes 100 dollars. Cabin 20 dollars, say a forty-acre field broken up and fenced cabin, 200 dollars. The prairies are generally from one to six miles in width ; of course about three miles is the furthest distance from timber, and the prairie constitutes the finest natural road possible to haul on. The prairie lands are undoubtedly worth from ten dollars to fifteen dollars (£2. to £3.) more per acre for farming than those that are timbered throughout, not only because they are richer, but because it would take at least that sum per acre to put the timbered lands of Ohio and Indiana in the same advanced state for cultivation." The natural grass which covers the prairies in great abundance is tall and coarse in appearance. In the early stages of its growth it resembles young wheat, and in this state furnishes a succulent and rich food for cattle. The butter made from this grass is excellent. Cattle and horses that have lived unsheltered and without fodder through the winter, and which are consequently much out of condition, after feeding on this grass are speedily changed into thrifty and sleek animals, as if by a charm.

The geological structure of the upland prairies in the entire peninsula comprehended between the Mississippi on the west, and the Illinois and Lake Michigan on the south and east, embracing all the northern part of the state of Illinois, and the greater part of the southern portion of Wisconsin territory, is almost entirely the same — that is, first, vegetable mould formed by the decomposition of grass upon the original clay soil, eight to thirty inches deep ; second, pure yellow clay, three to eight feet ; third, gravelly clay mixed with pebbles, four to ten feet ; fourth, limestone rock, two to twelve feet ; fifth, shale covering a stratum of bitumenous coal, generally four to five feet thick ; sixth, soapstone, then sandstone. The bed of limestone seems to be univer-sally found in this region, it having been discovered in all the wells that have been dug, and in all the banks of water courses of any magnitude. We quote again the words of a writer from the spot. "The bottom lands (that is the flat meadows) of these streams, which are usually about a mile and a half wide, cannot be surpassed in fertility. Like the great American Bottom, (so called) below the mouth of the Illinois river, the fertility of the Upper Mississippi and its adjacent streams is indestructible. On such a soil, under proper cultivation, 100 bushels of Indian corn and forty bushels of wheat to the acre can be raised with facility. With the most careless kind of culture, where the farmers do not think of applying the hoe after planting, and even the plough through but once, the average corn (Indian) crop is about fifty or sixty bushels per acre. These bottoms are frequently interspersed with groves of timber, and altoge-ther form as fine a succession of farm sites as the eye ever saw, or the heart can desire, and immediately at the back of these sloping bottoms is a dense foliage of stately timber, froming a rich bordering to the verdant picture below."

The settler may safely disregard an objection which has sometimes been made by superficial observers to some prairie lands which have not much timber. Coal, which exists in the bluffs, so called, (that is the high lands or banks) of the rivers and streams in almost every part of the country, will be his fuel, and he will grow the hedge thorn and the black locust for his fencings. So soon as timber or orchards are planted, they grow with unexampled luxuriance. A correspondent from Adam's county, in Illinois writes thus :—"Locust trees planted, or rather sown, on prairie land, near Quincy, attained, in four years, a height of 26 feet, and their trunks and diame-ter of from 1 to 5 inches. These grow in close crowded rows, affording a dense and arboury shade. In a few instances, where the same kind of trees had been planted in a more open manner, they grew, in the same period, to the thickness of 6 inches, and in from 7 to 10 years from their planting, have been known to attain sufficient bulk to make posts and rails."

The summer range for cattle in these upland prairies is inexhaustible, and the amount of excellent hay that may be made every season almost without limit. Horses, cattle, and sheep can be raised here with but little trouble and expense, com-pared with that necessarily incurred in the eastern states. The mildness of the cli-mate in many parts not unfrequently relieves the owners from all care and expense of feeding them through the whole year, but it is generally advisable to do so from the commencement of December until the latter part of March. When cattle are fed and attended to in the best manner by provident farmers, the expense is less by one half than wintering the same species of stock in the eastern states. The shortness and moderation of the winter seasons, and the abundant forage which may be gathered from the wild prairies, render the raising of stock both cheap and easy.

The grass, when cut from the upland prairies, and well cured, makes excellent hay, and cattle will keep in good order through the whole winter on this food alone. It has also been frequently remarked that both horses and cattle usually fatten quite as fast in spring and autumn on the wild grass of the prairies as upon the tame pastures of the east; and the richness and flavour of the beef thus fattened has been much esteemed at St. Louis and New Orleans, and generally considered of the finest quality.

Among the many agricultural products for the cultivation of which this country seems admirably adapted is the sugar beet-root, which, besides its great value in the manufacture of the beet sugar, is about to become a most important article in the feeding of cattle. The following account of what has been accomplished in this way by a single individual is extracted from a western paper of late date :—" Last year he (Mr. P——) raised fifty tons of beets to the acre, and his crop is much better the present season. The manager of the farm says, it requires but little more labour to raise fifty tons of beets than fifty bushels of Indian corn, while the former is quite as good for horses, much better for cattle, and rather better for stock hogs. He also asserts that sucking calves preferred beets, when properly prepared, to milk."

This letter shows that a new item of national wealth is about to be introduced into the western country. The culture of the beet-root has produced important results in France. It is well known that land in those districts where its growth has become general has increased in value from fifty to one hundred and fifty per cent., and the clear annual income per acre, after paying all expenses, ranges from seven to eight pounds. The profits would be equally great in the United States; for though the price of labour is cheaper in France, the difference would no doubt be amply compensated by the superior fertility of the western prairies, and the circumstance of dispensing with manure, which the depth and richness of the soil will render unnecessary for a long period. A considerable diminution of the annual profits in Europe consists in the expense of manuring the land, so as to make it sufficiently rich to produce a remunerating crop. In France from eight to twelve dollars rent per acre is annually paid, and yet large profits are made. An acre of good land will produce 44,000 pounds of beet-root, from which 2,400 pounds of sugar can be extracted, which, at ten cents a pound, amounts to 240 dollars (£48.) per acre.

But little has been done until very lately to introduce the cultivated grasses into the upper valley of the Mississippi; but timothy grass grows well, and produces heavy crops of hay for several years in succession, with proper cultivation, and clover and all the other European grasses grow luxuriantly.

Wheat yields a good and sure crop. It weighs upwards of sixty pounds per bushel. Winter wheat is sown about the middle of September; spring wheat as soon as the ground can be ploughed in the spring. The harvest is about the middle of July for winter wheat, and for spring wheat in August. The crop is frequently thirty-five bushels per acre; thirty may be pronounced the average. The average price is one dollar to one and a quarter per bushel, varying a little according to the competition of mills, and facilities to market. In many instances a single crop of wheat has paid the expenses of purchasing the land, fencing, breaking up the prairie, seed, putting in the crop, harvesting, threshing, and taking it to market. Wheat is frequently sown on the prairie lands as a first crop, and a great yield obtained. Common labourers on the farm obtain from twelve to fifteen dollars per month, including board. A young man of industrious, steady habits, who begins without a dollar, in a few years becomes a substantial farmer. A good hand in the harvest-field will earn from a dollar and a half to two dollars per day. Oats have not been raised till lately. They are productive, yielding from forty to fifty bushels the acre, and sell from twenty to thirty cents per bushel. The demand for them for food for stage and travellers' horses is much increasing, though the Indian corn still commands a preference with some. Hemp has not been extensively cultivated in the upper valley, but wherever tried has been found very productive, and of excellent quality.

The Indian corn, the pride and beauty of almost every part of the United States of America, is a staple production of the western states. It yields seventy-five bushels per acre, and in some instances has exceeded one hundred. It is planted about the 1st of May.

Among the indigenous fruits may be mentioned the plum, which grows in great abundance. The colour is generally red, the flavour somewhat tart, but delicious. In some places the quantities of this fruit are prodigious. Wild cherries are abundant, but are only fit for making a liqueur. The persimmon is a delicious fruit after the frost has destroyed its astringent properties, as is also the pawpaw. The black mulberry grows in most parts, and is used for the feeding of silk-worms, which appear to thrive as well as those fed on the Italian mulberry. The gooseberry, strawberry, raspberry, and blackberry grow wild, and in great profusion.

Of the nuts, the hiccory, black walnut, and peccan deserve notice, which last is a native of Illinois, and very delicious.

Coal, salt, lime, lead, iron, and copper are among the mineral productions of this country; but the soil has not yet been extensively explored for its hidden treasures. Coal, secondary limestone, and sandstone exist in almost every quarter. Lead is found in the north-western part of the State of Illinois, and in that part of Wisconsin adjacent to it, in vast quantities. Native copper in large quantities is found on the Pekatonica, and also on the Grant and Cincinna rivers; and at Mineral Point, and other localities on or near the Pekatonica, mines of the richest character are wrought with industry and success. Copper ore has already been raised from these mines to a considerable extent.

The woods and prairies of the Wisconsin Territory abound in game of every description, grouse or prairie hen, pheasants, partridges, wild turkeys, and deer; the latter are so abundant, that few of the settlers think of sitting down to dinner without a venison steak.

The domestic animals are the same as elsewhere in the United States: the wild prairies, everywhere covered with grass, invite the raising of cattle. Many of the farmers possess large droves, and, as before-mentioned, they may be multiplied to an almost indefinite extent. The neat cattle are usually inferior in size to those of the old States, but this is entirely owing to bad management: the cows are not penned up in pasture-fields, but suffered to run at large over the open prairies, and, if suffered to lose their milk in August, become sufficiently fat for the table by October. Farrow heifers and steers are good beef, and fit for the knife at any period after the middle of May. A cow in the spring is worth from 12 to 20 dollars; some of the best quality will sell higher. Cows in general do not produce the same amount of milk, nor of as rich a quality as in older States, but this again is to be attributed to the causes already assigned. If ever a land might be justly characterized as flowing with milk and honey, it is the Western country generally.

From the springing of the grass till September, butter is made in great abundance. It sells at that season in market for about 20 cents (about 11d.) per pound.

Much has lately been done to improve the breed of horses. Some farmers keep a stallion and eight or ten brood mares, the latter being a very profitable stock, as the cost of their keep is a mere trifle; their labour is always needed, and their colts, when well grown, always command a ready market. A good farm horse can be purchased for 50 dollars (£10.) A great proportion of the ploughing of the West is performed by horse labour instead of that of the ox, which latter animal seems to be generally preferred for that species of labour in the Eastern States.

Hogs are a staple of the West, and Cincinnati, in the State of Ohio, as has been before stated, is the great mart for them in the West. The slaughtering of hogs is an immense business in that town, and excites the attention of travellers from the wonderful and almost incredible expedition with which the animal is slaughtered and prepared for market in the shape of pork. Thousands of them are raised without any expense, except a few breeders to start with, and a little attention to keeping them tame. This kind of pork, made from animals that have been running wild in the prairies, is by no means equal to that raised and fatted in a domestic way. It is soft and oily, and will not bear inspection; at New Orleans and other markets on the Mississippi, and elsewhere, it usually sells for three dollars a hundred weight, whilst domestic pork will sell from four to five dollars, according to size, quality, and the time when it is delivered. With a pasture of clover or blue grass, a well-filled corn crib, a dairy and slop barrel, and the usual care that a New-Englander or English farmer bestows on his pigs, pork may be raised from the sow, fatted and killed, and weigh from two hundred to two hundred and fifty pounds within twelve months.

The following extract from a letter of the Honourable H. L. Ellsworth, of Washington, gives a correct idea of the cost of cultivating the Western prairies, and we think any readers feeling an interest in the subject will be gratified with a perusal of it.

The letter is dated "Washington, January 1st, 1837.—Is it possible that lands yielding 40 bushels of wheat, 70 of Indian corn, 60 of oats, and 450 of potatoes, and distant only ten or twelve days transportation from New York or New Orleans' cities, can be less than 50 dollars (£10.) per acre? In making selections, I have, when practicable, procured both prairie and timber, though I am sure there has been a common error to pass the rich prairie because timber cannot be found adjoining.

Under this belief, many settlers have to their sorrow *entered** the timber and left the prairie, because they believed nobody would enter that without possessing the timber. The prairie has been entered lately, and such is the facility of raising timber on prairies by sowing the seed of black walnut and locust, that the demand for timber land has diminished. Those who doubt the comparative value of timber land, will do well to consider that twelve dollars is a fair price for clearing timber land. Timber land, when cleared in the usual manner, is left encumbered with roots and stumps. 12,000 dollars (£2,400.) will be required to clear 1,003 acres of timber land, whereas the 1,000 acres of prairie can be put in tame grass, without ploughing.

" A prairie farm can be put in complete cultivation at from three dollars seventy-five cents, to nine dollars per acre, according to the computation of my son Edward, who has been extensively engaged in cultivating the prairie for the last year. From a personal examination of the land in France, and in the Wabash Valley, I feel no hesitation in pronouncing the latter decidedly the best for the beet sugar manufacture. In France, eight, ten, and twelve dollars per acre are paid for rent, and yet great profits are made. An acre of good land will yield 44,000 pounds of sugar beet, from which 2,400 pounds of sugar can be extracted, which, at ten cents a pound, amounts to 240 dollars per acre.

" In England paper is now made from the residuum of beets, after the saccharine matter is extracted. An application for a similar patent is now pending in the patent-office here. The sample of paper exhibited is very good, and the rapidity with which it is made must reduce materially the price of the article. Many labour-saving machines are introduced to aid in the cultivation of new lands. In a few years it is possible that ploughing on smooth lands will be effected by steam, and even now mowing and reaping are successfully done by horse power. Such are the profits of cultivation, that I would advise all who can to improve some parts of their lands. A small improvement will repay expenditure, and greatly enhance the value of the whole investment. Three benefits may be expected:—1st, the crops will pay expenses and yield a great profit; 2nd, the land cultivated and the land adjoining will be advanced several hundred per cent.; 3rd, if stock is put on the farm, the same is numerically increased, and greatly enhanced in value, by improving the breed.

" Either of these considerations is sufficient to justify cultivation, and guarantee a large return. I mention the successful cultivation of the hay in the west, from one and a half to two tons is a fair crop. This can be cut and pressed without any labour-saving machinery, at two dollars per ton; and if the grass were cut by horse power, the expence would be still less. The profits of one hundred heifers, at five dollars, might easily be supposed. Fifty breeding sows would probably bring seven hundred pigs per annum, and by these means a large farm could be stocked with little capital advanced. The price of hay at New Orleans varies from twenty to fifty dollars (£4. to £10.) per ton; an average for the last three years may be thirty dollars (£6). The cost of floating down hay, in flat boats, to New Orleans, may be eight dollars per ton.

" Indian corn is so easily raised, that it is found advantageous to turn hogs into a field of this grain, without gathering it. It has long been the practice in New York to raise oats and peas together, and turn in the swine to harvest the same when ripe. Experiments this summer in Connecticut, show a great profit in raising spring wheat and oats together, and feeding out the same to hogs. Farmers in Indiana and Illinois are successfully enclosing their farms by ditching, which has cost from fifty to seventy cents per rod, or 5½ yards. The law of those states compel the owners of lands adjoining to pay one-half of fencing, when they make use of or derive any benefit from the fences—this lessens the expences of fencing one-half."

With the present possession and perspective control of advantages such as have been partially stated in the foregoing pages, it is not a difficult task to determine the future condition of this country; and few who have ever visited it have failed to understand and appreciate its peculiar advantages. If the agricultural interest be the great basis of all wealth, that country must be the richest which is most capable of supporting the largest agricultural population.

The rich and fertile soil, the temperate and healthy climate, and the vast mineral products of this country, particularly of that part of it last referred to, have excited an earnest and intense interest among the people of the United States of America— an interest which will never flag till the whole of the Valley of the Mississippi shall become one garden; and such it is becoming with great and unexampled rapidity.

---

* To *enter* is an expression generally used in the west signifying " to select" or settle upon."

The increase of its population and resources are so wonderful as scarcely to be believed till witnessed. It was but as yesterday that the whole Valley of the Mississippi was one wilderness, and now it is fast becoming the most important part of the great nation to which it belongs, whose destinies it will control in ten years by its numerical votes. American statesmen know and acknowledge this truth, which, indeed, is so susceptible of demonstration as to be plain to ordinary minds. The Germans, of all European nations, have hitherto taken the lead of all emigrants into this country. For the last few years they have gone over in countless numbers. If the writer of these remarks could believe that the inhabitants of Great Britain would read and profit by them, he will have attained the object he had in view in writing them.

[*From Judge Hall, as quoted by Buckingham.*]

The settler may always select on our prairies, land as fertile as the richest river bottoms; and by settling in the edge of the timber, combine every advantage afforded by the latter. He finds the land already cleared, and has only to enclose it. The labour of bringing it into cultivation is already trifling. A heavy plough and a strong team are required the first year, to turn over the soil. The corn is dropped in the furrows, and covered with a hoe, and no other labour is bestowed upon it until it is fit to gather; because during that year the corn cannot be tended in the ordinary way, as the sod, already bound together by the fibrous roots of the grass, is merely turned, and not pulverized so as to admit of tillage. But by turning the grass down, exposing the roots to the sun, and leaving the sod undisturbed, it becomes mellow in one season, and while undergoing the process of decomposition, it affords nourishment to the growing corn. The crop thus raised is not abundant, nor is the grain very good; but something like half the usual crop is raised, which amply pays for the labour of planting and gathering. By the ensuing spring, the roots of the wild grass are found to be completely rotted, and the plough is put into a rich light mould, fit for all the purposes of husbandry. The ordinary operations of farming may now be conducted in the usual way; and the labour of cultivating a light soil, unencumbered with rocks and stumps, is so trifling as to leave time for the farmer to improve his land and buildings. The plough runs on a level plain of rich mould, and may be managed by a half-grown lad as well as in the other by the strongest ploughman.

In timber lands newly cleared, ploughing requires both strength and skill; the plough must be sharpened frequently, and is often broken; and at the last the ploughing goes on slowly. The difference in the greater facility of working prairie lands, the saving in the wear of all implements of husbandry, the economy of time, and of course the greater degree of certainty in the farmer's calculations, and the enjoyment of health, are so great as, in our opinion, to outweigh any inconvenience which can possibly be experienced in this country, for the want of timber, even under the most unfavourable circumstances. A farmer had better settle in the midst of a prairie, and haul his fuel and rails *five miles*, than undertake to clear a farm in the forest. The farmers of Illinois are beginning to be aware of this, and there are now many instances in which farmers, having purchased a small piece of land for timber, in the woodland, make their farm in the prairie. It is only necessary to make a nice calculation of the time consumed in the transportation of wood for fuel and other purposes, and to observe how small a proportion it bears to the other labours of a farm, in order to satisfy himself, or any one at all acquainted with the subject, that it is really a matter of no importance when brought into competition with the advantages of a prairie country.

[*Extracts from Letters from Emigrants.*]

Racine, Wisconsin, North America, Oct. 25, 1841.

I should not trouble myself to recommend this place, were I not so convinced that it is by far the best in the world for an English farmer or rural mechanic with a small capital. I have travelled through Pennsylvania, New York State, both the Canadas Ohio, Indiana, and Illinois, and west by the Mississippi river. There is now plenty, of government land close to this handsome seaport town to be sold at 5s. an acre (title deeds included), and plenty of improved farms within three or four miles for sale, at from three to six dollars an acre, with house, outbuildings, fenced in, and partly in cultivation; their reason for selling is, they came here four years ago, without money, borrowed of a company of money-lenders to purchase the land, at forty to fifty per

31

cent. interest, and there being no market till last year, they cannot pay for them, and will sell to go further back, on government lands, not yet in market. The land here is the best I have ever seen, black loam from six inches to two feet deep, all prairie, with timber in clumbs or groves, and in appearance, like a gentleman's park in England, and the soil is suited for every kind of grain; garden vegetables grow in the greatest perfection, as well as all the English flowers and fruits, and it is the best country in America for game, fish and good water, and there is plenty of living water on every farm; wells can be got any where by digging from six to twelve feet, and there is, I believe, every kind of timber growing here that is to be found in America. The wild fruits are grapes, apples, cherries, plumbs, rasberries, strawberries, goose-berries, currants, cranberries, wortleberries, blackberries, and various others, and nuts of various kinds. The land produces from thirty to forty bushels of wheat the acre, thirty to sixty of Indian corn, forty to sixty of oats, thirty to forty of barley, buck-wheat and flax in proportion. And the prairies furnish the best pasturage for cattle and sheep, which is the most profitable kind of farming here, the wolves having all disappeared, and the meadows or flat prairies produce at least three tons of hay on the acre, so you may keep and winter as much stock as you like, with very little trou-ble. Many persons have been prevented coming here, hearing the place is sickly, and no market for produce. Now, I declare, there is no country upon earth can be more healthy, being an open high prairie country in a northern latitude. I have seen or heard of no person being ill from the effects of the climate, the only disease is the ague, and this is only in swampy places. We have a good cash market for every kind of produce; hay from two to four dollars a ton; working cattle £8 to £12; cows twelve dollars; sheep six to eight shillings, flour five dollars a barrel; wheat three shillings and four-pence and one dollar a bushel; Indian corn one shilling and nine-pence; barley two shillings; oats fifteen-pence; buckwheat two shillings; pork two-pence; beef three-pence; mutton two-pence half-penny; veal three-pence; butter eight-pence; cheese four pence; potatoes one shilling per bushel; other vegetables no sale—too plentiful.   JOHN COLE.

Milwaukee, July 10, 1842.

My dear Daughters—I was very glad to hear from you, but the expense was enor-mous: the Americans are certainly behind you in postage plans. Never envelope your letters; they are charged double and treble. I have entered 170 acres of land, and engaged to build a house, and when finished to live in. You fill up a paper at the land-office, which is dated from the day you go into your house; you have then twelve months to pay it in. I shall have to pay £44 for mine, at five shillings and a fraction an acre. In the 170 acres there is 130 acres as good land as ever I saw; the rest will do for pasture, it is so situated along with some rough land that will not be taken up for years to come. There is a marsh close by, where you may cut as much hay as you like. This is as fine a country as ever I saw, as healthy as any country on earth; it has been settled about six years, and there have only died in this time three persons. The country round here is settling very fast, and a great many emigrants have arrived here this year. It is quite equal to the Cotswold Hills for sheep—any number might be kept. I work very hard, and must earn as much as I can between this and June; but I am in good health—never better. I think I was sixty-three the last day of May. E. has got an excellent business with her millinery and dressmaking, and earns four and sometimes five dollars a week. Milwaukee has 3000 inhabitants, although it has only been settled six years. It will be the largest place on the Lakes. There has been brought to this place, from Mineral Point, near 1000 tons of lead up to this time. You say, when you can muster £500 you will come out. That sum would make you as independant as a lord in England; you may get twenty per cent., and it would be a great income here. The average of meat is threepence a pound, eggs threepence a dozen. I have bought wheat at three shillings a bushel. It costs very little to live here. We miss a drop of good beer. Here there is neither beer nor cider. Our love to all friends.   J. H.

Eaglestown, Wisconsin, Sept. 26, 1842.

My dear Family—Mine is some of the best land you ever saw. Wheat is fifty cents a bushel, or two and a penny sterling, barley about one shilling, oats tenpence. One of my neighbours had at the least sixty bushels of barley to an acre: I helped to harvest it at three shillings a day and my board. What think you of that? Meat I find on the average threepence a pound, cheese fourpence, butter fourpence to five-pence per pound. I believe this the most healthy country yet discovered. Dry black loom, sandy limestone soil: from what I learn it is never too dry. It has not been a hot season, they say. The glass stood the highest at ninety-five Farenheit: the glass now stands at seventy-six. E. still gets on well. There is no tailor near us. We are twenty-six miles from Milwaukee. A journeyman shoemaker earns a dollar a day with board and lodging. The houses are from a quarter to half a mile apart. Newspapers cost a penny each. We landowners have no blacksmith yet: we must have patience. I know this step of mine in coming here is the best thing I ever did for my family. Paying for the land is the difficulty. Capital would do wonders here. Any one might do well who would be industrious. We have not many Indians here, but those we have are very civil. If they know you to be English, they make a great fuss with you, and call you brothers and sisters.

J. H.

Extract of a letter from Dr. John Smyles, of Albany, New York, to Mr. Pitkethly, late of Huddersfield, Yorkshire:—" But I must now reply more directly to your letter, or you will tire of my philosophising. In regard to Wisconsin Territory, I never was there, but many of my countrymen and friends from this quarter have visited it. From the account given by all, it must be a noble country, with a soil and climate fitting it admirably for English settlers. Its situation on the map is such, that you can ship either to New York or New Orleans, and receive from either place supplies in return. In climate, it approximates nearer to England than any other part of America. The section I now live in is too cold, full six months of winter, and I dislike this very much. This is a dreary time for us farmers to sit by the fire-side. As you remark in your letter, any kind of land may be had in Wisconsin—prairie, wooded, or part wet, although I fancy not much of the last. All of it is said to be better adapted for growing wheat than any other part of the Union. In population it is rapidly increasing, and will, in a year or two, become a state. By all means come and see the country before you determine on anything; but from a knowledge of your former active life, I should predict it would not suit your disposition to settle down in the wilderness of the far west to the cultivation of the soil. There would not be sufficient to keep in play your active mind, unless, indeed, you brought 1000 people with you—combined their labour in agricultural pursuits for your mutual benefit—you to reap for the capital advanced a fair return, and they for the labour spent an equal equivalent; and if you even gave to the last, as it ought to have, the largest share, in the end you would reap a rich reward."

Extract of a letter, dated Charleston, Peoria County, Illinois, August 17, 1842:— "The day after we arrived at New Orleans, we set sail up the Mississippi river, and landed at St. Louis in seven days. In another steamer we ascended the Illinois, and reached Peoria in a day and a half. Here we remained a fortnight, while I examined the neighbouring country, and finally purchased a farm at this place, which is twenty miles from Peoria. I have 80 acres of prairie land, 40 of which are cultivated, and grain in the ground, viz. wheat, Indian corn, oats, potatoes, peas, beans, pumpkins, &c. The house, which is exactly in the centre of the 80 acres, is of two stories, twelve yards by seven, and divided into four apartments below, viz. kitchen, pantry, and two other rooms. There is a good piazza in front, eight yards by twenty, where we frequently dine in the hot weather. The land is enclosed with a wood fence, eight feet high. There is a good well of water a dozen yards from the house, and five or six good springs on the land. For the whole I gave 1000 dollars."

Extract of a letter, dated Evansville, Indiana, July 16, 1842:—"Mr. William Y——, formerly with you, has already purchased a farm, containing 120 acres of land, about 35 acres of the same cleared and in good cultivation, with three good springs on it, with a very fair apple, peach, and cherry orchard; two substantial log cabins, and a good log barn, stable, corn-crib, thrashing floor, and smoke house. He also included in the purchase the growing crops, and those already cut and harvested, consisting of six acres of Indian corn, five acres of wheat, cut and in the barn; four acres of oats, ready for cutting; three-quarters of an acre of potatoes, seven acres of hay, with a sufficiency of garden stuff for the whole of the family; eleven head of horned cattle, thirty-one hogs, more than one hundred fowls, seven ducks, four geese, two dogs, one horse, one waggon, one winnowing machine, one plough, two sets of harness, with many other things connected with farming that it would be too tedious to mention; and also some household furniture. All this was purchased for the sum of £140 sterling, or 700 dollars."

COMMUNITY OF ICARIE.

A LARGE body of Communists, called Icarians, is spread over France, and has ramifications extending to other countries. They have always depended on legal and peaceful means to propagate their opinions, but that has not prevented them from being persecuted by the government, nor defended them from unjust aspersions. Thus their opposition to revolutionary measures, and especially to secret political societies, has not only been useless to them, but has laid then open to the attacks of the democratic party, which has declared in no measured terms unceasing hostility to communism; this not being sufficient, they are attacked by the ultra-communists, who advocate the right of obtaining by violence, that which the unjust system of society denies to them, and who are not easy under the indirect reproof which the opposite principles of the Icarians administer. M. Cabet who has devoted 40 years to the firm and constant advocacy of popular interests, and has occupied a high station in the state, is at the head of the Icarians; the *Populaire*, a weekly paper of which he is the editor, is their organ, and the "Travels in Icarie," and "True Christianity," written by him, contain their ideas on social organization, and their profession of faith, all of which are founded on the word "Fraternity," and comprehended in it.

MR. CABET'S ADDRESS, INVITING HIS DISCIPLES TO GO TO ICARIE.

M. Cabet, after alluding to the precept of the great Christian lawgiver, (whose disciples the communists (Icarians) proclaim themselves), "When they persecute you in this city flee ye to another," proclaims the intention of the body in question, under the direction, and influenced by his writings and principles, to leave France, and settle in a part of the United States, to be called "Icarie."

He says, "This is not to be a partial essay, nor a small emigration, for if our calculation does not deceive us, we may count on from 10 to 20,000 Icarians able to go and desirous of going, on an army of workmen of all professions, who will establish a people and a nation.

It will not be a mob without ideas, induced by misery and the wish of bettering their personal condition; they will be workmen full of heart, intelligence, and instruction, men chosen, examined, and proved, guided by one faith, warmed by one devotion and one enthusiasm.

During the time necessary for the preparations for the first departure we will examine the necessary questions, and having called to our assistance the council and experience of all the friends of humanity, we shall go with a plan prepared and perfected beforehand.

Nothing will be the result of chance —each for all, all for each—from every one according to his means, to every one according to his need,—first, that which is necessary, next that which is useful, afterwards that which is agreeable, without other limits than those of reason, equality, and possibility.

The strongest objection made to our plans is—how can you graft a new state of society upon the old one, resisting all that is opposed to its prejudices and customs? This objection will not exist with us; there will not be any obstacle to our commencing everything on the most perfect systems which modern science can offer to us; the plans and positions of our roads, towns, and manufactories, will be laid out from the beginning in the most advantageous manner; we shall aim at perfection in our workshops, our dwellings, furniture, clothing—in fact in everything.

"For the instruction of the adults, there will be perfect liberty of meeting and of discussion; all the professors, books, and journals necessary; as to the educa-

2

tion of the children, we shall prove what can be done with the intelligence and heart of man by communist teachers, having the best methods of teaching, and all possible means of rendering study agreeable and education perfect. Our opponents tell us, that without inequality of fortunes, without individual property unlimited and hereditary, without emulation, a state of communism would be a state of servitude, misery, and barbarism. We deny it; it is re-asserted—the denial is repeated. This might go on for ever, but for the future we will not have assertions, denials, or discussions. We will prove and manifest the truth by experiment. Let those who are doubtful wait the result."

In Icarie the domestic ties, and first of all marriage, will exist in all their purity and all their force, which will be self derived, and not depending on extraneous aid; there will not be any marriage portions, nor any forced celibacy. Woman will be established in her rights and dignity. There will not exist either slavery or domestic servitude; perfect democracy, with universal sufferage. The Icarians will not on any pretext carry war into their neighbour's home, consequently they will not know or need to know any thing of the military servitude. The love of their independence, institutions, and country, will cause them to be prepared to defend themselves from any aggression; that this defence may be the best possible, all the male citizens will be armed and disciplined.

There, machinery will be the friend of the workers; labour will by all possible means be divested of danger and excessive fatigue, and rendered attractive; the fine arts carried to the greatest degree of perfection.

Reflect, then, Icarians; we shall have a climate and sky at least equal to our own, a fruitful soil covered by a powerful vegitation, producing with little labour the same plants and animals.

Having left France we will not forget that she was our mother; however hardly she may have dealt with us, we will not cease to desire her happiness, nor to commiserate our persecutors, because "they know not what they do;" and are, as well as ourselves, the victims of the bad social organization which governs them from their birth.

We will, from this time, accustom ourselves to a language still more moderate, kindly, and fraternal; and increase our efforts to command the esteem of our adversaries.

Those among you who cannot follow us (and whose number will increase) will form part of the great Icarian family, and be regarded as brethren.

We have the words dream and Utopia continually thrown in our face; let us, in answer, establish and realize Icarie.

Here (France), workers, your destiny in infancy is privation and ignorance; that of many of you rags, dirt, and superstition—the example of vice and labour imposed as a condemnation before your physical force is developed.

Your destiny in youth and manhood is excessive labour, or the want of it; this labour often disgusting or perilous, and insufficiently paid, produces disease and premature old age; the conscription, the livret, perpetual uneasiness, real slavery, without prospect as without rights; deprivation of the pleasures of domestic life, or if you dare enjoy them, an increase of agony.

And in old age, how many of you, after a life of services to the country, are neglected and abandoned, until a hastened death ends your sufferings.

And this is contrasted by the opulence of your exploiters and masters, the privileged, who consume all and produce nothing.

Nevertheless, let us adhere to truth and justice; let us not bear towards the classes supposed to be fortunate, either envy, or above all, hate; for they also have their tribulations, ruins, and miseries; they are, perhaps, still more than we, the victims of a detestable social organization, rendering all men slaves and antagonistic, and depriving all of security and happiness. But if they are not happy that does not advantage us, our situation is no less intolerable; a radical remedy is no less necessary.

Let us examine what will be the condition of the workers in Icarie.

We shall not there see the people wanting all things, and the privileged regorging with superfluities, but all the citizens will be co-proprietors of an undivided national property; consequently there will not be any property with its cares and agonies, nor opulence with its oppressive and disturbing vices; there will be an assured livelihood, ease and abundance for all; the conditions equal labour in proportion to their physical and intellectual powers. There will not be either journeyman or master, but partners; labour will be the duty of all to the public; it will be equally a public function, whether guiding a plough or the state.

No wages, but an equal enjoyment of the produce. No distress from want of employment, no opposition, labour organised in the best possible manner, by experience, the public opinion, and the will of the workmen themselves.

3

Agriculture will be carried on on the largest scale possible, and the trades in immense manufactories. The labour will be so distributed that no one will be idle, no one overworked.

The manufactories will be clean, commodious, wholesome, and all possible means taken, by the most extensive machinery and otherwise to protect the workers. The professions chosen as much as possible according to taste and aptitude.

All the governmental positions will be elective, temporary, recoverable; all the citizens will be electors and eligible to all the positions.

The community will guarantee to supply all, with lodging, food, clothing, hygyenic, and medical care, and education, with the means of marrying and bringing up children, and progressively with all the reasonable enjoyments of civilisation.

There will not be any aristocracy, privilege, or inequality: but the purest democracy, equality everywhere and in everything, according to the principles of fraternity; an equality, relative and proportionate to the physical and intellectual powers, for the duties; relative and proportionate to the wants, for the distribution; so that as far as depends on the state, all may be equally happy.

In a word, in Icarie the workers are the people, the nation, society; they will themselves govern themselves for the interest of each and all; and when the most perfect education shall have given to the intelligence of a new generation all the development of which it is susceptible. Humanity will advance rapidly, by all the means possible, towards the degree of perfection assigned as its limit by Nature or Providence.

Workers here exploited, bondsmen without right and unrespected, without occupation or food, seek elsewhere the treasures beneficially offored us: Let us establish Icarie in America.

I will go with you, I will participate in your condition; I will be fed, clothed, lodged, and treated as yourselves; without any other privilege than that of being burthened with the greatest portion of care, watchfulness, and responsibility.

The effect of this address on the Icarians, and on those who oppose them, has been immense; and although of course absolutely opposite on each party, still it is such as might have been and was anticipated, with this exception, that the warmest hopes of the most ardent of M. Cabet's friends have been surpassed by the enthusiasm and devotion with which the Icarians received it, as will be evident from extracts from the correspondence which has been the result.

The animosity of the republican party may be best inferred from the fact, that M.

Cabet and the *Populaire* have since been acquitted by the Court of Rouen from an accusation of the Procureur Général for délit de la Presse (offence against the laws regulating the press), and that although we might have supposed that any journal professing liberal opinions would have rejoiced in the acquittal of any journal whatever, this has been so far from the truth that the *National*, the *Reforme*, and the *Démocratie Pacifique*—the two first being respectively the organs of the middle class and popular republicanism, and the latter professing to to be the "ne plus ultra" of Communism, have not either of them deigned to notice the judgment.

To learn the true measure of the acrimony of M. Cabet's opposers, it must be known that the most ridiculous accusations are made against him; for instance, he is paid 1,000,000 of francs by Louis Philippe, and 4,000,000 by the Emperor Nicholas, to rid Europe of the Communists; the Government pays him to go and cut a canal across the Isthmus of Panama, or that of Suez; he is an agent of the police; the Prince Joinville has given a large tract of land in Brazil; he is a coward, a traitor, a renegade, selfish, &c., &c. To all these prettinesses the opposers add, " that they will enter the ranks of the Icariens, and compromise them by bepraying them to evil, or by doing evil in their name." Although we know that the gentlemen connected with the above-named papers are incapable of much of the folly or or grossness described, they should not excite it from others, or they will be blamed in consequence.

It will be asked, what can cause such opposition? The answer will be found in the following faithful quotation from a pamphlet, published with a view of counteracting M. Cabet's address:—

"Everywhere it is said this state of things cannot last. Every one has the presentiment of a revolution. And this is the moment which you (M. Cabet) choose to take from France the purest of her children, the most intelligent and the most devoted of her patriots. It is taking from an army, an hour before the battle, its best and bravest regiments."

" Hinc illæ lachrymæ;" the revolution is impending, and the Icariens will not be the cat's-paw for the republicans; and why should they? The leaders of the republican party have on every occasion denounced Communism, and declared their determined opposition to it now and for ever; they have, besides, thrown the odium of all that is evil on some sects of Communists on the Icariens, and now they regret the loss, not of friends whom they esteem, but of allies, who are valued only because their admitted qualities would render them useful on the day of combat. **A 2**

EXTRACTS FROM LETTERS TO M. CABET.

This letter being the first received is given at length :—

" I have read your address with much pleasure : I thank you sincerely; it is the best news you could have given to your Icarien children ; I have shed many tears of pleasure in reading it, in thinking of the happiness we shall enjoy in the new country which we will establish far from France, where we are so miserable : is it possible to reflect cooly of such a happiness after having suffered so much ?

" After the theory the practice,—to work then : show to our detractors what we are capable of by unity and fraternity : let us go to work as true Christians for the time has come to put in practice the principles of Jesus and our first fathers ; let us lay the foundations of Icarie ; from there with fraternal love we will call the world to us : let us not weary of saying, Let us go to Icarie.

" My life is free of reproach, I am esteemed by those who know me, I have courage and 2,000 francs at your service.

" All that I can say will but imperfectly describe my thoughts. I have a good heart, courage, and hands, and several thousand francs. Count on me."

" I have read over and over again your call, and could not hinder myself from crying with joy each time."

" Your address has produced an effect impossible to describe, we did not expect the realisation of our dearest hopes."

" I lose no time in sending this good news. Mr. D. came :o see me; his wife is enchanted; he offers *to join with* 100,000 *francs;* he knows America well. The satisfaction produced by your address is complete; what consolation to be able to end our persecutions ! Will our enemies at last open their eyes ? Will they understand our incontestable truths ?—the more we reflect on them the more we are sorry that they cannot quit their darkness to enjoy the light of our felicity."

." My wife desires me to say she is transported with joy; she saw the future full of trouble for her children and for humanity, now she is like one risen from the dead, a light beyond that of the sun

seems to shine on her; she desires to arrive in Icarie even at the price of her life."

" The happy news was necessary to sustain us against the persecutions of power, the clergy, the gentry, and masters, who seem to have agreed together to pursue us without ceasing. Are we not told, ' put not a piece of new cloth on an old garment ?' let us observe the precepts. Here are tilers, brickmakers, quarriers, and masons, ardently desiring to contribute their best help."

" Yes, dear citizen, but for you, but for your advice, how many had last winter proclaimed the terrible device, 'bread or death;' may you be a thousand times blessed, you who had the courage to oppose yourself to the torrent of revolutionary passions. We owe to you our gratitude and respect ; you are our friend, our guide, our protector, to you we owe our first ray of hope; you have preserved many a husband and a father to their wives and children."

" Brethren can we believe our eyes ? Can it be true that by this simple and divine plan, the hour of departure for the promised land will sound for us ?"

" Your proposition is received with demonstrations of happiness which I cannot describe; all read with avidity, but let us remember we can succeed only by disinterestedness and perseverance, and doing as we would be done by."

" Apostles of social regeneration we will lay the first stones of the building announced by Christ, but let us be prudent, we must have men who will give up all for their fellow-creatures; the quality is preferable to the quantity. I am impatient to see the brightest day of my life, when I put foot on board-ship, for we shall quit living among the tombs for the promised land and the sun of light; we are already five who unite more than 60,000 francs. I will send you a long list."

" We were like those who live not, but your courage has reanimated us."

" How many years have I remained in darkness ? but my eyes at length see the light, count on me."

THE CONDITION OF WOMEN IN ICARIE.

IT is already known that the Icorien nation is proposed to be an association of citizen brethren all equal in rights, the territory undivided and cultivated in the interest of all ; that the education of all will be as equal as circumstances and reason will permit, that all will be required to produce equally, relatively to their means; and the desires of all will be gratified equally, relatively to their wants.

The fundamental principle of this relative equality is the relative equality of the sexes; this being admitted, who then can deny that woman requires by her nature to be more favourably treated than man? Consequently, one of the first articles of the constitution asserts, that man owes to woman gratitude and respect, care and protection; that everywhere and always the first place and the first share shall be hers, that the legislation shall regard the laws which interest her as the most important.

Another article asserts that all owe gratitude, love, and veneration to their parents, but especially to their mothers; a loving friendship to their brothers and sisters, but especially to their sisters; love and devotion to their wives: love and protection to their children, but especially to daughters.

Another proclaims that as all should do as they would be done by, each man owes to all women, old or young, the same sentiments and respects which he desires others to have for his mother, sister, wife, or daughter. The aged woman must receive from all particular respect.

The whole system of education justifies these laws, and impresses them in the disposition and mind of youth; the manners and customs constantly present their application.

Man taking nature and reason for his guides will look on woman as the source of his happiness, will use all his efforts to embellish and perfect her, and to render her happy.

Consequently, it is necessary to show what care will be taken of her from birth, during infancy and youth to develope her health, graces, and beauty; to cultivate her intelligence and wit, to perfect her disposi-

tion, that she may be a companion worthy of man, and capable of making his felicity.

The first fifteen or sixteen years are consecrated to her physical, intellectual, and moral education. She will be taught (as well as the young men) the elements of all the sciences and arts, every means being taken to render the study easy and agreeable. Above all, she will be taught to be a good daughter, sister, wife, mother, housekeeper, and citizen.

All the women (except those likely to become mothers, or having young children, or those past the age of labour, these being the objects of the special care of the community,) will be occupied in the workshops, exercising a profession of their own choice; all that can be possible will be done by machines, andotherwise, to render the work agreeable and easy.

Marriage, and the domestic attachments, will exist in all their purity and all their force—we hold them to be the chief source of happiness in social life: this we think so evident that it is not necessary to prove it: the contrary is the opinion of but few, and appears so erroneous, false, imprudent, and contrary to the universal feeling, that it must spring either from folly or a perfidious hostility to Communism.

It is not marriage which is an evil, but its bad organization; its being contracted for all sorts of interested motives, the bad education of the husband and the wife, the danger of want to which the children are exposed, and its indissolubility. To remedy this it is not necessary to suppress marriage, but to organize it better, which will be done in community; there cannot be any seeking after fortune; the parties will be better educated, the children will be amply provided for; but, if it should be absolutely necessary, divorce (under very great and well-considered restrictions) will render both parties free to accept other legitimate offers.

DIVORCE.

IF it become *impossible* for a married couple to live together in peace, they may be divorced; let us here be rightly understood— let us protest against any misrepresentation, or misconception by which the doctrine on this subject may be twisted to a meaning which is not meant. The French communists do not intend that divorce shall be encouraged by its facility, but that it shall in extreme cases be a remedy attainable, in order to protect all, and especially women, from a life-long tyranny, admitting of no escape, except perhaps, by some lightly formed immoral connection leading to misery.

The Icariens do not advocate the abso-

lute independence of woman, for marriage and the domestic affections are the source of the relative equality before spoken of; woman will gain by them a power she could neither exercise nor enjoy without them, and her dependence in community would be lightly borne as the fiat of nature.

The young men will be disposed by education to become good husbands and fathers, the young women to fulfil all the duties of good wives and mothers. There will be no marriage settlements, therefore the choice will depend on personal fitness; the young people will have every proper facility of enjoying each other's society; everybody may marry without fear of being burthened by a family: celibacy, though permitted, will be under ordinary circumstances considered as contrary to the second law of nature.

I am of opinion that in Icarie the results of the proposed plans of education, of occupation, and of the domestic arrangements will be that the temptations and opportunities to sensual errors will be very greatly diminished, and therefore the long train of attendant evils prevented in equal proportion, and as woman is always the victim of these errors, every prevention of them will be especially to her benefit. I am of opinion, moreover, that it is woman above all who should desire this communitary state; the more she loves her children, the more uneasy must she be for their future destiny (especially that of her daughters) and therefore the more she ought to desire the accomplishment of a state of social organization which might insure the happiness of all, and especially that of her sex.

The *Démocratie Pacifique* has thus attacked M. Cabet on this subject:

" A monotonous society, where you would perish with *ennui*, is dreamed of by M. Cabet, who would deprive real life, and probably the theatre in Icarie, of the amorous intrigues which slip with marriage into civilized comedy; of the trio, husband, wife, and lover, he would suppress the lover, leaving the husband and wife to a perpetual *tete a tete* —the love of liberty which distinguishes Cabetist inventions, there suppresses celibacy; you are obliged to harness yourself to a wife who, as she has no portion, must please: besides the law ordains it. Each man being furnished with a woman, there will not be any love without matrimony, will there be any with it? Love in a cotton night cap, holding a chamber candlestick, will dictate his laws to Icarie. We will not swear that this will not be put in practice, since we see that a man publishing these innocencies has adherents. The Icariens might find a better *beau ideal* and and another leader."

The Icariens may thank the Phalansterian for the line drawn. They are simple enough to be satisfied with the state of *ennui* so much dreaded by him, they even prefer it to the romance of the lover in the family circle. They seek not a *beau ideal*, but practicable measures; and they hope their leader will remain at their head until they shall not want one. I will not enter into argument to controvert the writer's reasoning; I need not show that morals and taste are attacked with a petulence worthy of a fashionable *roue*, but ill becoming a teacher of the people; I offer not to parry the brilliant witticisms flashing from the philosopher's pen; I compare not the services rendered to society by this young man, to those of the old man he jeers; I leave all who may read this letter to judge between the two.

SOCIAL CONTRACT, OR DEED OF ASSOCIATION, FOR THE COMMUNITY OF ICARIE.

PRELIMINARY EXPLANATIONS.

Necessity of an Initiative.

IF it were possible, all who desire to establish Icarie would unite to examine, discuss, and decide every thing in common, but this being impossible, it is indispensable that some one take the initiative, the more so, as in a great operation there are many things to be decided upon and done; but nothing would be finished if convocations, meetings, discussions, and deliberations were the mode of action. This initiative is a necessity. I therefore take it on myself.

Foundation is temporary.

A triple mutual confidence is the first element of the success of our enterprise, without which all would fail. This is Confidence of the Members in the Direction.

Confidence of the Direction in the Members.

Confidence of the Members between themselves.

Those who go must neither hesitate nor doubt; their faith must be perfect; their determination firm from conviction, and not to be shaken; they must act without regret, and not suppose any cause of complaint to be possible, or any complaint to be lawful.

It is therefore necessary that the Direction take every means to inspire, to preserve, and to increase confidence and even enthusiasm, and cause every thing to be known and examined, discussed and approved, before the departure.

The engagement of the Members will only become definitive at the time of going, until then all will be provisional, and may be modified, rectified, and improved.

If I had not full confidence of our success, I would not give up my time, health, and life to commence an imperfect operation, which might be abandoned; but I am certain of my intentions, and resolved to do all to deserve a well-considered and solid confidence. I am convinced that our doctrine is *The Truth*, and that our enterprise is the *Safety of Humanity*; I have also the conviction that our system will lead public opinion, and excite sufficient interest to procure us all the necessary devotion and all the means of realisation; in a word I have in the success of our enterprise that *faith* which removes mountains. I devote myself without hesitation to this position, only proposing a certain basis for our Social Contract.

The Necessity of a Deed of Association.

A deed of Association is necessary to precise and fix our ideas. The necessity is urgent; because, if we desire to go as soon as possible, suppose next spring, we have many preparations to make, many questions to examine, and no time to lose.

What will be the Nature of the Association.

Of the several kinds of Associations regulated by the Civil Code, IX., the *Societé en nom collectif ou Solodaire* is the only one which is consistent with our principles of Fraternity, of Equality, and Mutuality; the two others, the *Societé anonyme* and the *Société en commandite* being founded on inequality. Our Icarien Association will therefore be *a society in which one name represents the body* and a *Mutual Society*, in which all the burthens and all the advantages will be mutual and equal.

Intention of the Association.

The intention of the Society is to acquire vast territories in a fitting climate, to cultivate and improve them; and to establish themselves by making all the necassary constructions; exercising different trades, and carrying on an exterior commerce for the common interest.

Number of Members.

The number of the Members is unlimited: it should be sufficient to form a People, a Nation, a State.

Capital.

The capital of the Society will consist of the fortune of all the Members, and of the gifts which will be made by the friends of our enterprise.

Will there be One Gerant or more.

Several Gerants, five or six for instance, seem to present at first sight, more warranty of success on all accounts: but the difficulty of finding several men entirely of one opinion and of the same sentiments; the necessity of harmony, unity, and celerity; the danger of division, hindrances, and delay seem absolutely to demand an unique Gerance, which will be the more useful as it will bear all the moral responsibility.

Who is to be the Gerant?

Since I am perfectly known by my numerous writings and by a long life of devotedness; since I am conscious of possessing strength to be the *servant of all*, and to bear all the fatigues and all the responsibility of that servitude, without any personal advantage; since the mass of Icarians has given undoubted proofs of their confidence in me, and since it is necessary to act with decision, and impossible to wait for a regular manifestation, I do not hesitate to say that M. Cabet will be the Gerant.

The consent of the Members will be an Election.

Each person is as perfectly free to refuse these propositions, as I am free not to accept others, which I am convinced would render success impossible.

If all are dissatisfied with a single gerant, or with the Gerant-director proposed, they will not accept, they will not sign, they will not go; the Gerant, the Gerance, and the act will not be constituted; but if, on the contrary all, or the great majority adhere to it, approve of it, sign and go, this adhesion and consent perfectly voluntary and free, will be equivalent to a true election, in fact the most just election possible, seeing that the minority are not obliged to submit to the majority, but can withdraw if the conditions do not please them.

Duration of the Gerance.

This enterprise, one of the greatest ever formed, necessitates vast plans, vast combinations, vast labours of all kinds; numerous and important negociations with governments and with great mercantile houses, consequently great confidence on the part of these governments, these firms and the public, consequently stability, security and sufficient time for the execution, therefore I do not hesitate to say M. Cabet should be Gérant during ten years.

Duties of the Gerant-Director.

His general duty is to consider himself as the brother of all the associates, as the servant and representant of the society, to have no other interest than the common interest, to consecrate and devote himself entirely to the common good, and to set the example of all the civic and social virtues.

And since he must set an example of devotedness, and of the practice of fraternity and equality, he must not have any salary or personal advantage, but must be fed, cloathed, and lodged as the other members without any privilege.

Responsibility of the Gerant-Director.

The Gerant-director being the servant and representant of the society is essentially responsible for his gerance. Having no other power than the approbation, the confidence and the affection of his co-associates; if these sentiments abandon him he would be powerless. For myself, being certain that this responsibility has nothing to be feared, I shall accept without hesitation the judgment of the society at the end of the gerance.

Prerogatives of the Gerant-Director.

He will have the direction and the administration of all things, but *must* act in conformity with the general principles of the Icarien community, (fraternity, equality, liberty, mutuality), as they are indicated in the Travels in Icarie, and as they will shortly be resumed in the Icarien prospectus. He will sign for the society Cabet & Co., will represent the society, and act and treat for it, and in its name. He will receive the funds which form the social capital, will contract the necessary loans, will purchase for cash or on credit. He may choose one or more Gerants to act with him or to replace him in case of necessity. He will also choose all the agents or employees necessary, causing them to be elected by the members whenever election can be usefully and easily practised. He will establish a council of gestion, and all the commissions which may be useful.

Formation of the Society.

When there are one hundred members the society will be formed.

Admission to the Society.

No one can be admitted into the community who does not possess the conditions already laid down, and those which will shortly be published; any person having a contagious, transmissible, or hereditary malady, need not offer himself.

All unmarried persons will promise not to marry with persons who have not the requisite qualifications for admission.

The Gerant will choose a second member, the two a third, and so on up to ten; the ten will choose ninety others, and the one hundred united will confirm these nominations. These one hundred will choose among themselves twenty as a committee of admission. The committee will divide itself into four sections of five each, which will meet alternatively to decide on other admissions. The Gerant may convoke separately several sections according to circumstances; he may also unite them.

In each section and in every re-union of sections unanimity of votes and the confirmation of the Gerant will be necessary for the admission of the postulant.

To avoid disagreeableness the names of the members of the committee will not be made public.

In France, elsewhere than in Paris, commissions organised by the Director-gerant will judge provisionally on the demands for admission, and transmit their opinions to the committee at Paris which will decide definitively.

In other countries committees organized by the D. G., will decide and transmit their opinions to the director, who will confirm the decision if he think fit.

Obligations of Members.

Each member will engage to act according to the principles and rules of the Icarien community. He must bring at the time of departure *all that he possesses*, and his capacity and his labour. On making his demand he will engage to pay on his admission ten francs for preliminary expenses, necessitated by the preparatives, comprehending correspondence, printing, journeys, &c; these ten francs will be left even if he should not eventually go. Besides this sum, each person should advance all that he conveniently can; this sum will be carried to the account of his investment, and will be returned if he should not go.

Rights of Members.

The rights of members are equal and mutual as are their duties, all are electors all are eligible; all are equally undivided co-proprietors; all must be equally well fed, cloathed, and lodged, they and their families; all have the same right to marry, and the children of all the right to the same education.

If a member leave Icarie, he will not have any right to claim his portion. He can only have a gratuitous assistance. Therefore let every one reflect before going; and if he have any doubts, or thinks any regret possible, let him remain where he is ; because we want those only who are resolutely determined that they will and must succeed.

Such is the basis of our Icarien Society, we shall labour daily to develope it, and to render it perfect.

ADMISSION TO THE SOCIAL CONTRACT OF THE COMMUNITY OF ICARIE.

OUR project of going far from home to found a model society for the interest of humanity, is assuredly a noble enterprise, but it is very difficult, and demands great courage and devotedness.

We would not attempt it except with chosen individuals.

They must be superior in many respects, for intelligence, conviction, devotedness, industry, and unshakable constancy.

We are all convinced, we have all said, *the quality is preferable to the number*.

But we want both *number* and *quality*.

Fortunately we are perhaps better able to unite these desiderata than any other party ; for even our adversaries acknowledge that the Icariens, taken as a body, are the most studious and best informed, the best conducted, the bravest, and most generous, in a word, the elite of the workmen.

And we will choose from this elite.

We will now examine how this choice may be well made.

First of all, let us take a rapid survey of the manner in which the early Christians were recruited and organized, this will be both interesting and instructive.

Organization of the First Christians.

There is a great analogy between us and them, we are their disciples and imitators.

The old social organization, or the old world before Christ, was individualism, for which the Saviour or the Liberator wished to substitute fraternity and communism.

This old world was Satan, with his corruption, his pomps and vanities, and his tyranny, for which Jesus wished to substitute the reign of God, of justice, and of love.

The old world was darkness, error, and death, and the new world was to be the light, the truth, the resurrection, and the life.

And to revive and regenerate the human race, Jesus said to his apostles and disciples: Go and teach on all the earth my doctrines of fraternity, of devotedness, and of solidarity.

But before separating regulate your association and your propagand.

After the death of Jesus, the women enthusiastic, devoted, and courageous, encouraged and brought back the Apostles who were at first frightened, discouraged, and dispersed.

But in a short time the Apostles, electrified by the example of the women, founded at Jerusalem, a first Church or society of Christians, and afterwards dispersed themselves to commence a more vast propagand, and to convert the world by organizing churches everywhere. To found a Church, the Apostle preached and expounded the doctrine, and chose some of the first converted, who afterwards choose or admitted others, under the condition of confirmation by the Apostle.

All the ceremonies for the admission of Christians, were in the course of time so altered and corrupted, they now excite only indifference or disdain ; let us see what they were in the beginning.

They began by catechising or instructing; the catechism was an oral instruction, which the catechist gave to the united catechumens, they were not children, but men and women, to whom the doctrine of fraternity, and christian or fraternal morality were taught ; they were, above all, exhorted to put them in practice.

This catechising, instruction, or preparation ordinarily lasted two years. During that time Christians were appointed to watch over the conduct of the catechumen, and to assure themselves that it was truly conformable to the new doctrine and morality.

The admission was then made with much solemnity and many ceremonies, (according to the general custom of the time), at two epoques ; Easter and Pentecost.

He who wished to be admitted caused his name to be inscribed some time before hand on the register of aspirants, or on the unenlightened.

He first of all made his *examination of conscience*, that is, he examined himself conscientiously, that he might be assured that he sincerely adopted the doctrine and mo-

rality of Jesus, with all their consequences, and that he had really cast off *the old
man* to become a *new man*, capable of all
the sacrifices demanded by fraternity.

Then as a new man, firm, intrepid,
without any false shame, he made his
confession in presence of the assembled
church, who listened respectfully and in
silence. He avowed his ancient prejudices, his errors, his defects, his vices,
and bad actions. He declared his repen-
tance of them, and that he was resolved to
repair and for the future to avoid them.
The assembled church then examined him,
commencing by asking if he renounced
Satan, his pomps and works; if he wished
to do so, and would engage to do so for
ever.

He was afterwards interrogated on his
opinions and belief, on the doctrine and
morality, and on the motives of his con-
version.

They next enquired of his conduct and
his actions, and of his firmness to endure
the persecution to which he might be
exposed.

The church then proceeded to the
ballot.

If admitted he was called an elect.

And then he was solemnly baptised,
with all the other elect at Easter or Pentecost.

How different was this baptism of men
and women as a proof of their admission
into the Christain Church, as being fit and
worthy, from that which is now administered in Latin to new-born children.

The new elect then striped himself and
plunged into running water, to indicate
that he shook off, washed, purified, and
drowned the old man.

When he left the water he was called
a *neophyte* (new born), and he put on a
white tunic or robe, to indicate that he was
washed, purified, arisen from the dead or
regenerated, born to be a new man in a
new world or new social organization.

Before and after the baptism a number
of little ceremonies, and of symbols or
emblems were made use of, (as salt, spittle,
milk, honey, balm, a candle, the sign of
the cross on different parts of the body,
the imposition of hands), to indicate the
duties, qualities, and virtues of a Christian, Eight days after the baptism he was
called a Christian.

The first duty of a Christian was to
practice Communism, to put all his property into the common stock, or to sell
them and put the price into the common
treasury.

We see that the method is already
traced for us, and we new Christians may
put aside the ceremonies and emblems,
and adopt all that is rational, useful,
great, and popular.

Conditions of Admission.

1st. The most essential condition is an
absolute and reasoned devotedness to the
cause of woman, the children, the people,
and humanity.

It is necessary to have the courage to
be guided in all things by this devotedness, to be able to support all its labours,
and to sacrifice all vanity and jealousy to
the success of the enterprize.

2ndly, It is neeessary to adopt completely and sincerely all the general principles of the Icarien system,—fraternity,
equality, liberty, solidarity, community
Consequently to know all the Icarien
writings. And consequently also, those
who do not know them must hasten to
study them.

3rdly. It is necessary to be industrious,
to know a useful trade, and to be ready to
work on the land if required.

4thly. Temperance.

5thly. A good reputation.

6thly. An absolute cession af all possessions to the community; the community
engaging to supply all wants.

This list of conditions is provisional;
the conditions will be made definitive as
soon as they can, by a committee which
will be organized for that purpose.

Many questions which concern young
people and women, will be decided separately. The women will be invited to
discuss the questions which particularly
concern them.

Mode of Admission.

Those who desire to be admitted into
the Association will give to a correspondent a declaration containing their names,
age, profession, height, residence; whether batchelor, married, or widower; what
children; the first three indications also
for his wife and each of the children. His
presumed capital in money or goods.
When he wishes to go. And a reference
to several well known Icariens.

Each correspondent will inscribe these
demands on a paper printed for this purpose.

A committee of admission will be organized at Paris.

Each correspondent will send about ten
names, from which a commission will be
chosen.

Each commission will transmit by the
correspondent, after having made the necessary inquiries, their opinion on each
declaration.

The committee of admission at Paris
will decide definitively.

Thus they will decide on the admission
of their companions.

The whole will form a society under
one name, for the exploitation of the
common estate, on which they will carry
on different trades for the general interest.

COMMUNIST CREED.

Nature.

I do not believe that the universe is the effect of chance; but I believe in a first cause, which I call *Nature.*

I think that it is useless and dangerous to endeavour to characterize this first cause, because human intelligence is not sufficiently perfect to perceive and understand it, and because discussion relative to it, ordinarily degenerates into disputes and divisions. But I believe Nature to be infinitely intelligent, fore-seeing, wise, just, good and beneficent.

I believe that Nature intended that man should be *happy* on earth.

I believe that all the objects created around Man, the organization given to him, and above all, his intelligence or reason, are sufficient to render him happy.

I believe that if man is miserable it is not the effect of the will of Nature, but that of the ignorance of human nature at the beginning, of its inexperience and its first errors, the effect of the bad institutions, and the bad social and political organization began in the times of barbarism.

Primitive Ignorance.

I believe that the human race was first in a savage state, that orginally man nearly resembled the brutes, and was entirely ignorant, like the savages in countries newly discovered.

I believe that the consequences of this universal ignorance have established every where; the right of the strongest, of war and of conquest, slavery, the power over the life and death of the slaves, women, and children; tortures, superstitions, religious proscriptions, castes and classes, the privileges of birth, the inequalities of rights, education, and fortune.

I believe that it is contrary to reason to appeal to the innocence, the experience, and the wisdom of ancient nations; because the younger the human race, the less it possessed of knowledge and experience, and because it is now older and more experienced than at any former period.

I believe that social and political organization is still every where extremely imperfect and vicious, but that humanity is too young for us to be astonished at it.

Reason.

I believe that man is essentially a reasoning, perfectable, and sociable being.

I believe the reason of but very few men is what it ought to be, and might be, if devoloped by a good social organization. But I believe that the intelligence or reason

which distinguish man from other beings, will suffice when enlightened by experience to perfect humanity.

Perfectability.

I believe that man is essentially perfectable by experience and education; that human nature has generally and constantly improved itself from the beginning to the present time, that it is now better instructed than at any former time, and that it is impossible to fix a limit to its future perfection.

Sociability.

I believe that man is essentially sociable; that he is destined to live in society; that he has every where and always existed in a society more or less numerous; that society is natural, and that what is called civil or political society is but the continuation, development, and improvement of natural society by the aid of reason and experience.

Natural Goodness.

I believe that man being essentially sociable, is therefore essentially drawn towards his fellows; that he is sympathetic, compassionate, affectionate, good, disposed to succour and aid his brethren; that fraternity, love and devotedness are his natural dispositions or instincts, confirmed and developed by reason and education.

I think that men's vices are generally the effect of the bad social and political organization, and above all, of inequality, which produces indifference and selfishness, envy and hate.

I believe that all the vices would disappear and give way to fraternity, love, and devotedness, if inequality were replaced by equality in political and social organization.

Fraternity.

I believe that Nature is the common mother of all men; that all are equally her children; that all are brethren; and that the human race forms but one family.

I believe that Nature has not divided her children in castes or classes, in corporations or categories; that she has not destined the ones to be masters, governors, rich and idle, having all the privileges without any burden, and living in superfluities; and the others to be slaves, governed, poor, weighed down by labour, supporting all the burdens, without enjoying any advantage, wanting necessaries, wretched.

I believe that on the contrary, that the fraternity of men will necessarily bring their equality.

Equality.

I believe that the diversity of size, form, strength, &c. does not by any means destroy the equality in rights, duties, and enjoyments, as the difference between children does not prevent them from having the same right to the love of their parents, as the difference between citizens does not prevent their equality before the laws and the tribunals.

I believe that Nature has created all that is on the earth for all the human race, *all for all;* that all have the same wants, and consequently the same right to the things necessary to satisfy them; that if she had divided between her children, she would have given portions according to the wants of each; but she has never made any division, she has given to each an equal right to the earth and all its productions, the same as to the air, light, and heat.

I do not believe that Nature has endowed man with reason, and rendered him sociable that reason and society might destroy fraternity and the equality of rights. I believe on the contrary, that he is created reasonable, perfectable, and sociable, that reason and society may realize and perfect the equality of enjoyment.

I believe that the establishment of social and political inequality is a violation of the laws of Nature.

I believe that this social inequality has been established in all nations only because human nature was at first rude and ignorant. I do not believe that monarchy is the real and only cause of the misery of the people, or that a republic is its real and only remedy, since history shews that wretchedness has existed in republics as well as in monarchies.

I believe that inequality, which produces opulence and domination for the minority, and misery and oppression for the majority of the human race, is the radical cause of all the vices of the rich, (selfishness, cupidity, avarice, insensibility, inhumanity), and of all the vices of the poor, (jealousy, envy, hatred).

I believe that it is also the cause of all the rivalries and antagonism, of all disorders and discords, conspiracies, and insurrections of all crimes and calamities.

I believe that the same effects will subsist so long as the cause remains, and that the only means of ending the ills of humanity is to do away with aristocracy, or social and political inequality, and to replace it by democracy or equality.

Property.

I believe that Nature destined the earth to be undivided and possessed in common, as are the air, light, and heat; that the only objects that should be divided are those necessary for the wants of each; and that the community of goods is natural.

I believe that property is entirely a human invention.

I believe that this institution could only be good and useful by the earth being equally divided between all, and by each person's portion being inalienable.

I believe that the institution of property, joined to its alienability and inequality, as adopted by almost all nations has been an error, and perhaps the worst of errors.

I believe that illimitted property has facilitated the inequality of fortunes; that it is the principal cause of opulence and misery of all the vices and of all the miseries of humanity.

I believe that these evils will subsist essentially, fatally, and inevitably as long as property lasts; that the only way to remove the effect is to destroy the cause.

I think that a state should be established between the opulence of the few, and the wretchedness of the many, that state is the ease of all; and I believe that to establish this universal ease the natural community of goods must be established and perfected.

Vices of the present Organization.

I believe that the vices of domestic, social, and political organization are too numerous, too evident, and too generally acknowledged for it to be necessary to mention them.

System of Community.

I believe that community should be considered in three respects; of persons, of goods, and of labour.

People in the Community.

I believe that the nation or the people should form but one family of brothers, or one society, of which the members are all equal in rights and duties, in enjoyment and labour.

I believe that the equality should be perfect, and have no other limit than that of its possibility.

I believe that all the brethren [or associates should be *equally* citizens, electors, and eligible; that all should receive the same general and elementary education; that all should be equally well nourished, well clothed, and lodged; that all should be equally obedient to the law, and that all should work equally.

Sovereignty.

I believe that the sovereignty belongs to the people, and that the people should exercise it by the constitution and the law.

Constitution.

I believe that the constitution should be made or approved by the whole people;

that it should fix all the fundamental bases of the community, by deciding all the principles which regulate the questions of food, cloathing, lodging, marriage, family, education, labour, &c.

I think that examples only can be at present proposed, that it is necessary to avoid all discussions which might degenerate into disputes, or have any other serious inconvenience, because the opinions on the bases of community can only be individual opinions; and it is the people alone who will decide all.

Law.

I believe that the law should be the expression of the general will, that it may be prepared by a populaar representatation, chosen by all the citizens, but that it should be as much as possible approved by the whole people.

I believe that the law, thus made by all, consented to and desired by all, will be necessarily in the interest of all, and that no one can have the least dislike to execute a law, agreed to by each, for the common interest.

Liberty.

I believe that the law, which is the reason and the will of all, should regulate all that is relative to order and the general happiness, and that liberty should consist in doing that which is not prohibited by the law, and in eschewing that which is prohibited by it.

I believe that in a state of inequality there does not exist any true liberty for the immense majority who do not co-operate in making the law, but that a state of community gives true liberty, because each is governed by the rules which he has considered necessary.

Marriage.

I believe that of all the sexual relations, that of marriage is the most conformable to the dignity of human nature and the most capable of assuring the happiness of individuals, and order in the community.

I believe that the inconveniencies at present attendant on marriage, are not the result of marriage itself, but of the system of dotation and inequality, and that in state of equality and community, with good education, with perfect liberty of choice, which will be determined by personal fitness and qualities only, with the possibility of divorce in case of necessity, marriage will be fraught with advantages and without inconveniences.

I believe that not only all should marry, but, that when community shall assure to all the means of existence with moderate exertion, all will be inclined to marry,

The Family.

I believe that a domestic life is more natural than the separation of children from their parents, that it is one of the greatest pleasures granted to man, and that the mutual affection of parents and children, however strong it may be, will not have any of the inconveniencies under the system of community, which it has under the present system of Antagonism.

Education.

I believe that in community education should be the base of every thing.

I believe that the result of education should be, the physical, moral and intellectual perfection of human nature.

Territory.

I believe that the national territory should be considered as one vast domain, belonging to the society undividedly.

I believe that the society or its representatives should manage the social or common domain, have it cultivated by the citizens, receive the produce, send it to the workshops and the warehouses, and distribute all the natural and manufactured produce.

I believe that the result of this kind of management would be the suppression of enclosures, the cultivation of all that is now waste, a more perfect mode of cultivation, an immense economy, and a double or perhaps a tenfold produce.

Manufactures.

I believe that all the different manufactures should be considered as forming but one social manufacture directed by one will.

I believe that the society should direct and organize the work, the workers and the workshops.

I believe that each workshop should be special, unite all the workers in that line, and produce every thing in large quantities.

I believe that machinery, often fatal to the poor under the present system, cannot be too multiplied in the community; that all laborious, dangerous, and disgusting labour should be done by machinery, and that means should be found that the workers shall be only the directors of the machines.

I believe that every thing should be done to render labour easy and agreeable.

I believe that as all work is ordained by the society, all kinds of work should be equally respected.

I believe that all the citizens should be workers, that as much as posible every one should choose the profession the most agreeable to him, and that all should work an equal length of time.

I believe that by this system many useless employments and losses would be avoided, immense economy realized, and a large increase of produce be made.

Happy Effects of Community.

I believe that the system of community, giving plenty and a good education to all, will prevent all disorders, vices, and crimes, will insure the most perfect public order, and the peace and happiness of the citizens.

I believe that far from producing an equality of misery, it will produce an equality of comfort.

I believe not only that there is not any objection against communism, which is not to be easily refuted, but also that no other system resolves so well all the social and political questions.

I believe that in the community there cannot be either theives, drunkards or idlers, law suits and bankruptcies will be unknown; tribunals, punishments, prisons, and police will be useless.

The Necessary, the Useful, the Agreeable.

I believe that it will be necessary at first to procure for all the citizens what is essential, afterwards all that is useful, and that when all shall possess that which is necessary and that which is useful, that which is only agreeable may be sought, on condition that all consent to it, and that all may equally profit by it, for the equality in the enjoyment should be always perfect.

Fine Arts.

I believe that far from extinguishing the Fine Arts, this system on the contrary is the best adapted to improve and develope them, because no other system concentrates all the national power so much as Communism, because it does not meet with any obstacle to the use of all the magnificence of the arts in the public monuments, and all their elegance in all the objects which the Citizens enjoy mutually.

Possibility of the Application.

I believe that the opinion which rejects Communism as impossible and utopian is only as a prejudice which must give way to study and examination.

I believe, also, that the community needing a great creating and producing power to give an equality of comfort, it is more practicable in a great industrial and commercial nation, than in a small one without trade; that it is now easier than at any former epoque, because industry is now more powerful than ever, and that its facility will continue to increase.

Establishment.

I believe that Communism cannot be established by violence, and that a victo-

rious minority cannot impose it on a majority. I believe that if a minority would suppress the property of the large and small holders, and force the rich to work, the attempt which would break up all habits, customs, and modes of existence, would meet with more obstacles than any other social and political change has ever encountered. I believe that independently of open opposition, the opposition of inertia would cause it to fail.

I believe that community can be established only by the power of public opinion, by the national will, by the consent of all or of a great majority, in a word by the Law.

I believe that to form this public opinion, this national will, this consent, this majority, it is necessary to discuss, to tranquilise, please, persuade, and convince.

I believe that if the doctrine of community were false, it could never establish itself, because it would be easy to shew its fallacy; and that the communists who adopt it as the truest and the best, as they doubt not of its victory, should be the more ready to submit it to discussion.

I believe that threats and violence are in contradiction to our principles, that the communists should prove the superiority of their doctrine by tolerance and moderation, by goodwill and fraternity towards all, and especially towards those who are more or less advanced in the road of reform and of progress.

I believe that their greatest chances of success are in endeavouring to reform themselves, in avoiding carefully all that can bring divisions, in preaching by example, in practising all the social virtues, in proving that Communism will not cause misfortune to any, but happiness to all.

I believe that in presence of the events which are preparing an incalculable Revolution in Europe, which will destroy all the democratic sects, or will give great facilities to the progress of equality, the community should by patriotic devotedness and for the interest of communism itself, sacrifice all to the necessity of Union, whether among themselves or with any other Democrats.

I believe that to avoid difficulties, it will be necessary to render our adversaries disinterested, by proclaiming that the present generation cannot be deprived of its right to property nor forced to labour, and that the system of community can be obligatory only for the coming generation, which will be prepared for it by education.

Electoral Reform.

I believe that Electoral and Parliamentary Reform must come first, and that all democrats ought to adopt them as a means

15

of arriving pacifically at all reforms, social and political, even at the establishment of community, the final aim of democracy.

State of Transition.

I believe that even in the case of a Reform or a popular Revolution a preparatory Regime is necessary, and therefore must be accepted with resignation.

I believe that this transitory regime should be a democracy with all its consequences and all the measures necessary to prepare for community; admitting the principle of community, and continually tending to establish it by a successive decrease in every social and political inequality.

I believe that this transitory regime may without inconvenience take all available means to increase the national domaine without abolishing the right of property; for example, by suppressing collateral successions, testaments, and dotations, and by acquisitions by voluntary contracts, that it might establish a progressive income tax, facilitate large associations, and partial communities, organise labour, regulate salaries, destroy want, and generalise a common and gratuitous education.

I believe that this transitory Regime will be longer or shorter, according to the progress of public opinion in favour of community; and that it will immediately produce immense ameliorations for the people.

I believe, also, that communism is the system the most opposed to agrarianism; to pillage, injustice, and oppression, and that it tends more than any other to develope Fraternity, Devotedness, all the generous passions, and all the social virtues.

ADDRESS OF THE ICARIEN COMMITTEE

TO THOSE WHO DESIRE TO AMELIORATE THE CONDITION OF THE PEOPLE.

THERE are many persons who desire sincerely that the condition of the suffering portion of the people should be ameliorated. But they are so alarmed at the immensity and the atrocity of the evil, and the depth of its roots in the organization of society, that they know not how to remedy it, for they fear that by attacking the first cause, the social bond would be broken, they are nevertheless obliged by their humanity to make use of all the palliatives that can be thought of.

Our intention is to prove, experimentally, that individual property is *the cause of* the evil; and, by establishing a Communist State, to prove not only the possibility of its existence, but its superiority in all respects over any other form of government.

What (it may be asked) has our enterprise to do with the amelioration of the condition of any but ourselves? Our reply is, that it will be a more advantageous plan of emigration than any which your Legislators can either propose or carry out, we shall be able to ease the Population of your over-crowded factories, and we will not drown them in rotten unseaworthy vessels, nor by packing them like herrings in a barrel, cause hundreds to die of fever in one voyage. We will gather your orphans from your unions, your outcast children from your gutters, and instead of becoming acquainted with misery and vice in the streets and the prison, they shall be the Brethren of our Children, and shame your miscalled civilized society by their virtues, developed according to our doctrine of Fraternity, and by our system of Education.

All who have not given the necessary study to the subject of Communism must necessarily differ from us as to it, but if they examine our project ever so superficially, they must see that we are sincere, and that our principles and views deserve credit for high morality and a tendency to diminish vice by diminishing or destroying many of the temptations and opportunities which lead to it.

One truth especially must not be overlooked, which is, that we seek not to destroy but to build up, we know that Communism cannot be established in Europe without producing many evil consequences, our principle of Fraternity being opposed to such an effect, we intend going where there is not anything to destroy, and where we may build up our City and our Nation in Love and in Peace.

It may be thought that our plan is Utopian, visionary, unexecutable; we think, that we may without too much vanity claim an average portion of Intelligence and Instruction, we are deeply interested in finding the truth, we have studied the subject seriously for years, we have sifted thoroughly the arguments on both sides; we seek not to support an hypothesis which we have set up, but we have arrived analyitically at what we are convinced is the truth.

Is it then assuming too much to assert, that we are better able to judge in this matter, than others who, however great their knowledge and abilities, have not studied it as we have, and do not feel the same interest in it as we do.

Our experiment is the greatest ever undertaken, if we succeed, its effects on the destiny of our race must be advantageous, we therefore hesitate not to ask the well-wishers of humanity to aid us.

They may do so,

1stly. Morally by the influence of their Esteem and Countenance.

2dly. Intellectually by communicating friendly council as to obstacles which they may suppose of importance, by advice or documents on the subjects of Finance, Agriculture, Manufactures, Commerce, &c.

3dly. Materially, by gifts of working drawings, prints, or models of Instruments, machinery, buildings, &c., by sending us books, tools, arms, or other useful objects.

The first number of " The Populaire"* for each month, will contain acknowledgements of all objects received during the month precedent, with the names, initials, or other signatures of the persons who have presented them.

We are desirous of rendering ourselves useful to the scientific world, by adding to the Collections of Natural History, Geology, &c.; by Meteorological and other observations; and we will attend to the instructions of Scientific bodies or individuals, as to the best means of aiding their labours.

ICARIEN COMMITTEE,
13, *Newman Street, Oxford Street.*

---

* " The Populaire," is the Icarien Newspaper, it is published weekly at Paris.

LONDON:
Printed by F. I. Watson, 2, Red Lion Court.

British Labour Struggles:
Contemporary Pamphlets 1727-1850

An Arno Press/New York Times Collection

The Factory Act of 1833. 1833-1834.

Richard Oastler: King of Factory Children. 1835-1861.

The Battle for the Ten Hours Day Continues. 1837-1843.

The Factory Education Bill of 1843. 1843.

Prelude to Victory of the Ten Hours Movement. 1844.

Sunday Work. 1794-1856.

Demands for Early Closing Hours. 1843.

Conditions of Work and Living: The Reawakening of the English Conscience. 1838-1844.

Improving the Lot of the Chimney Sweeps. 1785-1840.

The Rising of the Agricultural Labourers. 1830-1831.

The Aftermath of the "Lost Labourers' Revolt". 1830-1831.